Tackling Controversial Issues in the

Can you help young children understand racism?

Can you avoid bringing your own prejudices into the classroom?

How do you broach family values with seven-year-olds?

Talking effectively about controversial issues with young children is a challenge facing every primary school teacher. *Tackling Controversial Issues in the Primary School* provides teachers with support and guidance as you engage with the more tricky questions and topics you and your pupils encounter.

Illuminated with case studies and examples of how teachers and children have confronted issues together, this book helps you understand your own perspectives and provides fresh approaches for the primary classroom.

It considers how best to work with parents and carers, whole-school policies for tackling issues, and ideas for circle time, setting up international links, school councils and buddying systems. The range of challenging topics covered includes:

- Family values
- Racism in mono- and multicultural settings
- Democracy and citizenship
- The environment and sustainability
- Consumerism, finances and media advertising
- Gender, health and identity
- Grief and loss.

For all student and practising primary teachers, *Tackling Controversial Issues in the Primary School* provides much needed support as you help your learners face complicated ideas, find their voice and get involved in the issues that they feel make a difference.

Richard Woolley is Senior Lecturer in Primary Education and Fellow in Learning and Teaching at Bishop Grosseteste University College Lincoln, UK.

Tackling Controversial Issues in the Primary School

Facing life's challenges with your learners

Richard Woolley

LONDON AND NEW YORK

First published 2010
by Routledge
2 Park Square, Milton Park, Abingdon, Oxon OX14 4RN

Simultaneously published in the USA and Canada
by Routledge
270 Madison Avenue, New York, NY 10016

Routledge is an imprint of the Taylor & Francis Group, an informa business

Typeset in Bembo by
Taylor & Francis Books
Printed and bound in Great Britain by
TJ International Ltd, Padstow, Cornwall

British Library Cataloguing in Publication Data
A catalogue record for this book is available from the British Library

Library of Congress Cataloging in Publication Data
Woolley, Richard.
Tackling controversial issues in the primary school : facing life's challenges with your learners / Richard Woolley.
p. cm.
Includes bibliographical references and index.
1. Education, Elementary–Social aspects–United States. 2. Educational equalization–United States. 3. Neoliberalism–United States. I. Title.
LC212.82.W66 2010
372.011'5–dc22 2010004281

ISBN 978-0-415-55017-8 (hbk)
ISBN 978-0-415-55018-5 (pbk)
ISBN 978-0-203-84832-6 (ebk)

With gratitude to Muriel Cantlay and Sophia Duncan

Contents

Tables

Preface

Tackling Controversial Issues is significant as it considers difficult and challenging topics faced in education purely from the perspective of primary schools. It explores issues in all three stages in the primary phase and may prove controversial in some quarters for including the *Early Years Foundation Stage* in the consideration of some subjects. I hope that readers will find this useful, both in developing a sense of progression in children's learning and also in considering the difficult issues encountered by some of our youngest pupils. It is not my intention to push the boundaries of professional practice purely for the sake of it, but rather to explore progression and continuity in learning from the early years until children enter secondary education.

Each chapter includes case studies and opportunities to consider research and practice; their format varies according to the needs of each subject. Each one includes a consideration of child development to help to explore progression: the degree of detail varies according to the needs and complexities of the subject being examined. It is hoped that this provides the opportunity to reflect on the experience of others and to apply the issues in realistic and relevant ways. Each of us has different experiences as a practitioner and will be at a different stage in our career. We will each interpret these examples in the light of our own values, attitudes and philosophies of education. At times, the content of this book may present challenges to our views or practice. This is not a bad thing: it would be far worse for it to elicit no response at all and would do a disservice to the importance of the issues it contains. Differences of opinion can be creative and constructive if approached in a manner of openness and collegiality. This book is certainly not offered as the perfect answer to each issue, based on a flawless career. Rather, it is founded in my own professional journey and offered as a starting point to help each of us consider our next steps towards inclusive and supportive practice. On some points, my own views will be very clear and, I hope, expressed with commitment and passion.

This book seeks to explore some key issues that will help us to enable our children to learn in safe, secure and supportive environments, enjoying their right to childhood and considering the increasing responsibilities that they have in the world, and for the world, as they learn and grow. It seeks to address the perennial issues of discrimination and injustice that permeate so many aspects of our society and to help us to consider how we can be a part of educating for a fairer, more inclusive and just society. That aim may be idealistic, but if we can move a little further along the journey in our communities we will prepare our learners to face the challenges of the world, both today and in their futures.

Richard Woolley
Bishop Grosseteste University College Lincoln

Acknowledgements

An interest in difficult and controversial issues has permeated my career. As an undergraduate at the College of Ripon and York St John, Brian Howard's seminars on contemporary moral and social problems introduced me to new ways of thinking and challenged my perspectives on many of the needs of society. That he was also my first mentor as I prepared to train for the teaching profession was highly significant and his influence remains with me as I work with my own students. He introduced me to Phil Scott, who led my PGCE course at the same college. She inspired me to see the best in each child and to work towards social justice through the processes of both formal and informal education. More recently, my interest in subjects which often remain taboo in education was fuelled by Clive Harber and Jeff Serf, whom I first met at the TIDE~ Centre in Birmingham. I am grateful to all four for their influence.

I express my gratitude to colleagues at Bishop Grosseteste University College Lincoln for their support during this project. Particular thanks go to Kathleen Taylor and the whole programme team working on the BA (Hons) Primary Education with QTS. Chapter 5 was supported by work on community cohesion with Frank Hanson and colleagues in primary schools in the Boston area of Lincolnshire. Chapter 6 was informed by work on family diversities with colleagues in Lincoln: I express particular thanks to Janice Morris, Children's Literature Librarian. I am grateful to the University College for its role in facilitating these activities.

Chapter 8 was developed with the support of an Imperial War Museum Fellowship in Holocaust Education (www.iwm.org.uk/holocaust/education). Thanks are expressed to Emma O'Brien at the Imperial War Museum; Yifach Meiri and Lea Roshkovsky at the International School for Holocaust Studies at Yad Vashem, Jerusalem; Ruth-Anne Lenga and Paul Salmons at the Institute of Education; and Marian McQueen and other colleagues who shared in my learning journey on the fellowship programme.

I am grateful to all those who have commented on draft chapters, and particularly to Marion Mence, Mike Cole, Darryl Humble, Sacha Mason and Donald Woolley; my thanks also to Helen Pritt at Routledge for her support and guidance over recent months. It goes without saying that all shortcomings in the text are my own. Every effort has been made to contact copyright holders for their permission to reprint material in this book. The publishers would be grateful to hear from any copyright holder who is not here acknowledged and will undertake to rectify any errors or omissions in future editions of this book.

Finally, my most sincere thanks are expressed to all the teachers, children, students, carers and parents who shared their insights and experiences with me. Without their input this book would lack some of its reality. In all cases, their contributions have been anonymised.

Chapter 1

Introducing controversial issues

Concepts and challenges

> After a meeting, I was engaged in conversation with a woman who suddenly turned her interest to my own background: 'Do you have a family?' she asked. 'Yes, I do,' I replied, 'my mum and dad live locally and I have a brother.' 'No,' she replied, 'I meant do you have a family of *your own*?'

Teachers face a range of issues, often raised directly by their learners, on a regular basis. They need to be prepared for unexpected questions and crises (whether personal to the children, national or international). This introduction sets the scene for what will follow and provides signposts to different sections within the book. It raises a range of issues and considers what constitutes a controversial issue. Our understanding of issues is based on the way in which we perceive the world. At times those around us see things from different perspectives and in very different ways, as shown in the vignette at the start of this chapter. We can find our opinions, values, attitudes and beliefs challenged; sometimes we are misunderstood and at times we misunderstand others.

The source of controversial issues

The issues addressed in this book are controversial for a range of reasons. Many relate to Cole's notion of *'isms' and phobias* (Cole 2008b) that include classism, racism/xeno-racism and xenophobia, sexism, disablism, homophobia and Islamophobia. These issues each appear at various points throughout this book. Teachers and other child-care professionals need to be aware of isms and phobias in order to create classrooms founded on equity, the value of pupil voice and the principles of democracy.

Why are issues controversial?

Issues concerning the market (Chapter 9) and democracy (Chapter 5) will be controversial for some because they involve discussing political issues with children. An increasing focus on enterprise education means that children are being introduced to economic systems from a young age. This needs to be questioned and evaluated. In British society the suggestion that capitalism's free-market economics and the dominance of global multi-national companies (Chapter 4) should be balanced with a consideration of alternatives, such as socialism, is controversial. Sometimes controversy comes from suggesting something different to the norm.

Issues of 'race' (Chapter 2), identity and gender (Chapter 6) may be controversial because they challenge the status quo. To suggest, as antiracist educators do, that society perpetuates racism unless it makes a direct stance against it, stimulates discussion. Similarly, whilst most people would agree that we should value children's families and home backgrounds

(Chapter 3), they may shrink from their children knowing about same-sex parents. Introducing an understanding about sexual orientation to primary school children can prove controversial, yet they have an existing awareness of such relationships from the media and other sources. Controversy can come from ideas that make us feel uncomfortable.

Bereavement (Chapter 7) is not controversial in itself: it is a fact of life. However, it is a difficult issue to face and without a willingness to engage with it we will never be able to face life's challenges with our learners. It is astounding that it is an issue largely neglected within the formal curriculum, even when learning about life processes. Whilst some will feel that this is an area to be addressed by parents and carers, as educators we will work with bereaved children and their families at various points in our careers. Similarly, the Holocaust (Chapter 8) is not controversial: it is fact. But when some primary schools choose to include it in their curriculum or to mark *Holocaust Memorial Day*, important questions must be raised about the appropriateness and effectiveness of this. Some issues are controversial for age-appropriate reasons.

Thus, controversy can arise from the unexpected, from a lack of understanding, from personal discomfort or from questioning the age-appropriateness of subject content. Having said this, an issue is not controversial solely because it causes debate. It is, thus, important to explore what constitutes a 'controversial' issue.

Defining controversial issues

A controversial issue is one that presents challenge and stimulates debate; it involves no universally held or fixed point of view. Almost any issue can feel controversial when people hold different beliefs, views or values. Some issues are controversial because of their subject matter, for example whether experimentation should take place on human embryos. Others present a challenge because of their inclusion in the school setting, for example whether sex education is appropriate in a primary school classroom. In each instance, there will be differing and, sometimes, contradictory views arising from the issue or its presentation. The Crick Report (QCA, 1998) suggests that children need to address controversial issues in order for them to develop the skills necessary to deal with them knowledgeably, sensibly, tolerantly and morally.

By definition, a controversial issue must be addressed through means of reasoned and informed reflection, debate and evaluation. One may believe that the earth is flat, but this view does not stand up to reasoned scrutiny. Thus, it is not controversial – no matter how hard one may argue for it. *The Education Act* (1996) aims to ensure that children are not presented with just one side of a controversial issue by teachers; there should be a balanced presentation including views from different sides. However, in some matters, for example those pertaining to human rights, it may not be appropriate to present an unbiased view. It is important to identify and explain the reasons for any bias so that children understand how an issue is being approached and the reasons for this. Developing reasoned arguments, based on evidence, is a key part of exploring controversial issues and provides an essential life skill for children.

Why address controversial issues?

It is important to address controversial issues with children for several reasons. First, they will be aware of many issues and situations (from their families, the news media and other sources) that are of concern and that may challenge their thinking. To deny the opportunity to raise these in school is to remove its role in education (the ability to think, reflect, analyse and evaluate) and replace it with that of training (knowing the mechanics of grammar, mathematical processes and facts). Whilst information is important, being able to use and apply it is more so. Second, without the opportunity for discussion, children will have significant gaps in their learning in terms of knowledge, skills, concepts and understanding, which are needed to equip them for life: children need to be presented with opportunities for critical thinking (Oxfam, 2006b). Third, children need opportunities to develop and express their opinions, whilst listening to and understanding those of others: a classroom can provide an ideal setting to do this in a supportive and safe environment (Citizenship Foundation, undated). It is important to remember that controversial issues can be sensitive and require carefully thought-through strategies for their consideration. Generic strategies are introduced below, and further specific strategies are explored in each subsequent chapter.

The significance of this book is that it explores controversial issues in primary education, both those that are challenging because of their content and others that prove sensitive because of their inclusion in a school environment, seeking to support teachers in considering their own approaches. It considers how teachers can tackle issues that are relevant to the interests and experiences of their learners, the strategies that can be effective in classroom settings, and how children can learn to make informed choices as to how they can exercise their own rights and their responsibilities (Oxfam 2006b). This approach is rooted in examples from classroom practice to enable teachers to consider pedagogical issues through the experience of others.

I hope that readers will disagree with some of the ideas and arguments in this book: to do otherwise would be to fail to engage with the sometimes sensitive, controversial and subjective content. In places, my own views and biases will come through; I think that this is inevitable when exploring subject matter about which I care deeply. However, I hope that I am appropriately open and honest about any biases and that these will make the text all the more engaging.

Identifying controversial issues

It is now over 20 years since the first major texts on teaching controversial issues were published (for example, Stradling et al., 1984; Wellington, 1986; and Carrington and Troyna, 1988), and over ten years since the Crick Report (QCA, 1998) set out the case for citizenship education. In addition, 2009 marked a significant anniversary of the United Nations' *Convention on the Rights of the Child*, the first legally binding international instrument to incorporate the full range of human rights – civil, cultural, economic, political and social (UN, 1989). This is a timely point at which to review teachers' views on issues-based education.

An examination of the issues included in texts on controversial issues twenty years ago shows that concerns have changed. Wellington (1986) included a chapter on nuclear armaments, an issue that still hits the headlines today (e.g. concerning whether to renew *Trident*), but concerns about the threat of nuclear war seem to have diminished since the end of the Cold War. You may wish to consider what issues you anticipate being controversial in primary schools and those that you feel apprehensive about facing. For some, existing experience will already have informed these views. The views of student teachers outlined below will provide prompts for comparison. They were gathered through a survey of students in eight universities in England during 2008–9 (including pre- and post-1992, Russell Group, Guild HE and 1994 group universities) that varied in size of provision and setting. An online questionnaire was used to discover:

- the personal importance placed on key social issues in primary education;
- the issues that had been covered in students' training programmes;
- the issues that students expected to encounter in their first teaching post; and
- the issues they anticipated finding most difficult to address in school, with reasons.

Graded scales were used to elicit responses to the first three elements, and the fourth provided an opportunity for open responses accompanied by unlimited free-flow text input. Responses were gained from around 12 per cent of the target group. Students were approached by e-mail from a member of faculty in their institution or by an announcement on a virtual learning environment (and in some cases both). All contributions were anonymous and no individual institution can be identified in the findings.

The views of student teachers

The choice of subjects for the book's content has been informed by this exploratory study, which was undertaken during the first semester of 2008 with students in primary initial teacher education. These students, in their final year of undergraduate study on courses leading to QTS (Qualified Teacher Status) and on PGCE programmes, completed an online survey. The students were asked to rate issues according to the personal importance they placed on each in primary education. They were also asked whether they thought they would encounter these issues early in their careers. Some 55.6 per cent of respondents were on undergraduate courses and the others were undertaking a PGCE course.

Table 1.1 shows the answers in ranked order according to the highest importance that students placed on each issue. It is interesting to note that, with one exception, the student teachers felt that each issue had some degree of importance. Nearly all were felt to have at least a medium level of importance by over four-fifths of respondents. Such a judgement is clearly subjective, but it does suggest that, for these students at least, issues-based education has a place within the primary school.

Students identified areas of concern in response to the open question: *Which three issues do you anticipate finding most difficult to address in school?* Their responses have been grouped, with the most common categories being:

Sex and relationship issues	64.3%
Death and bereavement	55.7%
Family issues	38.6%
Spirituality and religion	27.1%
Racism	25.7%
Media influence	21.4%
Financial capability	12.9%

It is interesting to note the individual and sometimes private nature of the first four categories. Relationships, bereavement, the family and religion can each be intensely personal and they can be the subjects that we avoid discussing. How we feel when talking

Table 1.1 The importance student teachers placed on each of a range of areas in response to the question: *Personally, what importance do you place on each of these issues in primary education?*

% of respondents	*High*	*Medium*	*Low*	*None*
Multicultural and antiracist education	85.9	14.1	0.0	0.0
Issues about families (separation, divorce, same-sex parents etc.)	66.7	29.5	3.8	0.0
Education for global citizenship	59.0	35.9	5.1	0.0
Issues relating to democracy (e.g. school councils, children's voice)	57.7	38.5	3.8	0.0
How to develop community cohesion	56.4	35.9	7.7	0.0
Environmental issues (e.g. sustainability, use of resources, climate change etc.)	53.8	43.6	2.6	0.0
Growing up (e.g. physical changes and puberty)	53.8	42.3	3.8	0.0
Bereavement (e.g. supporting bereaved children and coping with loss in the school community)	53.8	39.7	6.4	0.0
Addressing issues in the news (e.g. war, famine)	46.2	50.0	3.8	0.0
Children's spiritual development	43.6	44.9	10.3	1.3
Approaching Holocaust Memorial Day and Remembrance Day	32.1	53.8	14.1	0.0
Children's developing sexualities	24.4	57.7	17.9	0.0
The impact of advertising and the media on children	14.3	64.9	20.8	0.0
Developing children's financial capability	11.7	64.9	23.4	0.0

about such issues as adults will, inevitably, affect how we feel about the possibility of exploring them with our learners. Media influences and financial capability are judged to be less of a concern, and were also the areas that students felt to be of least importance (as shown in Table 1.1). This book seeks to provide strategies to support discussions about such issues so that they can be approached with increased confidence and with appropriate boundaries to help everyone involved to feel safe and respected.

Throughout this book, practical examples and summaries are used to promote discussion and reflection. Each chapter includes a *Developing Practice* box to help us consider how to apply key elements to our professional practice. This is also done through *Pause for Thought* and *Tackling Issues* activities. Here, the first considers students' concerns about the possibility of facing difficult issues with their learners.

Pause for thought

Reasons for student views

When giving reasons for their choice of the issues they expect to find most difficult to address in school, students commented that:

> I have encountered parents who are not interested. This makes it hard as you feel like you are working against the parents, and it is hard to gain continuity if

what you are doing is not supported at home ... However, I think this is the most exciting and fulfilling area of teaching: not just looking at attainment, [but taking an] holistic approach to children and teaching about real things and not just 1+1.

(Undergraduate student, South East)

The influence that the media has on children is huge, and largely biased towards what the reporter, television programme etc. wants to get across. Children already come into lessons with a preconceived idea about something that has often been reinforced by peers/parents/carers. Sometimes, through their ignorance, they already have ingrained prejudices that as a teacher I feel I would be failing if I did not try to readdress, and try to allow the child through careful discussion to look at both sides of the argument, and maybe reconsider their views.

(Undergraduate student, East Midlands)

In a lot of the schools I've been in there has been either wide multiculturalism within the school itself or at least within the community at large. Especially in schools in less privileged areas this has translated into problems with racism between children from different communities. These problems can be pervasive and often, especially in the younger children, originate at home and from parental/ family attitudes; therefore it can be very hard to alter children's views.

(PGCE student, West Midlands)

Consider the issues raised by these student teachers:

- How do their concerns compare with your own, and with your own experience?
- How might past experience have affected the concerns raised? Do you identify any misconceptions or stereotypes in their views?
- How might these student teachers begin to address such issues and to build their own knowledge, skills and confidence?

Some respondents commented that they had not received much information during their course of study, and sometimes no detail at all, on how to approach the issues they raised as causing them concern. These answers may reflect the students' perceptions of the content of their course, rather than the coverage of issues, and, as all were still in training, they might have had input coming later in the year.

The students' comments add weight to the need for issues to be addressed in initial teacher education and for schools to be supportive as newly qualified teachers face new experiences. Typical examples of such responses are on the subject of Sex and Relationship Education, the area that students anticipated to be the most difficult to face in schools:

> I have had no college input on this matter and have no idea how I would approach it within the primary school.
>
> (Undergraduate student, East Midlands)

> I think this links in with sexuality as families are so varied in our society and I have apprehensions about contradicting the views children may have taken on from their families about what is the 'norm'. It is really that classic thing of children going home having listened to their teacher and repeating it to the parent and the parent replying, 'I don't care what your teacher says this ... is the way it is!'
>
> (Undergraduate student, North East)

> I would be happy to discuss anything [about sexuality] honestly with children, but would worry about how their parents/carers would react.
>
> (PGCE student, South East)

Table 1.2 The level of detail in which students felt their course had addressed each of the key areas raised in the survey

% of all responses (% of undergraduate responses)	*In detail*	*Some*	*Little*	*Not at all*
The impact of advertising and the media on children	1.2 (1.8)	35.8 (49.1)	30.9 (29.8)	32.1 (19.3)
Issues relating to democracy (e.g. school councils, children's voice)	22.0 (29.3)	41.5 (41.4)	29.3 (25.9)	7.3 (3.4)
Education for global citizenship	51.9 (66.7)	24.7 (17.5)	14.8 (12.3)	8.6 (3.5)
Environmental issues (e.g. sustainability, use of resources, climate change etc.)	17.1 (12.1)	46.3 (51.7)	23.2 (22.4)	13.4 (13.8)
Multicultural and antiracist education	60.5 (82.8)	25.9 (15.5)	13.6 (1.7)	0.0 (0.0)
Issues about families (separation, divorce, same-sex parents etc.)	20.7 (29.3)	36.6 (46.6)	20.7 (13.8)	22.0 (10.3)
Growing up (e.g. physical changes and puberty)	3.7 (5.2)	28.0 (37.9)	42.7 (39.7)	25.6 (17.2)
Children's developing sexualities	1.2 (1.7)	18.3 (25.9)	29.3 (32.8)	51.2 (39.7)
Addressing issues in the news (e.g. war, famine)	11.1 (14.0)	24.7 (29.8)	38.3 (38.6)	25.9 (17.5)
Bereavement (e.g. supporting bereaved children and coping with loss in the school community)	3.7 (5.2)	25.6 (34.5)	26.8 (27.6)	43.9 (32.8)
Children's spiritual development	28.0 (39.7)	28.0 (31.0)	25.6 (20.7)	18.3 (8.6)
Approaching Holocaust Memorial Day and Remembrance Day	7.3 (10.3)	24.4 (32.8)	30.5 (31.0)	37.8 (25.9)
How to develop community cohesion	13.6 (19.3)	35.8 (43.9)	24.7 (19.3)	25.9 (17.5)
Developing children's financial capability	0.0 (0.0)	12.2 (13.8)	45.1 (50.0)	42.7 (36.2)

The concerns about working alongside parents/carers are important and I address this area in detail later in this chapter.

Whilst I did not undertake documentary analysis of the content of each training programme to establish what was yet to be covered, Table 1.2 shows the level of detail in which students felt their course had addressed each of the key areas raised in the survey. The fact that the survey took place before the mid-point in PGCE courses means that the data from students on three- and four-year undergraduate programmes may be most useful here, although in many instances there is not a great degree of variance between the order in which their answers are ranked and those of the full survey.

The figures in this survey provide an indication of the perceptions of a sample of student teachers. However, it must be stressed that this was an exploratory study and its range and scope, whilst providing interesting data, do not have sufficient breadth for any generalisation to be made. They provide a snapshot of the views of a particular cross-section of students. Readers will want to consider their own views on the students' perceptions and to evaluate these views in the light of the broader context and generic strategies outlined in the next sections of the chapter.

The context of controversial issues

Key documents provide a context for our consideration of controversial issues in primary education. The *United Nation's Convention on the Rights of the Child* (UN, 1989) provides an international perspective; *The National Curriculum* (DfEE and QCA, 1999) and a range of associated strategies and documents provide a national perspective. These are the elements that inform our practice at a local level. They give useful background and set out the legal situation for those working in England. Each is explored at various points within this book. At this point, it is important to comment specifically on *The National Curriculum* and current developments in its form and focus. Readers in other contexts will want to consider how these points relate to the curriculum in their own setting.

The National Curriculum

The *National Curriculum* (DfEE and QCA, 1999) is now taken as a given by most teachers in England. Certainly, its implementation is a legal requirement. Those who trained to teach after I entered the profession (I began my first job in September 1989) have not experienced the classroom without a statutory national curriculum. Although it was revised in 2000 and its emphases have been affected by a range of strategies in recent years, particularly the Literacy hour (from 1998) and Numeracy lesson (from 1999) and subsequently the Primary National Strategy (DfES, 2003), the fundamental notion of the importance of a nationally prescribed curriculum remains in place. The *Rose Review* of the primary curriculum has reinforced this view (DCSF, 2009). For many teachers, the introduction of the *National Curriculum* (DfEE and QCA, 1999) diminished the opportunity for controversial issues to be included in primary education by filling curriculum time to the extent that no space seemed to remain for flexibility.

Readers will want to consider their own views on whether effective cross-curricular teaching can create time in primary school classrooms for those activities that teachers believe to be important. That the *Rose Review* (DCSF, 2009) has endorsed this approach to classroom organisation is positive and supports schools in developing creative ways of organising learning. This opportunity has always been open to schools, but pressures from league tables and inspections led to many primary schools operating a timetable compartmentalised into discrete subject areas. The design of the *National Curriculum* (DfEE and QCA, 1999) suggests such an organisation of learning, but does not require it. I have worked under such pressures and fully appreciate the issues associated with them. Current developments in how the curriculum is approached offer more flexibility and freedom, and, I believe, are to be welcomed.

The revised primary curriculum (DCSF, 2009), intended to be implemented from September 2011, has three core aims; these aims are to develop:

- successful learners
- confident individuals, and
- responsible citizens.

In many ways these are allied to the previous aims, to enable all children to learn and achieve and to facilitate social, moral, spiritual and cultural development (DfEE and QCA, 1999: 11). The addition of confidence and citizenship make a consideration of the issues in this book all the more important. This is further supported by the plan to introduce Personal, Social, Health and Economic education (PSHE) as a statutory subject in primary schools and an increased curriculum focus through programmes of learning that include children's health and well-being. Those working with different curricula will, no doubt, identify similar strands and emphases within their own setting.

Strategies for tackling controversial issues

Having set the scene in terms of defining controversial issues, highlighting needs identified by student teachers and exploring developments in the curriculum, it is now important to examine some generic strategies. Readers will want to consider how these might be used in their own classrooms as each specific issue is explored in subsequent chapters. First, I highlight strategies that relate to whole-school approaches to learning about controversial issues. In the next section there is a consideration of experiential learning and a range of approaches to take with your learners. Later, I suggest strategies to support relationships with parents/carers.

Whole-school approaches

Whole-school approaches to support the exploration of controversial issues include a number of strategies.

Policies must make clear how potentially controversial issues are to be addressed within the school community. They need to indicate to staff members how to deal with any complex or challenging questions that arise and how to find support. Policies should also make sure that parents/carers are aware of the approaches that are being employed and that they are engaged as partners in the education process. As the governors of the school review all policies regularly, this provides one means of ensuring that teachers feel confident and supported by other stakeholders in the school.

In-service training, whether on courses external to the school or through staff meetings and training days, may provide one means of developing expertise in specific areas and disseminating knowledge and strategies. However, the areas of PSHE and Citizenship, to which much of this book may be felt to relate, do not always have a high priority and budgets are limited. It may be that this book provides some stimulus for in-house training, accompanied by the supporting materials included in the bibliography and the resources at the end of each chapter.

Lessons within the school curriculum can be used to address controversial and difficult issues. However, it is essential that these are not seen as isolated 'bolt-on' elements of learning, as this will significantly diminish their benefit. For example, it may be appropriate to discuss bereavement, using the stimulus of children's literature or picture books, and this might be best done at a time when children are not dealing with an immediate loss. However, other issues may be covered best at the point of need. As is suggested at several points in this book, it is important that issues are discussed in context so that children can apply them to their own experience and internalise the learning. Lessons will arise from whole-school long- and medium-term planning, some of which may relate to specific programmes.

Programmes provided by a variety of organisations may be useful in raising issues and addressing children's attitudes. One example is the DARE programme, which addresses the issues of drugs, alcohol and violence (www.dare-uk.com). However, once again there needs to be a context in order for learning to have any application. Schools need to consider how such programmes fit in to the continuum of learning: how they will be prepared for and followed up. The DfES introduced another programme, used increasingly in schools, in 2005. This series of booklets outlines the guidance for *Excellence and Enjoyment: social and emotional aspects of learning* (commonly know as the SEAL materials). There are four sets of booklets with accompanying CD-Roms addressing the Foundation Stage, Years 1/2, 3/4 and 5/6. It is intended as a whole-school approach and provides opportunities for continuity and progression in learning (DfES, 2005). Seven themes follow through the series, exploring personal and interpersonal skills:

- New beginnings (empathy, self-awareness, social skills and motivation)
- Getting on and falling out (friendship, cooperation, anger management and conflict resolution)
- Say no to bullying (self-awareness, empathy, managing feelings and social skills)
- Going for goals (focusing on motivation and self-awareness)
- Good to be me (managing feelings and empathy)
- Relationships (using the context of family and friends)
- Changes (managing feelings, motivation and social skills).

These aspects help to support children's social development, which is a precursor to cognitive development, revisiting ideas and skills in a spiral curriculum throughout primary education.

Class and school councils are considered as a part of Chapter 5. The issues that they consider can be more wide-reaching than matters pertaining to the school's internal organisation. For example, considering whether to support a charity, discussing where the school's resources are purchased and originate, or identifying national or global themes for forthcoming assemblies, can add a greater dimension to their role.

Experiential learning

Experiential learning involves providing children with experiences that enable them to reflect on concepts and ideas. Whilst some issues are global and possibly distant, teachers can provide activities that enable learners to think through ideas and to begin to formulate their own opinions and outlooks. This stands in contrast to didactic teaching, which is more likely to close children's minds to alternative views and to have little effect (Oxfam, 2006b). However, experience is not usually enough in itself: it is possible to make a mistake and to repeat it, sometimes several times. What is required is an opportunity for reflection: to consider how our experience, feelings and senses have impacted on our existing knowledge and understanding and how that experience calls for us to modify our outlook. This leads to application as one's practice is impacted by experience and reflection. Experiential learning does not only involve providing children with experiences, it also involves using their existing experience as a basis for learning.

Strategies to facilitate experiential learning include the eight possibilities that are outlined below.

Engaging in a campaign can provide a real life opportunity to make a difference. I suggest that this is a useful strategy, but with the caveats outlined in Chapters 6 and 9, particularly the need to avoid stereotyping any recipients. Campaigning can involve much more than fundraising. Children might research the aims and roles of non-governmental organisations (NGOs), including Action for Children, Age Concern and Oxfam, or write to their local councillors and Member of Parliament. Requesting information to evaluate can be as useful as making contact to share a point of view.

Visits and visitors can provide a rich range of resources. Meeting people who have first-hand experience of issues can help children to develop their own views. Visitors need to be briefed carefully so that the content of any discussion is age-appropriate and reflects the equality policies of the school. There also needs to be due care shown to child protection issues. Visits require a great deal of planning and risk assessment, but can offer children new and stimulating experiences. Whether travelling to a local place of worship or site of environmental interest, or heading further afield, teachers have the opportunity to give children experiences that otherwise they would not access.

Role play provides the opportunity to 'experience' the world through simulation. Having the chance to gain some sense of being in the 'shoes' of another person provides a stimulus for thought and reflection. It can help to bring an insight into another point of view or way of life. Whilst it is impossible to know what it is truly like to be another person, this strategy can help along the journey.

International links are increasingly popular and have been supported/facilitated by a number of government initiatives. They require an ongoing commitment from the school, which can be particularly important if a key member of staff responsible for driving the project forward leaves. Schools need to be clear about what they expect from the relationship with another school and to appreciate that learning will be reciprocal. Such links provide the opportunity to learn about others and also to learn from them. Of course, such links can also be local or regional.

Visualisation can help children to plan ahead for issues that they will encounter. Imagining a situation and exploring possible outcomes can offer some children the opportunity to rehearse a range of options and solutions. It can be easy to presume that children have choices when faced with a difficult situation. However, some do not have the experience to draw upon alternatives. I worked with one child who always resolved disagreements by hitting others. Over time, we discussed and planned alternatives (for example, walking away, talking to a peer or 'running off' his anger) and gradually he was able to understand that a range of options were available to him.

Communities of enquiry are core to the approach known as *Philosophy for Children* (discussed further in Chapter 5). They support the skills of enquiry, reasoning and evaluation, and facilitate information-processing and creative thinking. This enables children to explore meanings, beliefs and values within a supportive and secure community of co-learners (for an overview, see DfES, 2005: 56–57). Similarly, *debates* offer the opportunity to develop an understanding of the spectrum of views on a subject. Topics need to be chosen carefully and some issues are inappropriate. For example, discussing the pros and cons of racism would not be productive, but considering options for how to develop the school environment might be. It is important to consider how any element of competition might impact on the learning to be developed through this process. It would be counterproductive for the process to undermine the skills of cooperation or of developing mutual understanding that the activities are seeking to promote: it is not as important to win the debate as to learn through the process.

Buddying provides opportunities to support others and to develop friendships. It provides the opportunity to model and practise the behaviours and values that support the development of a sense of community. It can also enable a child to gain a sense of the needs and perspectives of someone else. As is noted in Chapter 5, whilst it is true that pupils don't just learn about democracy, they live it, they also need to learn about it. Teachers need to consider whether buddying involves a befriending role or whether children need specific support or guidance to undertake this responsibility: we need to be careful not to presume that a child has an innate ability to be a buddy. Taking this a stage further, *peer mediation* requires training and the support of staff in order to help it function safely and effectively. It provides an opportunity for children to work together to resolve disagreements and tensions and thus models a degree of democracy in school. It also provides a mechanism to resolve difficulties that arise from children discussing controversial issues or exhibiting inappropriate behaviours relating to them. This may lead to intervention from the teacher, using other strategies to address attitudes or views that are the underlying cause of cause conflict (see Farrington, 1999; Cremin, 2007; and Hopkins, 2007).

Circle time can provide a valuable opportunity to pause for thought, to address specific needs (e.g. bullying) or to discuss issues of interest to children. The latter is the element particularly relevant to this discussion, although sometimes the issue that prompts the need for a circle time discussion will itself identify a more general need. For example, an instance of bullying might lead to a wider conversation about respect, *'isms' or phobias*, and equality; this may take place on another occasion. Whilst activities such as circle time take time out of the school day, which some would argue is already pressurised, they do give the opportunity to help the school or class community to run more smoothly and can thus create a more productive learning environment in the time remaining (for an overview of approaches to circle time, see DfES, 2005: 51–55; Mosley 2005a; 2005b;

2006; and White, 2008). Planning such opportunities into the timetable for a class can allow teachers to develop progression in learning and to address needs at a point where issues feel less immediate than the moment when they arise.

One strategy that is used throughout this book is that of small-scale case studies. These appear frequently to provide classroom-based situations or research materials that raise or address issues. Several of them are accompanied by key questions. The intention is to use the experience of teachers and other child-care professionals to support our reflections on controversial and challenging issues.

Case study

In one Year 6 class, Dawn asked: 'Why do some people do things that are really bad?' She had brought a newspaper article about a suicide bomber to a discussion of the 'news board'. Each week the class updated this display and had time to talk about issues that caught their interest. Other articles on display included one about a child who had gone missing and another about deforestation in South America. Dawn's teacher commented:

> The children have a keen awareness of issues around the world. Sometimes they bring clippings from the local press, but on the whole they focus on national and international stories. Some have access to newspapers at home and others print articles from the Internet or write their own summary of stories from television bulletins. At first, I found this a daunting experience because I did not know what issues would be brought for discussion. But now that we have established a regular routine, the news board provides a very natural focus and a way to air our concerns and interests. Recently, we had a spate of stories about young people and knife crime. It provided a useful opportunity to talk about how people can be stereotyped as a homogenous group. We now have a ground rule that reminds us not to talk about groups of people as though they are all the same. This was useful when Dawn brought her article today. We are careful to remind ourselves that however the media labels a person, they are not representative of all people in that grouping. I used to emphasise this through my use of questions, but now children make the comment themselves.

The situation in Dawn's classroom raises some key questions that are addressed repeatedly throughout this book:

- How do we help to evaluate news stories and to address any worries or apprehensions that they cause our learners?
- How do we avoid stereotyping and challenge the stereotypes used in some media products?
- Can the interests of children be incorporated into the curriculum, particularly with regard to current, real life situations that concern them?
- How can learners gain some sense of empowerment so that they do not feel helpless in the face of major disasters or tragedies?

- How can a balance be achieved between creating a safe and secure environment in the classroom, whilst also acknowledging the existence of the children's wider worlds?
- What strategies might enhance or augment this approach?

It will be useful to bear these questions in mind as each issue in this book is considered. Each reader will want to apply the examples and questions raised to their own setting and experience.

Working with parents and carers

A key concern identified by 36 per cent of the student teachers in my survey about controversial issues (introduced earlier) is how parents and carers might react to some issues being raised with their children. Using free-flow answers, they identified some significant apprehensions concerning the ways in which the views of parents and carers affect children's views, particularly on matters of sexuality, spirituality/religion and racism. These concerns are particularly important, as there was no prompt within the survey to raise issues relating to parents and carers.

To alleviate these concerns I suggest some strategies, some proactive and some reactive:

- *Keeping parents/carers informed.* If you know in advance that you plan to address an issue with your class, why not alert parents and carers to this through a class newsletter? You can suggest that if parents/carers have concerns, they can contact you to share these. Sometimes, being proactive in this way removes concerns.
- *Sharing the bigger picture.* In the school newsletter and on its website the head teacher can alert parents/carers to the school policy for PSHE and Citizenship and inform them that, at certain times, difficult issues will arise in class and need to be addressed in order to maintain a harmonious atmosphere in the school. They could invite the parents/carers to discuss this at a coffee morning, or have the policy available to read at an open evening. Giving parents/carers the opportunity to raise and discuss concerns in advance, and asking for their support, can help to build a sense of partnership. Some parents/carers will be grateful that the school is willing to address issues that they, themselves, find hard to talk about with their children.
- *Checking school policies* to make sure that you are aware of any guidance on how to approach issues with your learners. This is a key part of keeping yourself professionally safe and making sure you are supporting the aims and ethos of the school. The best way to develop policies in school is through discussion, not by doing what you believe to be right despite what policies say. If you have concerns about the nature of any policies, you can raise these with the head teacher or another supportive colleague.
- *Putting yourself in the parent/carer's shoes.* Empathy can be an effective means of diffusing a situation when a parent raises a concern, and an even better means of thinking ahead and anticipating any difficulties.
- *Responding quickly* to any concerns or comments from parents/carers. Leaving issues aside because they feel too challenging is likely to make them grow rather than subside. If you are concerned about speaking with a parent/carer, why not ask a colleague to

accompany you or at least to be close by? If you cannot address a need immediately, a prompt message asking a parent/carer to call in to have a discussion with you shows that you are taking their views seriously and acting on them.

- *Building relationships* before issues arise. It is always better to meet a parent/carer for the first time on a positive footing rather than having to make initial introductions when there is a problem. This is not always easy or even possible. However, having an open afternoon or just sending a note early in the term to introduce yourself, or to make a positive comment about a child's achievement, can make a link that establishes a positive footing.
- *Asking questions* to clarify the situation when you speak with the parent/carer. Showing that you are willing to listen and hear their viewpoint may help to resolve any difficulties. Try not to launch in on the defensive from the start. Offering a seat and a drink may also ease the start of any meeting.

These suggestions may fail, but they provide starting points for the possibility of cooperation and partnership. If a problem persists or you find that you are involved in a prolonged conversation that is not going anywhere, consider referring the parent/carer to a member of the school's management team and be prepared to join them in a conversation. If possible, you might want to prepare the ground for this before a meeting happens so that your colleague is aware of the situation.

Summary and key points

Over thirty years ago, Rushton outlined the official goals of teacher education in general and in the United Kingdom in particular. He observed that: 'Nowhere are moral, ethical or value goals of teacher training at university level mentioned' (Rushton, 1976 cited in Katz, 1996: 411). Three decades later, and over two decades after the Education Act of 1988 and the introduction of the national curriculum for England, research by Harber and Serf (2006) suggests that trainee teachers in England are still ill-prepared to tackle difficult and controversial issues. From a comparative study based in the UK and South Africa, they argue that student experience does not reflect the claims made by teacher educators in relation to the prominence and delivery of education for democratic citizenship (including issues relating to gender, sexual orientation and 'race').

Although the standards for Qualified Teacher Status (QTS) (TDA, 2007) stipulate that student teachers must be able to create safe and secure environments in which learning can flourish, it would appear that students generally are not being prepared to tackle issues of identity and diversity. Certainly my survey of students suggests a lack of awareness of, and a genuine concern about, these issues. Teacher education needs to support the development of co-operation, mutual respect and open mindedness, 'and make possible the experience of a harmonious and caring environment in which learning can take place' (Voiels, 1996: 159). This is not only an issue for initial teacher education; the need to prepare to deal with sensitive issues also relates to teachers' continuing professional development. It stands in stark contrast to a system that is driven by targets, tests and league tables. One may question whether only what is easily measurable is seen as valuable in the current education system.

The Crick Report (QCA, 1998), which laid the foundations for the citizenship curriculum, suggests two strong reasons for teachers being prepared to tackle difficult and controversial issues. First, without a discussion of controversial issues we fail to address an important element in the educational experience of children and young people. Second, such an omission fails to prepare them for adult life. It argues that children ought to know about the moral, political and religious issues of the day, as they may either be directly affected by them or have some opportunity to make a difference to their communities and affect outcomes. It is important to consider how such issues are dealt with in practice.

The General Teaching Council for England has stated that teachers will be guilty of unacceptable professional conduct if they 'seriously demean or undermine pupils, their parents, carers or colleagues, or act towards them in a manner which is discriminatory in relation to gender, marital status, religion, belief, colour, race, ethnicity, class, sexual orientation, disability or age' (GTC, 2007: 4). This makes a careful consideration of the issues in this book essential. In addition, in a UNICEF report of 21 industrialised countries issued on St. Valentine's Day (UNICEF, 2007), the UK came joint-last with the United States for 'child well-being' (see Cole, 2008d for a discussion). That this is the case, and why it is the case, should be part of every school's implementation of *Every Child Matters*.

It is impossible to implement the *Every Child Matters* agenda (DfES, 2004) without recourse to controversial issues in education and in wider society. To do otherwise is to deny the life experience of the children in our care and to fail to prepare them either for life in the present or their future. Children are facing difficult issues every day, whether they be those relating to finances (including concerns at home about unemployment, bills and debt), bullying (including that relating to 'race', gender and sexuality), worries about environmental issues (such as carbon emissions and global warming), working out how to relate to peers, family issues (for example, arguments with parents/carers and siblings, divorce, parental/carer re-marriage), or bereavement. They are concerned about how they can be listened to and really heard. They are also interested in how they can make a difference to the world and get involved. To ignore this experience and such interests/concerns is to try to educate a child without considering who they really are. To break ECM into its five strands (DfES, 2004), to:

- be healthy
- enjoy and achieve
- achieve economic well-being
- make a positive contribution
- stay safe

without considering the needs of the whole child is to fail to remember that every child matters. I have seen this list re-ordered to form the acronym SHEEP (stay safe, healthy, enjoy and achieve, economic well-being and positive contribution). Sheep may be famous for being followers, but I am sure that an aspiration for our learners is that they become free thinkers and innovators. Readers will note that I have ordered the five elements so that the initial letter of each line forms the acronym BEAMS, a more positive and uplifting *aide memoire* that focuses on the active verbs. Whether these 'beams' are the major planks of effective child development and education or the resulting smiles of our children is for you to decide.

Chapter 2

Living together

Antiracist education in mono and multicultural settings

> When I was seven my dad took me to my first football match. Huddersfield Town was playing Bolton Wanderers at home. We arrived late, without a ticket, and ended up at the back of the cop. I was never a tall child, and at such a young age I only gained short glimpses of the match when I was lifted onto my father's shoulders. Standing near us was a black man trying to sell refreshments. I could not understand the jeers he received from the spectators about the price of the chocolate he was selling, its quality or the need for him to 'take it back to where he came from'. It was the first time I encountered racism and the first time I recall being aware of 'race'.

Antiracist multicultural education is essential in preparing children for life in twenty-first century Britain. Whether children live in diverse or seemingly mono-cultural settings, it is important to explore issues and to help children to appreciate others of different backgrounds, cultures and religions. Central to this is the need to explore racism and xenophobia; with regular headlines about migrant workers entering the UK it is important to appreciate that racism may appear in forms that teachers may not anticipate (for example through attitudes to those from Eastern European countries). This chapter includes issues relating to the families of migrant workers (based around research in the Boston area of South Lincolnshire), refugees and asylum seekers. Fundamental to this is a discussion of human rights; an appreciation of diversity; the need to address myths and misconceptions that have grown up around new populations; and a need to address the recurring debate about 'British' values and culture.

'Race' and racism

The term 'race' is problematic, and for this reason it is used here in inverted commas. In general, social scientists and some geneticists regard 'race' to be a social construct rather than a biological given (Cole, 2008a; 2008b; Rose and Rose, 2005). Indeed Rose and Rose (2005) argue that as a scientific term, 'race' is well past its sell-by date: greater contemporary understanding of DNA suggests that *biogeographical ancestry* might be a more appropriate term. Traditional categorisations of 'race' fail to acknowledge the complexities of the way in which people are made up, and they can lead to large groups being stereotyped. The more that is understood about the complexity of human genetics, the smaller the sub-populations that could be described as 'races'; for example,

> there are average gene differences between the populations of north and south Wales, which contribute to different geographically distributed disease susceptibilities, but it would be a bold scientist or politician who would argue that here are two distinct races.
>
> (Rose and Rose, 2005)

Racism is not problematic as a term: its occurrence is divisive and destructive. It can appear in many forms: at institutional or personal levels; in overt or covert ways; through direct and oppressive (dominative) or exclusive and isolating (aversive) practices; through notions relating to biological factors and those associated with cultural differences; and it can be intentional or unintentional (Cole, 2008b). Racism is any occurrence of the term that is perceived to be racist by a victim or any other person (Home Office, 2001). *The Race Relations Act* 1976 as amended by the *Race Relations (Amendment) Act* 2000 sets out a general duty in three parts (in section 71(1) of the Act): to eliminate unlawful racial discrimination; to promote equal opportunities (although this concept is limiting and will be explored in more detail in Chapter 3); and to promote good relations between people from different racial groups (Home Office, 2001). These three aspects are interrelated and complement one another. It is essential that teachers have a conceptual awareness of what racism is and of their duty to combat it.

It is important to clarify what constitutes unlawful racial discrimination. It is unlawful to discriminate, directly or indirectly, against someone on the grounds of 'race'. Under the act, 'racial grounds' means reasons of race, colour, nationality (including citizenship) or ethnic or national origins (Home Office, 2001). Direct racial discrimination means treating one person less favourably than another on racial grounds. An example of direct discrimination is applying harsher discipline to black pupils because they are black. Indirect racial discrimination means that a requirement or condition that is applied equally to everyone:

- can only be met by a considerably smaller proportion of people from a particular racial group;
- is to their detriment; and
- cannot be justified on non-racial grounds.

All three parts must apply. An example of unlawful indirect discrimination might be where a school's rules on uniform do not allow for a particular racial group's customs and cannot be justified in terms of the school's needs (CRE, 2002: 36). Whatever the controversy surrounding the term 'race', this definition of racism provides a clearer picture.

Case study

It is important to be aware of the stereotypes that can be associated with different groups, including those relating to 'race'. One example serves to illustrate this idea:

> John worked in a large multicultural school in a major town. 'I love working here,' he commented, 'the children come from such varied backgrounds. I have a large proportion of Asian children in my class, and their parents are always so supportive. You can't fault them; you just know that they will be ambitious for their children and make sure they work hard at school.'
>
> (Teacher, Year 6)

These assumptions, that Asian parents/carers are supportive and that their children will be hardworking, reveal a stereotype that leads to presumptions and assumptions that may not be rooted in evidence.

Other stereotypes may include the ideas that some racial groups are good at sport, some are disinterested in school or learning, or that some parents/carers have little interest in being involved in the life of a school. Whilst some children and parents/carers will exhibit these traits, they should not be regarded as a result of their genetic make-up. All stereotypes are invariably problematic and where they relate to ethnic groups are at least potentially racist (Cole, 2009):

> Underlying racism, there is often a more general intolerant attitude to people who are different for reasons other than race (e.g. religion, language, gender, sexual orientation, age, physique, or even dress style or hair style, to mention some of the more obvious).
>
> (Anti-Racist Alliance, undated)

It is important to remember that racism will be encountered by different people in different ways: it is not a homogenous experience. Factors that will affect people's experience, include:

- age
- social class
- disability
- gender
- religion/belief, and
- sexual orientation.

It is self evident, but none-the-less important, to state that the experience of a heterosexual black Caribbean woman will be different from a gay South Asian man. Similarly, when studies consider the often publicised under-achievement of black boys, they need to consider not only whether or not being black impacts upon achievement, but how social class, gender, sexual orientation, economic well-being and age affect achievement. Each person needs to be addressed in their own right and in the light of their own experience. This is true in all instances of discrimination and bullying, not only those relating to 'race'. Furthermore, it is important to challenge the use of the term 'monocultural' wherever it appears. Usually this is used to refer to a setting that is categorised as being white working or middle class. This, itself, is a stereotype that refuses to recognise the diversity within a community.

Pause for thought

Consider the definition of racism provided by legislation as outlined above.

- How does this reflect, or differ from, your existing understanding of the term?
- Do the policies and practices you have experienced in school(s) reinforce this broad definition?
- What is your response to the rejection of the term 'monocultural' in the light of the equality issues outlined above?

Institutional racism

Following the Macpherson report on the Stephen Lawrence Inquiry (1999), the notion of institutional racism gained public prominence. Institutional racism is defined in the Report as:

> The collective failure of an organisation to provide an appropriate and professional service to people because of their colour, culture, or ethnic origin. It can be seen or detected in processes, attitudes and behaviour which amount to discrimination through unwitting prejudice, ignorance, thoughtlessness and racist stereotyping which disadvantage minority ethnic people.
>
> (Macpherson, 1999: 6.34)

Macpherson noted that racism was not only found in the police service, but was also to be found in education and other systems. As professionals, it is our role to make informed judgements based on evidence: we assess children, note their achievements and identify next steps for their development. It is essential that such formative assessments are not affected by preconceptions based on gender, 'race', social class or any other factor. One example serves to illustrate the point.

Case study

When the Foundation Stage became a part of *The National Curriculum* (DfEE and QCA, 1999) in 2002, the existing baseline assessment was replaced with a profile, based on the early learning goals, which involves practitioners' ongoing assessment of the six areas of learning. Many of us will be familiar with this process, where summary profiles have to be completed for each child reaching the end of the Foundation Stage (at age 5 years) in England. An evaluation of this new process, undertaken by Ofsted (2004), found that it was less sophisticated than the previous method and did not provide the same information. It is based on the day-to-day observations that a professional makes of individual children when they are involved in activities in the usual classroom environment; there are no tests or set tasks for the Foundation Stage Profile. Assessment is thus based on professional judgement, which can be subjective. Gillborn (2008) argues that black pupils were judged to be less successful using this process than under the previous system.

This would suggest that, in some cases, teacher stereotypes were affecting the assessment of learners. This idea was supported by Diane Abbott MP, speaking in a debate on black and minority ethnic pupils in the House of Commons (Abbott, 2008):

> In relation to base-line entry tests, black pupils outperform their white peers at the start of school, but the new observation-based foundation stage profile reverses that pattern. Black pupils are disproportionately put in bottom sets, and as someone whose child went through the school system and went to a state primary close to my home in Hackney, I have seen that with my own eyes. The following is an

> interesting quote from a Department for Education and Skills report, *Evaluation of Aiming High: African Caribbean Achievement Project*: 'Whilst many teachers ... believed setting to be based solely on ability, data indicated that African Caribbean pupils were sometimes relegated to lower sets due to their behaviour, rather than their ability.'

It is possible that assessment can establish inequality and that it can maintain it. It is essential to value all learners and to ensure that our teaching and assessment methods take into account their learning styles and needs so that a sense of community where all are valued and equal is established and maintained. We need to identify and challenge stereotypes and to reflect on our own values and attitudes to ensure that we model the fairness and acceptance that we seek to engender in our learners. This is fundamental to enabling all children to learn and to achieve (DfES, 2004). Sometimes this can lead to soul searching and, whilst this process is not easy or pain free, ultimately, it can lead to more inclusive practice. That these ideas echo the *Swann Report* (DES, 1985), considered in more detail below, suggests that the issue of institutional racism is still entrenched in the education system and there remains a significant amount of work to be done.

Islamophobia and xeno-racism

Since the attacks of 9/11 in New York and Washington DC (11 September 2001) and 7/7 in London (7 July 2005), there has been a rise in Islamophobia. Muslims have been racialised and the national media has stirred up a frenzy in which anyone appearing to be Muslim is more likely to be treated with distrust. Debate continues to arise in the media concerning government plans to intern suspected terrorists for prolonged periods of time without charge. Wearing cultural or religious garments causes suspicion and pupils and staff members in schools have become the focus of newspaper headlines as a result (for example *The Sun*, 2006; Pyatt, 2007). Teachers in schools have faced opposition from parents/carers when introducing Islam in Religious Education lessons and have found children withdrawn from participation in visits to mosques. Children are thus faced not only with racialised presentations on the television news, but also racism expressed by their families. In this context it is more important than ever that schools address racism and help children to appreciate that the stereotyping of any religious group is inappropriate. It is crucial to note this racialisation of a religious group, which falls outside the terms of 'race' relations legislation (Home Office, 2001) defined above, but is covered by the *European Convention on Human Rights* (included in the *Human Rights Act*, 1998) and the *Equality Act* (2006) that include discrimination in education settings.

At the same time, some elements of the popular press are demonising migrant workers from Eastern Europe in a new form of racism. Traditionally termed xenophobia (which may be defined as a deep dislike of foreigners) this labelling relates to the categories of nationality, citizenship or national origin as identified in the *Race Relations (Amendment) Act* (Home Office, 2001). As such, this is racism and to term it xenophobia is to seek to dilute its impact and distract from its reality. Sivanandan (2001) terms it xeno-racism; Cole (2009) terms the way in which such workers and their children become racialised as xeno-racialisation: 'a process whereby refugees, economic migrants and asylum-seekers become racialised' (Cole 2008a: 124).

Case study

The example of Karl (aged ten) serves to illustrate one example of xeno-racism:

> I was nervous when I started my new school. It wasn't that different from my old school, but I didn't fully understand what the teacher and the children were saying. They spoke so quickly, but the teacher did put some Polish words around the classroom so that I felt at home ... On the playground I am able to join in playing football – which I love. I love Manchester United and have done for ages. But whether I play badly or well I get called Pole boy and Sauerkraut. It feels like everyone is trying to trip me up and I have to fight to get the ball or shoot a goal. I think I play pretty well, but I am always the last to be picked when we line up ... At home I was always the team captain. It's like they wish I wasn't here.

Schools have an important role to play in helping to integrate refugees, asylum-seekers and the children of migrant workers so that they are able to learn and achieve without fear of racism. Since the Macpherson report (1999), schools have been working to address racism in its overt and covert forms and to face up to accusations of institutionalised racism. The rise of Islamophobia and xeno-racism presents a test for any progress that has been achieved and any policies and practices that have been established. Despite Macpherson, the *Race Relations (Amendment) Act* and official material from the DCSF (and its predecessors) making clear that racist language is unacceptable and abusive, there is still evidence of low level racism in mainly white communities (Gaine, 2005) and a persisting myth that the problems lie elsewhere. There can be an assumption that racism is to be found in urban settings where the population is more diverse (Gaine, 2005; Lewis, 2001; Jones, 1999). There can also be a fear of speaking about racism and of saying the wrong thing. Unless racism is acknowledged and discussed, the problem will remain ignored. There is a danger that racism is associated with violence, which can lead to other examples becoming trivialised or ignored. Varma-Joshi (2007: 161) suggests that:

> Challenging racism forces predominantly white communities to question that which is taken for granted. It demands that we be critical and creative. If we see no evil and speak no evil, we lose opportunities for growth and development.

If we ignore racism, or fail to discuss it because 'it doesn't happen here', we effectively maintain the status quo in which the majority population maintains power (hooks, 2003).

Antiracist education

Education has a major role to play in challenging and eradicating racism. This is termed *antiracist education*:

> An antiracist education examines past and present historical inequalities, slavery, colonialism, fear and hatred, unequal relations and structures of power, negative beliefs and attitudes, learned behaviour, institutional and organisational racism and discrimination,

> both direct and indirect. Racism is frequently unrecognised and, as a set of beliefs and attitudes, it is frequently unconscious.
>
> (London Borough of Tower Hamlets, undated)

Alastair Bonnett (2000: 84–86) suggests six forms of antiracist practice, which he describes as:

- *everyday antiracism*: tackling the occurrence of inequality and racism that forms a part of everyday popular culture;
- *multicultural antiracism*: the affirmation of multicultural diversity as a way of addressing racism;
- *psychological antiracism*: the identification and challenging of racism within structures of individual and collective consciousness;
- *radical antiracism*: the identification and challenging of structures of socio-economic power and privilege that foster and reproduce racism (which I suggest includes challenging stereotypes and assumptions based on social class);
- *anti-Nazi and anti-fascist antiracism*: challenging extreme right organisations and ideas (which may include views held by some parents/carers and views communicated to their children);
- *the representative organisation*: the policy and practice of seeking to create organisations representative of the 'wider community' and, therefore, actively favouring the entry and promotion of previously excluded 'races' (sometimes termed 'positive discrimination' or 'affirmative action').

In all of this, it is essential to ensure that antiracist education does not portray non-white people or particular nationalities as passive or disadvantaged. It is essential to enable people to speak for themselves and to make their own views known. It is also essential to avoid the assumption that the 'white' population is a homogenous group. It is itself made up of many groupings and people from varied backgrounds who, even though white, can be racialised – falsely classified as belonging to a distinct 'race' (Miles, 1982; Cole, 2009) – and thus subject to racism (as exemplified by the story of Karl, above). Antiracist education is not solely about addressing the needs of 'non-white' people; it has a far broader remit and purpose. In some senses it may be better termed *anti-discrimination education*, but the prevalence of racism necessitates its specific focus. It is important to keep returning to the definition of racism presented in the legislation (outlined above).

Case study

One head teacher commented:

> *All our children are white and most are from middle-class backgrounds. Multicultural education is not relevant to them. They don't have the experience of people from different ethnic groups or different religions. It might be important to cover those issues in an inner-city school, but they have no relevance to our children.*

This raises the question as to how this school is preparing its children for life in a twenty-first century world. All the children will encounter a diverse world through the broadcast and paper media and all of them will move from this setting to secondary schools, different neighbourhoods and workplaces, which will reflect a more diverse society. To suggest that antiracist education has no place in this school is isolating, narrow-minded and exclusive. It denies the children the opportunity – and their right – to learn from the rich diversity of the world they inhabit and it fails to engender respect for, and appreciation of, others who are and will become part of the children's lives.

Multicultural and antiracist education

Multicultural antiracism is the affirmation of multicultural diversity as a way of addressing equality. It combines two approaches, which in the past have been in tension. In the 1980s, multiculturalism came to the fore, and was encouraged by the Swann Report (DES, 1985). It was based on the premise that prejudice will be diminished if children learn about each other's cultures. However, the study of music, food and clothing from different cultures did more to create a sense of separateness and division than to build bridges. The approach was often superficial and tokenistic, and was characterised as the 3 Ss: saris, samosas and steel bands (Troyna and Carrington, 1990). In contrast, antiracist education

> starts from the premise that the society is institutionally racist, and that, in the area of 'race' and culture, the purpose of education is to challenge and undermine that racism.
>
> (Cole, 2009: 72–73)

Whilst multiculturalists aim to enrich the curriculum by exploring examples from a variety of cultures and seeking to engender a less ethnocentric perspective, antiracists are concerned more with identifying and challenging racist attitudes and practices. Multiculturalists thus celebrate the value of diversity, whilst antiracists stress the need to promote equality (Craft, 1986). The two approaches need not be mutually exclusive and can be complementary. It is unlikely that racism will end unless diversity is appreciated and valued, but a tokenistic celebration of diversity can prove patronising and even engender racism. Managed sensitively, the two are potentially components of an effective whole.

Teachers may take a variety of different approaches to diversity across a spectrum of practice, including being:

- monocultural practitioners: who see cultural diversity as an obstacle;
- benign multicultural practitioners: who see obvious cultural differences but go little further;
- critical multicultural practitioners: who deal with different ways of life in proactive ways;
- intercultural teachers: who see cultural diversity as a way of enriching the curriculum and build bridges;
- antiracist multicultural practitioners: who value diversity and challenge racism.

I suggest that the final category is the most effective, if it combines the best elements of both multicultural and antiracist approaches. Cole (2009) argues that developments in technology that now allow people to speak for themselves (for example through websites, blogs and e-mails) make it possible to hear authentic voices in ways that make possible antiracist multicultural education. This allows a move away from the patronising and superficial elements, noted above, that undermined multiculturalism in the past. Combining effective multicultural practice with antiracism highlights the important additional dimension of equality.

Tackling issues

Effective antiracist education

Effective antiracist education may include several of the following characteristics:

- *receptivity and being reflective*: being open to new ideas and being willing to evaluate one's own practice and practices within schools form an essential part of minimising racist incidents and of promoting diversity and inclusion. This can include the ways in which parents/carers are welcomed into a school and in which their views are appreciated and acted upon;
- *willingness to identify racism, xeno-racism and Islamophobia*: teachers need to be confident, willing to take note of events that they observe and ready to listen to those who have concerns. This can include being prepared to reflect on oneself and one's own values, attitudes and beliefs;
- *willingness to act*: identifying racism is not in itself an end or a criterion of success. Whilst it is important, more important are the actions that follow and the preparedness to address issues and work for change;
- *being open to change and development*: whatever the current situation in a school, a readiness to develop effective practice in increasingly creative ways is essential to maintain and further antiracist education. A school that can say, 'We have no racism here,' may be in danger of becoming complacent;
- *being proactive and not reactive*: schools need to consider not only how to deal with racist incidents but also how to develop a culture and an ethos in which racism is unacceptable. This may include considering how inclusive displays, posters and children's literature are and addressing issues through the curriculum and assemblies so that they are considered before incidents occur.

Community cohesion

The *Education and Inspections Act* (2006) introduced a duty on all maintained schools in England to promote community cohesion and on Ofsted to report on the contributions made in this area. This duty on schools came into effect in September 2007 and the duty on Ofsted commenced in September 2008. In July 2007 the government issued *Guidance on the Duty to Promote Community Cohesion*. This guidance states that:

> As all children and young people can benefit from meaningful interaction, schools will need to consider how to give their pupils the opportunity to mix with and learn

> with, from and about those from different backgrounds, for example through links with other schools and community organisations.
>
> (DCSF, 2007a: 1)

Such links may come through contact with other schools in a cluster or family of schools, or through links in different locations nationally or internationally. They require a good degree of commitment so that they become well established and they need to be reciprocal. There is a danger that an international link with a school in a less economically developed area can lead to a sense of 'supporting' the partner school, which can in turn reinforce notions of need and dependency rather than challenging stereotypes and recognising commonalities.

If community cohesion meant that 'they' must become like 'us' to form a single homogenised society (whoever 'they' and 'we' may be), any sense of meaningful contact between people would be diminished, if not eradicated. In contrast, the *Diversity and Citizenship Curriculum Review,* written for secondary schools but equally applicable to primary schools, states that

> we passionately believe that it is the duty of all schools to address issues of 'how we live together' and 'dealing with difference' however controversial and difficult they might sometimes seem.
>
> (DfES, 2007: 78)

The guidance identifies different elements associated with the term community. The initial two elements explore diversity within a school community and within the wider community in which a school is set. They form the main concern of this chapter. The focus on meeting with members of the community is particularly key to this process. Such interactions need to work on more than a superficial level if they are to have any meaningful impact. The *Commission on Integration and Cohesion* (CIC 2007: 112) identifies meaningful contact between people from different groups as important in the process of breaking down stereotypes and prejudice. It suggests that contact is meaningful when:

- conversations go beyond surface friendliness;
- people exchange personal information or talk about each other's differences and identities;
- people share a common goal or share an interest; and
- it is sustained long-term (so one-off or chance meetings are unlikely to make much difference).

I would add that it also needs to address issues of equality, otherwise power imbalances will undermine any real relationship building. In addition, the commission suggests that:

> keeping difference in the forefront of people's minds when they are interacting across groups helps them to generalise what they have experienced – so they will take from their encounter not just a revised view of an individual, but of a whole group.
>
> (CIC, 2007: 112)

This focus on difference needs to be linked to considerations of similarity and equality. Appreciating differences can lead to mutual respect and understanding, but it has the potential to become divisive. Appreciating both similarities and differences can help to foster mutual understanding and the sense that we are all similar and different to some extent. In this context it is important to consider how racism can be manifest in contemporary society. The definition of racism (above) includes nationality, citizenship and culture. In this sense the legislation applies equally to white migrants to the UK. It is important that schools do not narrow their definition of racism to such an extent that it fails to encompass the broad definition in the legislation. Promoting community cohesion provides one means of addressing racism (for further discussion on community cohesion and antiracism, see Cole, 2009: 74–75; 86 and 162).

Case study

A pilot project in Lincolnshire schools provided the opportunity for children and members of the local community to come together to share memories of childhood. The *Personal Histories Project* provided a chance for those from very different backgrounds, or varied ages and experiences, to share a common experience, remembering the toys, music, food and games that they enjoyed when younger. It was a chance to bridge differences and to create links. Full details of the project are included at the end of this chapter. Whilst one-off projects may have limited impact, as a part of ongoing work within schools they can stimulate dialogue and help to develop an increasing sense of community cohesion.

Schools have the opportunity to work at a variety of levels in order to develop and promote community cohesion. These can include:

- *school to school* (through collaboration between staff in developing activities and by bringing together schools to share ideas, conversations and experiences);
- *school to parents/carers and the wider community* (through interviews, the use of visitors and research undertaken by children);
- *school to community services* (through interviews and research undertaken by children, e.g. with local councillors, a local newspaper, police officers, etc.);
- *school to other partners* (by developing links with other organisations, e.g. Community Service Volunteers or local companies willing to make links so that staff can listen to children read, or assist with classroom and extra-curricular activities).

Considerations for schools

The following elements arose from the evaluation of the project to develop community cohesion that is detailed in the case study box, above (Woolley and Hanson, 2008). Full details of the project, including its aims, rationale and processes, are available at www.bishopg.ac.uk/personalhistories. The elements provide points of focus for consideration when developing curriculum and community projects to address cohesion and antiracist education.

Preparation

As with all matters pertaining to the school curriculum, preparation is key to a successful activity or project. Any project undertaken in schools will need to consider:

- the amount of curriculum time to be committed to the project;
- the need for an appropriate run-up, including time to identify those willing to work with or meet the children and to consider how the project will fit into and build upon existing curriculum activities/plans;
- how existing school plans can be adapted to use the project to develop the required skills, knowledge and understanding;
- how all members of staff can be made aware of the aims and purposes of the project/activity, and the ways it can be organised, to promote shared vision and ownership and consistency in delivery.

Collaboration

A curriculum-based project in school can provide the opportunity to develop links with members of the community. Schools can do this in a variety of ways, including the use of questionnaires and visits by members of the local community. It may be useful to consider:

- how classes in a school, or children from different schools, can work together to share different experiences, outlooks and backgrounds;
- how the catchment areas of schools vary, and how schools can help each other to access visitors from different backgrounds (including from different agencies/organisations and those originally from different geographical locations and of different nationalities);
- how community cohesion can be developed by schools working together, linking those with different or shared experiences in the same geographical area (i.e. cohesion between groups of children);
- how parents/carers and other community members can be encouraged to participate (in school or through questionnaires, homework activities etc.) to ensure that the project has an impact beyond the school itself.

Integration

Ideally any project or series of activities will be integrated into a wider programme of study within a school. Community cohesion and antiracist education are not a bolt on to the curriculum but need to be a part of the overall ethos. Best practice suggests:

- that community cohesion needs to be addressed before, during and after a project;
- that a project should build upon existing work, or act as a catalyst to further community links and an appreciation of diversity on an ongoing basis;
- that the impact of a project needs to be monitored, e.g. by evaluating children's learning, by monitoring the occurrence of racist incidents/bullying, and by monitoring which sections of the community take part by meeting with children, attending an exhibition or event and whether this reflects the community as a whole;
- that the project should not be the responsibility of one member of staff, so that its themes continue if staffing changes occur.

Sustainability

Finally, sustainability builds on the notion of integration. A school-based project or development in the curriculum needs to be sustainable and to avoid being a one-off week or series of days, which can lead to tokenism. This may be achieved in a number of ways including:

- linking to assemblies at various times in the year;
- building community cohesion into plans for ongoing/future topics;
- identifying possibilities for future (perhaps smaller) activities or events to refocus on community cohesion;
- considering how to build upon progress as cohorts of children move through (and leave) the school.

These points will enable schools to develop a continuum of activities helping to nurture a commitment to antiracism, respect for diversity and an appreciation of the different backgrounds and experiences represented in the school and the wider community.

The notion of 'Britishness'

Key to any consideration of community cohesion is the notion of 'Britishness', which regularly appears in newspaper headlines. It is a concept that provokes heated debate and, whilst it is not a new concept, it is difficult to define and may defy definition. How people understand and respond to this concept has a significant impact on community cohesion and harmony. Readers in other contexts will want to consider whether there are similarities with issues in their own settings.

In the last century, Winston Churchill (1940) famously stylised the British as an 'island race', commenting that Hitler was seeking

> to try to break our famous Island race by a process of indiscriminate slaughter and destruction. What [Hitler] has done is to kindle a fire in British hearts, here and all over the world, which will glow long after all traces of the conflagration he has caused in London have been removed.

This use of 'race' as synonymous with nationality is interesting, and reflects a part of the definition from the *Race Relations (Amendment) Act* already outlined. More recently, during the conflict of 1982, Margaret Thatcher referred to the people of the Falklands/Malvinas as 'an island race' whose 'way of life was British' (Short and Carrington, 1996: 66; see also Cole, 2008a: 117). Later, in 1993, John Major described Britishness saying that in 50 years time Britain would still be a country of:

> long shadows on county [cricket] grounds, warm beer, invincible green suburbs, dog lovers and as George Orwell said, old maids bicycling to Holy Communion through the morning mist.
>
> (Major, 1999: 376)

This comment may have been aimed more at addressing a perceived growing integration into the European Union than the growth in the number of migrant workers in the UK. It paints a picture that seems to reflect Churchill's Britain more than that of Major's own day, if it actually reflects anything more than a fictionalised or idealised vision of a Britain of yesteryear. In October 2008, Prime Minister Gordon Brown dropped plans for a Britishness day, along with suggestions from immigration minister Liam Byrne that it could be marked by such national 'distinctives' as drinking, watching television and appreciating both the weather and Morris dancing (Tibbetts, 2008; Whitehead, 2008). One may wonder what the British people think to such a description of their key pastimes.

Tackling issues

Consider the term *Britishness*.

- What does the term mean to you?
- Are there characteristics or traits that identify someone as British?
- How does the term contrast with others, e.g. Scottish, Welsh or European?
- What might be positive or negative about defining the term clearly?
- How might attitudes to Britishness (from children, parents/carers or colleagues) affect discussions about racism or diversity in your own classroom?

A more recent comment on Britishness was made in response to an article on the website of the *Independent* newspaper (2008):

> Being British is about driving a German car [to] an Irish pub [for] a Belgian beer, then ... grabbing an Indian curry & Turkish kebab, [once at] home sit on Swedish furniture & watch USA shows on a Japanese TV. And the most British thing of all? Suspicion of anything foreign.

This comment reflects the inter-relatedness of people in a global world. These issues are discussed in Chapter 4. It is perhaps important here to note that a reliance on people from across the world for the provision of food, textiles, electrical goods and other services is not a new phenomenon; such links go back decades or centuries, yet still result in headline-grabbing media coverage. There is some sense that to be British means to depend on people the whole world over for our quality of life and the lifestyles we enjoy.

The scientific literature of the nineteenth century is replete with terms such as 'the English race' and 'the Scottish race', implying a relationship between biological and national differences (Rose and Rose, 2005). It is interesting that whilst discussions about contemporary Britishness do not focus on past histories of the empire, at times they do focus on the relationship between the constituent parts of the nation: certainly humour and sporting events reveal the tensions inherent to this relationship. The founding of contemporary Britain under the 1707 Articles of Union passed without major celebration on its three-hundredth anniversary. Perhaps this is one indication of the complex and sometimes indistinct identity of this composite nation (for a discussion of issues relating to personal identity, see Chapter 6). One might hope that a nation made up of the separate entities of Wales, Scotland, Northern Ireland and England might have an appreciation of multiculturalism, although in recent years moves have been more towards devolution than unity. In addition, its history includes settlement from Ireland and elsewhere in Europe. Cole (2008c) notes that there were Africans in Britain, both slaves and soldiers, during the Roman occupation; that Europe has had strong links with India going back 10,000 years; and that migrants have been arriving from China since the mid-nineteenth century (see also Fryer, 1984; Visram, 1986). British multiculturalism is not a new phenomenon.

The notion of nationhood

It is important to consider that the notion of 'nation' is itself a human construct. Whilst geographical features may occur naturally, and may form a part of a nation's borders, the idea of a principality, state or nation is not natural and can change over time. Nationhood can be divisive as well as engendering a sense of pride. National pride often comes at the expense of others, as it can imply superiority and accentuate difference. One only has to consider the traditional preponderance of jokes aimed by the English towards those from Ireland, Scotland, Wales, India or Pakistan to identify inherent attitudes based upon 'race'. Such allegedly harmless humour belies a tension between people from different locations separated only by the establishment of legislation or protocols. It contrasts with the idea of cosmopolitanism, which is outlined in Chapter 4.

Nationality may be important in terms of living under a rule of law, receiving protection and exercising rights and responsibilities. Article 15 of the *Universal Declaration of Human Rights* (UN, 1948a) states that:

- Everyone has the right to a nationality.
- No one shall be arbitrarily deprived of [their] nationality nor denied the right to change [their] nationality.

However, these principles are set out in order to protect persons from genocide (see Chapter 8) and dispossession, rather than to divide and promote distrust.

The notion of 'British values', so often in the headlines of the popular press, itself throws up many issues. To define a sense of such values in a unique way, which is distinct from other countries or groups of people, is difficult if not impossible. Honesty, loyalty, truthfulness, pride, respect, indeed any term one can list, cannot be claimed any more by Britons than they can by Brazilians, Venezuelans or the French. Whilst some elements of culture may be distinctive to a nation, values are not. If values have any relationship to 'race' then it is solely to the human race. Rather than developing a curriculum to celebrate Britishness in our schools, we should be exploring the value of what it means to be human in an interdependent and cooperative world.

Developing practice

Addressing racism can be a complex process and some readers will feel apprehensive about it. In order to develop effective practice, we need to:

- be aware of the procedure for recording racist incidents in our school;

- evaluate how our curriculum and resources combat misconceptions and stereotypes about groups of people and/or individuals;
- consider what place the notion of Britishness has in schools;
- evaluate the balance between being proactive and reactive to racism and discrimination in our classrooms;
- add to the diversity represented in our classrooms through the use of resources (what is currently represented and what is missing?);
- consider how the duty to promote community cohesion has impacted on our teaching and our school ethos, and;
- discuss how to tackle issues from outside the school (e.g. in the media or the views of parents/carers) in positive and effective ways.

As with so many issues, it is only by putting ideas into practice that we truly begin to learn and to develop effective practice. Being open and honest about our concerns and sharing our experience with fellow professionals provide means by which to reflect and progress.

Summary and key points

This chapter has explored 'race' as a social construct, rejected by sociologists and many geneticists. Whilst 'race' may have become discredited as a term, racism is still endemic in social structures and appears in many forms, overt and covert. In contemporary society it has arisen in new forms, including Islamophobia and xeno-racism. Policies and practices in schools can seek to address institutionalised and societal (xeno-) racism, using the combined approaches of multicultural and antiracist education.

Working to genuinely celebrate diversity and to combat inequalities provides opportunities to combat racism and to develop harmonious relationships that accept differences and reject division. This is more than a process of educating our children; it also involves personal reflection and self-evaluation: we will only be successful in challenging racism with our learners if we are willing to engage in the process ourselves (Connolly, 2003). Our own backgrounds and experiences will impact on this process, as has my own journey that started with the vignette included at the start of this chapter. Reflecting on the sources of our own views, values and attitudes is not an easy process, but it is a fundamental part of being a learner as well as an educator. As teachers we have a key place as role models demonstrating the values we seek to nurture in our learners. We also have a role in challenging the notion of 'monoculturalism' that seeks to homogenise communities, which are, in reality, diverse and multifaceted. Multicultural education is not enough in itself: we must challenge racism across the spectrum of its existence and discuss racism to ensure that we do not become complacent and thus allow it to flourish.

Useful resources

Institute of Race Relations: an independent educational charity: www.irr.org.uk

Multiverse: a range of resources on issues relating to cultural diversity and inclusion available at www.multiverse.ac.uk

New Arrivals Excellence Programme: information on working with newly-arrived isolated pupils with English as an Additional Language (EAL) in settings that may have little access to Ethnic Minority Achievement (EMA) support: www.standards.dcsf.gov.uk/primary/publications/inclusion/newarrivals

Personal Histories: a project to develop community cohesion: www.bishopg.ac.uk/personalhistories

The Runnymede Trust: an independent policy research organisation focusing on issues of equality and justice: www.runnymedetrust.org

Further reading

Bonnett, A. (2000) *Anti-Racism*, London: Routledge.

CIC (2007) *Our Shared Future*, sine loco: Commission on Integration and Cohesion.

CRE (2002) *The Duty to Promote Racial Equality: a Guide for Schools (Non-Statutory)*, London: Commission for Racial Equality.

DCSF (2007) *Guidance on the Duty to Promote Community Cohesion*, Nottingham: DCSF.

Gaine, C. (2005) *We're all white thanks: the persisting myth about white schools*, Stoke on Trent: Trentham.

Chapter 3

Family values

What and who makes a family?

> Sarah lives with her mum and her grandma in a small village in Lancashire. Her dad died after being injured by sniper fire during the Gulf war, days before Sarah was born. Now at university, she recalls how, when she started school, she began to realise that her family was different to others. 'I found that I was the only one living with my mum and grandma. Some children just had mums at home but their dads would visit at the weekend to take them out. I couldn't understand why my dad couldn't visit. I used to cry at night when I thought about him never even seeing me. At school everyone seemed to assume that we all had a dad ... at least somewhere.'

Children come from a range of home and family backgrounds. Schools sometimes present an assumption that families are nuclear, through the stories and images they display, through teacher language and through the images that are present in and absent from classrooms. This chapter explores how an inclusive approach to family life can be developed so that children from diverse and varied backgrounds feel that their lives and experiences are valued and appreciated.

As educators it is important to consider that whatever our own experience may be, and whatever our views on the ways in which families should be constructed or function, the children in our care did not choose the circumstances of their birth and have probably not been able to choose their own family or with whom they live. However, by the ways in which teachers relate to parents and carers, the ways in which they develop their classroom environments and the attitudes they exhibit they can send out very significant messages about the importance of family life and the values they place on different kinds of families. This includes attitudes to same sex parents/carers, those from different social classes and ethnic backgrounds or those with disabilities. This chapter considers this powerful position and explores opportunities to ensure that all children are welcomed and respected and that diversity is valued. Importantly, it considers how classrooms and schools can reflect the diversity of society in order to promote understanding and respect.

Pause for thought

Consider what words come to mind immediately when you think of the word family.

- Look at the balance of words: how many are positive, neutral or negative?
- How might your views of family (ideal or otherwise) affect the ways in which you relate to children and their families?

- What do you believe the purpose of family to be? Do you believe that this requires a particular pattern of relationships, or is it based more in values and attitudes?

Families can include one, two or more parents, carers, and members of an extended family; families can be stable, transient or temporary. Change can come suddenly and it is important to consider how to support children when change does occur. In addition, schools need to reflect on how they will support and appreciate the different models of family experience that children bring to the classroom. This chapter considers examples of experience from primary school classrooms and ways of using children's literature to value home and family life.

The diversity of family life

To think of children's families as being a source of controversial issues in primary schools is challenging: we do not choose where or when we are born; we do not select our birth parents; and we may have little control over the circumstances that affect our patterns of home life as we grow up.

Children may live with one or two parents/carers; their parents may live separately and have new partners or spouses giving them more than two parents. They may have been adopted and be aware of this and have questions about their birth parents and the circumstances surrounding their adoption. Their parents or carers may be bisexual, gay, lesbian or transgender. Children may live in circumstances that are different from their peers: in houses of varying sizes, in flats, on boats or in trailers, in urban or rural locations, or in temporary accommodation. Children may live in a family of two people – comprising themselves and an adult; they may have siblings or step-siblings or may live in an extended family made up of different generations. Some children will live apart from their brothers or sisters. Other children will live in more than one location, sharing their time between different adults. Some are looked after by a foster carer and may or may not have contact with their parent(s). Some children are separated from a parent/carer who works away regularly, works very long hours, is serving in the armed services, is in prison, or has died (Morris and Woolley, 2008).

Classrooms include children with diverse experiences of family life. Sometimes these circumstances change dramatically and unexpectedly and this raises many questions in their minds (for issues relating to bereavement, see Chapter 7). The level of security and care experienced by children can vary over time. It is in this context that teachers and other professionals seek to nurture individual development and to promote learning. How we as teachers seek to maximise learning is affected by the ways in which we appreciate the backgrounds and life experiences of the children in our care.

It is often the differences between children that impact on the ways in which they relate to one another. Bullying can arise from perceived differences in family income, social class, ethnicity, attitudes to school, ability and disability, sexuality, personality traits, confidence, family background – indeed any difference whether real or perceived. At times teachers have to diffuse and address situations associated with these issues. However, such conversations cannot be marginalised to circle time; they need to be addressed through an inclusive ethos within the classroom and across the whole school. In other words, schools need to be proactive rather than reactive. Respect for difference cannot appear in isolated pockets of time; it has to permeate all that we do, and indeed who we are, on an ongoing basis.

Sometimes we communicate what we value through our words, actions, attitudes and the resources we make available in our classrooms. However, we can also reveal what we value by the things that we omit. If the texts that we share with children always show families as having two parents/carers of different gender, how does this impact on those living with another model of family life? If a child is being raised by their grandmother or by an uncle, how can they find positive images of that setting that give reassurance and value their experience? I sometimes hear teachers say to their classes, 'Don't forget to tell your mum and dad when you get home ... ' How is this heard by those living with one parent/carer or with another pattern of family life? How might this affect Sarah, whose story started this chapter? Should children have to filter and reinterpret our words so that they apply to their home situations?

Considering attitudes

How we work with children, young people and their families will be affected by our own values and attitudes; it is important to reflect on how these impact on our practice (Woolley, 2008b). The key objectives of education, that children stay safe, are healthy, enjoy and achieve, make a positive contribution and achieve economic well-being (as outlined in the *Every Child Matters* agenda for England, DfES, 2004) can only be achieved through effective communication between schools, families and a range of child-care and support services. Most children spend significantly more time with their family than at school. Valuing the contribution of carers and parents, their knowledge of their child, their skills and expertise and their views about educational provision for their child is an important aspect of schooling (Bastiani & Wolfendale, 1996; Sage & Wilkie, 2004; Abbott & Langston, 2006). The development of the *Every Child Matters* agenda in England has created a system that seeks to promote joined-up thinking between the various agencies that seek to care for children and young people from birth to nineteen years. Some teachers will argue that they have been working in these ways for years; however, this does not remove the opportunity to celebrate the possibilities provided by *Every Child Matters*. Teachers in other contexts may recognise these values and ways of working and may also be exploring how to apply them in their own schools.

In order to qualify as a teacher in England, teachers must demonstrate that they 'have high expectations of children and young people including a commitment to ensuring that they can achieve their full educational potential and to establishing a fair, respectful, trusting, supportive and constructive relationship with them' (Standard Q1, TDA, 2007: 4). This reflects the first aim of the National Curriculum for England, that 'the school curriculum should aim to provide opportunities for all pupils to learn and achieve' (DfEE & QCA, 1999: 11). That the first standard for qualifying teachers and the first aim of the National Curriculum both relate to valuing children in order to help them to develop, learn and achieve is no coincidence. This stresses that equality is not an optional extra or an extra strand to be squeezed into an already crowded curriculum: rather, it is an integral part of the process of learning and teaching. These values are reflected in the *Code of Conduct and Practice* for teachers, issued by the General Teaching Council for England and discussed in the conclusion to this book.

The distinction between equality and equal opportunity is important and warrants brief comment: equal opportunity relates to the chances afforded to people; equality relates to outcomes. In theory, we may all have the opportunity to dine at a Michelin starred restaurant, but in reality it is only accessible to those with sufficient wealth to make the outcome possible. Similarly, it is important to ensure that the education system not only offers the potential for children to access opportunities, but that it also develops a system in which all are valued so that their circumstances do not mitigate against them being able to achieve their full educational potential. For a more detailed discussion of equality issues in education (with particular reference to 'race', gender, disability, sexuality and social class) see the introduction to *Professional Attributes and Practice* (Cole, 2008b).

Valuing families

There can be a tension between our personal values, beliefs and attitudes as teachers and those of the client groups with which we work. This raises questions of personal attitudes versus professional values. One relates to the ways in which we choose to live ourselves, and the other to the ways in which we operate within the work environment. For some of us this will create a tension, especially if we hold passionate or very specific views on the ways in which the world should operate. It is important that our personal views, values and preferences do not get in the way of appreciating the lived experience of the children in our care. We also need to consider what influences our personal and professional attitudes, how they change over time and what identities we have as a teacher (Day et al., 2006). Two examples serve to illustrate the point.

Pause for thought

> When Celina and Shaun speak of all living together with their two mums, how can I [as their teacher] support their experience of family life? One way is by providing positive images and stories that show that their family is valued; another is by making sure that their family is welcomed and by making sure that my language in the classroom includes the variety of home situations that the children come from. In my own classroom I talked of the children's 'adult at home' and of 'your family' rather than 'mum and dad' to ensure that all the children were included. I believe that we need to take an approach that appreciates the diversity of the experience of our learners and includes them all.
>
> (Woolley, 2008b: 115)

A former colleague recounted to me the story of a child in Year 1 who drew his family during a lesson focusing on 'Our Homes':

> He drew his mum, with whom he lived, and his two dads; mum and dad had separated not long after he was born, and dad now lived with his male partner. His teacher asked who the second man was, and when told responded: 'We don't want to see that here.' She told the child to rub out his father's partner (Woolley, 2008b: 115). The devastating effects of such a situation must not be underestimated. Whatever the personal views of the teacher, their professional

role is to support and nurture the child. They are not in a position to judge the child's home circumstances and should not reject or devalue the child's experience of family life.

- Consider your own personal responses to these two examples.
- How appropriate do you consider the strategies to support children (outlined in the first example)?
- What would be an appropriate response to the second example by: the head teacher; a colleague; the child's parents/carers; the class teacher?

It is important that when we talk with children about *families*, we consider the image that we have in our own minds. It may be that we think of our own family, however that may be constructed. We may have positive or negative perceptions of the term derived from our own experience and influenced by the media. However, we need to ensure that our own view is not projected onto the lives of the children in our classes, for their experience will vary from our own in a variety of ways. However we feel that families should be constructed in an ideal (or other) world, it is inappropriate for us to use our own worldview to undermine the experience of the children and young people in our care. The two examples above illustrate how a teacher's view can either value or undermine a child's experience. Such attitudes can nurture or weaken the relationships with children that support learning.

Families in children's literature

One way of addressing diversity in family life is through children's literature. Using picture books can provide a way to discuss ideas, whilst distancing oneself from the immediacy of the issues (see also Chapter 7).

A text that may be useful when talking about families with same-sex parents/carers is *One Dad, Two Dads, Brown Dads, Blue Dads* (Valentine, 1994). It tells the story of the parents of Lou, who are both male and blue. The dads are shown engaging in a range of day-to-day activities. The fact that Lou has two dads is not an issue in the story. Throughout the book his friend asks Lou if his dads are different to her dad, and then his friend wonders why they are blue. The answer is simple: they just are. The book is cleverly written so that the issue is that the dads are blue: the fact that they are both male is incidental. This makes it possible to consider diversity in families, focusing on an aspect of difference that does not require an immediate consideration of sexuality or gender. It provides a positive and humorous illustration of same-sex parents with which some children will identify.

Another text that shows children with same-sex parents is *Josh and Jazz Have Three Mums* (Argent, 2007). It tells the story of twins Joshua and Jasmine. They have two mums, Mummy Sue and Mummy Fran, and a puppy called Bumps. Josh and Jaz's teacher explains that all the children in the class are going to draw their family trees. This unsettles the twins: they lose their appetites and don't want to play when they get home. Eventually they are able to explain to their mums why they are upset – as they are concerned because everyone else at school seems to have a mum and a dad and they are different. The mums retell the story of how the twins were adopted. Their birth mum and dad had been unable to learn how to take care of them; they talk about the different kinds of families in which children grow up. The children realise that they actually have three mums and a dad. Together, the family draws out the children's family tree. The children take it to school and feel accepted and valued by their teacher and classmates. This is an affirming story about adoption and same-sex parents, which also affirms other models of family life. It highlights the need for teachers to be sensitive to the needs and experiences of the children in their care.

A further quality text with this theme is *If I Had a Hundred Mummies* (Carter, 2006). It considers the trials and tribulations that would be faced if a child had just that – a hundred mothers! There would be endless bedtime stories, masses of kisses and people to care, the need for a huge house and a whole range of clutter and junk. There might also be plenty of holidays, lots of sweets and plenty of ice creams. There would be a hundred people to keep an eye on the child and to make sure that she ate her greens. The prospect of one hundred mothers seems daunting and to bring a mixed range of positives and drawbacks. The punch line is that one hundred mothers is not an exciting prospect, but having two is just fine. This is an unexpected end to the book: it provides an affirming message to children with two mums.

These texts suggest that it is possible to present positive images of children's experience of family life in primary school classrooms. Bastiani (1989) considers the ways in which different models or patterns of family life may impact on the classroom, for example the variety of parenting and caring arrangements and styles; particular needs arising from family breakdown (including communicating with parents/carers and issues raised by remarriage); the problems raised by long-term unemployment; and issues raised by different patterns of family life resulting from religion and culture. It is important that as teachers we appreciate the diverse experiences of the children in our classes and take these into account; it is also important that we understand that there will be many issues in children's homes of which we are not aware. Effective home-school communication, and the valuing of children's families that is implicit to this, is highly important (Bastiani and Wolfendale, 1996; DfES, 2003; Abbott and Langston, 2004; Sage and Wilkie, 2004; Woolley, 2008a). It is essential that teachers value and appreciate children's families, in order to make such effective communication possible.

Pause for thought

Consider the following lesson idea for children aged 4–7 years.

Lesson focus: Families are different

Points for discussion:

- Who is in our family? Ask pupils to draw pictures of their family.
- Talk about the differences between families – why are families different? How are they different?
- What other sorts of families are there?
- Ask the class to draw imaginary families and display them.

(DCSF, 2007b: 98)

A suggestion for older primary school children is to look at families in the media. How are they similar or different to our own? What families are not represented?

- Consider how the above activities might help to promote children's understanding of difference and their appreciation of similarity.
- How might knowing about children's home backgrounds help you to be more supportive? How can you create an inclusive and welcoming atmosphere in your classroom and develop relationships of trust with parents/carers?
- How can you ensure that you are inclusive in activities generally?

It is important that as teachers we consider how and why we discuss family life with children in a realistic way. There are several reasons why we may be nervous about this. First, there may be the chance that children share personal issues from the home that the teacher and other children might find uncomfortable; second, there may be the chance that children repeat what each other has said about their respective families, which may cause awkwardness or embarrassment; third, the teacher may wish to promote a particular model of family life or to focus on its more positive aspects (e.g. mutual care, respect, tolerance and love); and finally, teachers may be cautious about the possibility of children asking them personal questions about their own family life. Whatever our reservations, teachers need to consider how to value children's families, and how to represent them in their classrooms, whilst avoiding a tendency to idealise the notion of family: all families disagree or face difficulties at times; it is unrealistic to portray or discuss family life without accepting this (Passey, 2005). If family life and values are only presented in a supposedly idealised manner, then children may assume that something is wrong or inferior with their own family and this may lead to anxiety.

Sharing values

A key value is the belief that children should be brought up in safe, secure and loving environments. I suspect that none of us would reject such a view. The ways of working this out may be interpreted differently by each one of us, and by those we work with in school: colleagues and carers/parents, children and young people. However, the overarching principle provides common ground that goes beyond our personal values and provides a basis for the professional views that underpin our classroom practice. Research has shown that all parents are concerned with their child's education (Tizard, Mortimore & Burchell, 1981; Lareau, 1989; Reay, 1999). It is important to bear this in mind and not to make inappropriate judgements to the contrary.

Such professional views must also extend to the staffroom, where we need to remember that education workers also reflect the diversity of society whether or not they choose to share this with us. It is not only children who bring diverse life experiences into the school setting: teaching assistants, teachers, administrators and other support staff all have lives beyond the school walls. Some may share aspects of these with us and others will keep them private. Whether the diversity of family life is apparent within our staffroom is immaterial; we must act and react in ways that promote mutual respect, trust and professional relationships.

I heard the story of a child that had been taught by their mum how to draw a house whenever the topic of 'homes' came up at school. The child learned to draw a square house with a pitched roof, four windows and a door (Tierney, 2007, speaking at a conference to launch the North Lincolnshire Inclusion Strategy). The parent felt that there would be a stigma attached to the fact that they lived in a trailer as a part of a traveller community. Some local authorities have developed picture books to present the lives of traveller children. One particularly appealing example is *Where's My Teddy?* (Hockey, undated), published by the Durham and Darlington Education Service for Travelling Children. In the current context, where some parents/carers choose not to disclose that they are from a traveller background for fear of discrimination by schools, it is important to show that their background is valued and appreciated.

The accounts detailed so far in this chapter present a challenge for us to develop inclusive schools and inclusive classrooms. A great deal has been achieved in recent years in terms of developing inclusion for children and young people with special educational needs and in terms of addressing 'race'. This process of inclusion needs to continue in order to ensure that we support the development and well-being of all learners and also that of carers, parents and colleagues.

Busting the myth

How do we ensure children's well-being, if we perpetuate the myth that families are made up of two parents, one male and one female, with 2.4 children? This idea is not only outdated and outmoded but also provides the ammunition used by bullies on the playground or school yard (Woolley, 2008b). If we perpetuate such attitudes in our schools, then we are complicit with the bullies and fail to show our children that their backgrounds are valued whether they come from one or two parent/carer households, families with several parents/carers, adoptive or foster families, traveller or extended families, or families that include same-sex parents/carers. We need to challenge stereotypes from the earliest years of education. Key to *Every Child Matters* (DfES, 2004) is the idea that we should foster children's physical and mental health. If we do not organise our classrooms in ways that show that we value the diverse life experiences of the children, we are creating tensions that fail to promote mental health and will cause children to feel, at best, uncomfortable and undervalued.

Case study

One teacher admitted to me that he had never considered how families are shown in his Year 1 classroom (Woolley, 2008b). I asked how many children were from single parent/carer homes, and how many were from traveller or black and minority ethnic backgrounds or living with same-sex parents or carers. I also asked whether these children had access to any age-appropriate literature that showed that their family and background were valued by the school. It was an interesting conversation and he was surprised that he had not considered the issues before. It is important that schools consider such issues and essential that they create inclusive classrooms. In contrast, I am sure that we would wish to consider how children and young people access positive images of different types of family that are not represented within their classes, but that are still significant within the society in which they live.

Community cohesion and change

Increasingly, issues of community cohesion are making the headlines in the local and national press, particularly with regard to the impact of migrant workers and their families (discussed in Chapter 2). Diversity between families can be a key issue in schools and children are often confronted by strong opinions in their homes and local communities. *The Mice Next Door* (Knowles, 1991) tells the story of a group of mice, the Hardy family, which moves in next door to another family. The story outlines the stereotypes of having mice living next door – as perceived by the father and narrated by his children. The father has a negative attitude to the new neighbours, because they are different, yet the mother seems more positive and welcoming. She sees ignorance and sometimes hypocrisy in what the father is saying. In the end, because of the mice's helpfulness, the father's stance is altered and the families become friends. The mice could represent any new family moving into an area. The book challenges the stereotypes held by the father – and the focus on a family of mice makes it possible to apply the ideas to a range of settings and to discuss them in abstract ways that do not directly affect particular individuals. The book needs to be used sensitively as some of the expressions used by the father may be controversial, depending on the circumstances of the children reading the text. It may be best used as a shared text, rather than being read by individual children, so that a teacher can support discussion and address any stereotypes or prejudices held within a class. It may be particularly relevant to addressing issues of community cohesion and considering the coverage of issues in the news media.

Partnership with carers and parents

Vincent (2000) identifies three different roles for parents and carers. First, they can be consumers in receipt of a service for their child from the school or setting. This is an unequal relationship and sees the parent/carer taking a passive role. Second, they can be supporters. In this less passive relationship the parent/carer agrees to back the professionals educating their child. However, the use of their expertise and individual interests and skills is not maximised; rather, the parents/carers agree to affirm the school in its work. Third, they can be participants with a fully active role in partnership with children and professionals. Parents and carers may be partners in many ways: offering help in the setting; attending meetings and courses; running services such as a home-school association; serving as governors or committee members; and helping to produce and organise resources. They are also partners in terms of educating their child and appreciating the highly significant role that they play in this process. As Epstein (2005) notes, we should encourage parents and carers in their important role of 'encouraging, listening, reacting, praising, guiding, motivating and discussing'. This role enables them to fully exercise their rights and responsibilities.

Tackling issues

Research commissioned by DCSF (Peters et al., 2008) found that 51 per cent of parents feel very involved in their child's school life, an increase from 29 per cent in 2001 (based on two-parent households only to enable comparison). Almost half (45 per cent) saw education as being an equal responsibility shared by parents/ carers and schools, with 28 per cent feeling education to be mainly or wholly their responsibility. The survey found that over half the parents surveyed had been involved in helping at their child's school, with the Parent-Teacher Association, a homework club or a parents' forum. (Here I note that Home-School Association or Family Forum would provide more-inclusive terms for such organisations.)

- How do these figures reflect your own expectations and experience?
- What are the main purposes of developing effective home-school links?

It is now over forty years since the *Plowden Report* (Central Advisory Council for Education, 1967) highlighted the need for effective home-school collaboration. For over twenty years legislation and guidance from successive governments has strongly encouraged working in partnership with parents and carers. The 1988 Education Reform Act emphasised parental choice and schools' accountability to parents, and the Children Act of 1989 formalised the concept of parental responsibility. Subsequent documents and strategies have reinforced further this role (QCA, 2000; DfES, 2002; DfES, 2004), emphasising the importance of their involvement in achieving the desired outcomes for their children. Research suggests that parents/carers see the most useful method of communication with schools about their child's progress as being through informal discussions (Peters et al. 2008), with 28 per cent preferring this method. The benefits for parents and carers of such involvement include (Draper and Duffy, 2006; Johnston, 2009):

- gaining a broader perspective on their child's development;
- accessing professionals in order to share their concerns;
- enabling the professional to know their child well.

It is important to help parents and carers to understand the aims, purposes and processes of the education setting so that they can appreciate its provision. Some parents and carers will have negative feelings from their own education and these may affect how they feel when entering the setting. It is important to remember that learning settings may have changed a great deal since parents and carers were, themselves, at school. They may not be familiar with the curriculum or a variety of pedagogical approaches. Engaging parents and carers is not always an easy process and many factors can get in the way. However, the benefits of any progress, however slow or time-consuming, can far outweigh the persistent effort required. Further reading on involving parents and carers in their children's schooling can be found in Hornby (2000), Berk (2001), and Whalley (2001) and strategies are included in the introductory chapter to this book.

Developing practice

In order to develop effective practice, we need to consider:

- how aware we are of the home backgrounds and family patterns of our learners (whilst also respecting the right to privacy);
- how our own experiences of family life affect our values and attitudes;

- whether our resources include representations of the range of family patterns in our classroom and in society;
- how aware we are of promoting positive mental health and how we foster positive self-esteem and self-confidence;
- how the language we use in our classroom is inclusive of different families;
- whether we acknowledge that families share highs and lows or whether we present an ideal picture of families to our learners;
- whether our staffroom is an inclusive place where colleagues from all backgrounds feel welcomed and secure; and
- whether the strategies we use to welcome and involve carers and parents in our classrooms are effective.

Summary and key points

Rather than concentrating on 'family values', this chapter has focused on valuing families. All stakeholders in schools come from a range of family backgrounds and with a wealth of experience of family life. Whether positive or negative (and most likely a mixture of both), each person comes with experiences that shape their view of family and that inform their expectations and values. We now return to the question posed in the title of this chapter: 'What and who makes a family?' All those who value a child's home circumstances help to 'make' a family. A family is more than a legal or biological relationship between individuals; it involves an intangible connection based around relationship and relatedness. Appreciating that connection is a gift that a teacher or any person can bestow upon others: to let a child know that who they are, where they come from and the experiences they have encountered are important to us is fundamental to letting them know how much they matter.

Involving parents and carers in the education process is essential. However, this means that parents and carers must feel that schools are genuinely seeking their views and are seeking to establish genuine partnerships with them (Driessen, Smit & Sleegers, 2005). In addition, teachers and other staff members need to be sure of the benefits of working more closely with parents and carers and need to have the confidence to engage in this process. This can be challenging for those who feel that they were trained to work with children, not adults (Carnie, 2006), and may be particularly daunting for newly qualified teachers who find this a difficult aspect of their professional practice and who would prefer to avoid or limit such communication (Johnston, 2002). It can seem particularly difficult when parents and carers come from backgrounds very different to our own, but this is no reason to neglect building relationships with them.

As education professionals, it is important to remember that whatever our own experience may be, and whatever our views on the ways in which families should be constructed or function, the children in our care did not choose the circumstances of their birth and have probably not been able to choose their own family or with whom they live. However, by the ways in which we relate to parents and carers, the ways in which we develop our classroom environments and the attitudes we exhibit, we can send out very significant messages about the importance of family life and the values we place on different kinds of families. This is a powerful position of privilege and we have the opportunity to ensure that all children are welcomed, respected and valued, and that diversity is prized.

Useful resources

Family Diversities Reading Resource: 100+ picture books to value children's families, available at www.bishopg.ac.uk/fdrr

Griffiths, J. & Pilgrim, T. (2007) *Picnic in the Park*, London: British Association of Adoption and Fostering.

No Outsiders Project; see www.nooutsiders.sunderland.ac.uk

Further reading

Abbott, K. & Langston, A. (eds) (2004) *Birth to Three Matters: Supporting the Framework of Effective Practice*, Buckingham: Open University Press.

——(2006) *Parents Matter: Supporting the Birth to Three Matters Framework*, Maidenhead: Open University Press.

DCSF (2007b) *Safe to Learn: embedding anti-bullying work in schools*, London: Department for Children, Schools and Families.

Herlem, F. C. (2008) *Great Answers to Difficult Questions about Divorce: what children need to know*, London: Jessica Kingsley.

Chapter 4

Developing worldviews

Global citizenship and care for the environment

> Children in Year 2 were collecting information about where their food and clothing originated. Using packaging collected at home, and reading the labels on their clothes, they compiled a list of locations and indicated them with pins on a map of the world. They recorded short video clips thanking people for the contribution they had made to the life of the class, and e-mailed them to representatives from local councils and tourist information offices in each region and country along with a set of questions devised to find out more about life there. The letters, e-mails and brochures they received in return helped them to appreciate that people around the world make a contribution to daily life and to understand more detail about their localities.
>
> (Peter, Year 2 teacher)

Learning to appreciate others is an essential part of developing respect and empathy. This chapter explores human experience in different settings and suggests strategies to challenge stereotypes and misconceptions – both our own and those of children. Including a global dimension in learning (a significant part of which some term *Education for Global Citizenship*) does not only involve considering the lived experience of those in distant places; it also involves appreciating diversity in local communities and regions. Often the choices people make on a local level have a significant impact on distant and unknown others around the world. This chapter explores how to support children in understanding the implications of their choices:

> The lives of children and young people are increasingly shaped by what happens in other parts of the world. Education for Global Citizenship [E4GC] gives them the knowledge, understanding, skills and values that they need if they are to participate fully in ensuring their own, and others', well-being and to make a positive contribution, both locally and globally.
>
> (Oxfam GB, 2006a: 1)

Most of our choices have an impact on other people and on the environment. Environmental issues are concerned with more than 'being green': they include appreciating the social, cultural and physical settings encountered by a range of people on a daily basis. Whilst issues about caring for the planet are of importance, and are explored in this chapter, other issues include human rights, animal welfare and the purpose, role and appropriateness of charitable works. There is a danger that 'charity' can characterise people in distant places as powerless and needy. Whilst aid and charitable giving are important in times of crisis, there is a risk that children come to see those in the 'third' world as dependent and misunderstand their needs and cultures. In addition, it is important to help children to understand that the work of NGOs (non-government organisations) often seeks to help people in difficult circumstances to help themselves and to use their skills and talents in positive ways. It is also important to explore issues of the sustainability of aid projects, and of similar initiatives to develop communities in the UK.

What is global citizenship?

Developing a sense of being a global citizen enables children and young people to begin to appreciate their interconnectedness with others and to consider that there are many ways, both seen and unseen, in which they are related to other people in a range of locations. It takes the notion of a global dimension to learning and stresses an active element, citizenship, which involves engagement and participation. Beginning to feel a sense of the oneness of humanity is one way in which the shared spirit of humanity can be understood, albeit in a partial and evolving manner. Becoming aware of one's citizenship and one's place in the world opens up opportunities to begin to sense the often intangible, and yet very real, connection with others: it adds a global dimension to learning.

The term *citizenship* is often used to indicate membership of a nation state. Such membership involves duties and obligations, such as paying taxes and voting in elections, accepting the rule of law and the consequences of illegal activity. This implies that there can be a penalty for failing to fulfil one's responsibilities as a citizen and requires a framework for compliance and some kind of policing of behaviour. The term *global citizen* may conjure similar associations and raise questions about who or what polices the rights and responsibilities of such persons. One answer might be the United Nations, which has set out expectations for human rights and the rights of the child (UN, 1948a; UNHCHR, 1989). The UN deploys peacekeeping forces to seek to maintain some kind of rule of law in conflict zones around the world. However, this does not address more general day-to-day behaviours or actions by citizens.

There is an alternative view of global citizenship. It is not concerned with law, regulations or policing, nor is it concerned with the artificial human-made constructs and constraints of nation states and political boundaries (discussed in Chapter 2). For example, I may be a Yorkshireman by birth, live in England, Great Britain or the United Kingdom, and reside in the European Union, but these descriptions do not fully describe my experience of being human and, in some ways, seek to divide or separate me from my fellow human beings. We may be aware that our use of resources affects others outside these boundaries: our consumption of food, fuel and imported goods has an impact far beyond the state-based descriptions of who we are. Our sense of forces beyond our control, often brought to us through the broadcast media, means that we live in a context far broader than any demarcated by post code or nationality. Whether it be natural disaster, global warming, poverty, or the impact of HIV/AIDS and disease, we may have an awareness of our interconnectedness with unknown others and a knowledge that we enjoy a disproportionate share of the world's bounty through an accident of birth: had we been born in a different place or at a different time our lives would have been totally different. Whilst living within a nation state, and conforming to many of its expectations, we may thus also have a sense of being pan-national or trans-national. However, it is interesting to question the use of the term 'national' involved in these terms, because they legitimise or reinforce the separation between people and peoples caused by nationhood. The term 'global' seems more inclusive and less restrictive: we all share the planet, the globe, and are thus its citizens. Whilst the term *globalisation* often refers to the power of unwieldy and unaccountable multi-national corporations, this need not invalidate the word global. This is not an argument for a single *global state*; rather, it is an argument in favour of a *global state of mind*. Global citizenship may, in some senses, be a tautology but it is a concept with which it is worth wrestling.

Developing skills across the primary phase

Developing the skills associated with global citizenship across the primary phase of education starts with the local and works outwards to the wider world. Young children's egocentricity requires that learning be centred on themselves, their immediate surroundings and their experience. From this point, it is possible to consider increasing circles of influence and relationship as they grow and mature.

Early years foundation stage

From the age of three, children start to make increasing connections between the different spheres in which they encounter friendships or acquaintances (Papalia, Gross and Feldman, 2003). For example, they realise that Mrs Stevens, who works in the Post Office, also lives in the house opposite them. They are able to form positive relationships with a wider circle of people, including those who help them in their local community (e.g. the school administrator, the fire safety officer who visits school and the local police officer). From the age of 40 months, children have an increasing awareness of different cultures and beliefs (DCSF, 2008a). Taking time in their setting to mark special times of year from different cultures will reinforce children's experience of their own background and introduce them to new ones enjoyed by others. Talk about differences and similarities can help in the appreciation of others and professionals need to be sensitive to any negative comments or attitudes, and work to help children to value difference as being positive. Professionals can make sure that non-discriminatory practices are modelled and valued, by helping all children in a setting to participate in activities and by encouraging turn-taking and listening to one another (Berger, 2000; Dowling, 2005; Berk, 2006; Johnston et al., 2009). By the end of the Foundation Stage, children should be able to find out about past and present events in their own lives and those of their families and people they know; identify features in the natural world and in their locality; and begin to know about their own cultures and beliefs and those of other people. They should also 'understand that they can expect others to treat their needs, views, cultures and beliefs with respect' (DCSF, 2008a: 12). Thus, children in the Foundation Stage are developing both a sense of self and how that self fits into the world around them: they are beginning to understand that they are citizens within their local community and to appreciate that this affects how they treat others and how they should expect to be treated.

Key Stage I

In Key Stage 1, children are making increasing contributions to the development of a sense of community. Their individual interests, likes and dislikes all add to the variety of the experience of playing, working, socialising and learning together. In addition, they are able to share their experience of their home communities and to appreciate the different experience of others (Broadhead et al., 2010). As children grow up, they become more aware that people differ by ethnic origin. By the age of four or five, they may be able to identify basic differences, for example between people whom they identify as black or white. However, an awareness of the constancy of ethnicity does not come until the ages of eight or nine (about a year later than a sense of gender constancy, discussed in Chapter 6). For example, Aboud (1988) found that half the six-year-olds shown photographs of an Italian-Canadian boy putting on native-American clothes thought that the pictures were of different boys. There can be a misunderstanding about how appearance affects who we are or where we come from.

During Key Stage 1, children develop their knowledge, skills and understanding in geography through the study of the locality of the school and a contrasting locality (either in the UK or overseas) (DfEE & QCA, 1999: 111). In addition, the non-statutory guidelines for PSHE and Citizenship (DfEE & QCA, 1999: 137–38) include the need to consider belonging to different communities and to consider how to care for the local environment. Considering where our food and raw materials come from provides the opportunity to explore reliance on people from a range of settings. The sense of citizenship is thus enlarged and begins to include elements from the wider world.

Pause for thought

Consider the short vignette that opens this chapter.

- How might this experience help children to appreciate the experience of people around the world?
- Are there possibilities that stereotypes or misconceptions could be introduced or reinforced?
- How can the use of technology help children to access varied and diverse locations? Can such opportunities provide first-hand contact, which adds reality to their experience and learning?

Key Stage 2

During Key Stage 2, children study both a locality in the UK and a locality in a less-economically developed country (DfEE & QCA, 1999: 114). Their studies include the range of scales: local, regional, national and international. The non-statutory guidelines for PSHE and Citizenship (DfEE & QCA, 1999: 139–41) include: the need to discuss and debate topical issues, which will inevitably include topics from the international news; appreciating the national, regional, religious and ethnic identities in the UK; and considering the sustainability of the environment and the use of resources. The breadth of opportunities includes a suggestion to consider social and moral dilemmas that the children come across in life. Many of the issues that children raise will be drawn from the news media. It is important that their views of countries and localities beyond the UK are not solely informed by this source as it may lead to an impression skewed towards warfare, famine and natural disaster. Curriculum plans need to ensure that children can discover the range and diversity of life in settings other than their own and develop a balanced and realistic picture.

Case study

Children in Year 5 at a rural school communicated with a school in a rural area of South Africa via e-mail and using a web-cam. Initially the two schools exchanged a list of questions, and then children divided into groups to formulate their responses. The answers gave rise to further questions and the children began to develop a dialogue. One school developed an ongoing display of information and the other made a book showing how their experiences were similar and different.

Learners in Key Stage 2 can develop a wider understanding of citizenship, realising that this involves responsibilities toward others. They are able to appreciate that children in varied locations have experiences that are sometimes similar to their own. At this stage it is important to support them in questioning why this is the case and in considering how their actions on a manageable (and local) level can contribute to the well-being of others. (For a discussion of how my own students in primary initial teacher education developed awareness of E4GC, see Woolley, 2008c.)

Addressing preconceptions, misconceptions and stereotypes

Periodically, the citizenship curriculum receives significant media coverage, usually associated with the question of teaching British values (see Chapter 2). What it means to be British stimulates a great deal of debate. However, surely a more useful and constructive question is: what does it mean to be human? What values, attributes and behaviours mark out true humanity? This provides a far more inclusive and positive approach to citizenship education.

Such an approach involves the development of the whole child. It cannot be addressed solely through a single weekly lesson in schools, or even an occasional 'citizenship week', but rather must permeate the curriculum and the ethos of a school. A global dimension can be developed by making links across the primary school curriculum focusing on the development of skills and themes, rather than on specific or individual curriculum subjects. This approach is supported by the curriculum design advocated as a result of the *Rose Review* (DCSF, 2009). By developing children's knowledge, skills and understanding, it is possible to encourage them to explore their own preconceptions, misconceptions and stereotypes of others' beliefs, contexts and lives. This can be achieved by considering issues concerned with learning and by teaching about cultures outside the learners' own experiences, which differ in place, time, beliefs and values. This also links to spiritual, moral, cultural and social development (SMCS), one of the two fundamental aims of the *National Curriculum for England* (DfEE & QCA, 1999), exploring the ways in which we are dependent on others and how our actions and values impinge upon their experiences.

The importance of challenging preconceptions and misconceptions about the lives of others and the context in which they live is significant. Global citizenship provides a useful tool as a part of this process and enables learners to confront their own views and attitudes as well as considering how they can begin to formulate their own views of the world. It may provide one tool as a part of *multicultural antiracist education* (described in Chapter 2). It is essential to enable children to develop empathy with, and an active concern for, the planet and those with whom they share it. The notion of respect is central to this process: there needs to be a growing sense that if we are to take issues of respect seriously, then we need to address difficult and sometimes controversial issues within our teaching. This process also involves the teacher as learner.

Charitable works

Schools are regularly approached by charities and invited to engage in fundraising activities. In times of disaster, these may provide one means of enabling children to gain a sense of making a difference and contributing to the needs of others. These issues will be introduced in Chapter 9. However, it is important to help children to think beyond the immediate, or superficial face of, need so that they begin to question issues relating to human rights and some of the causes of human need.

Key questions to consider when engaging in such activities include:

- How can we avoid stereotyping the recipient group?
- Why does the need exist: should we question some of the causes of the need?
- What additional action can we take to make a difference (e.g. writing to our Member of Parliament, inviting the MP to visit the school or contacting a member of the government)?
- What can we learn about life in the recipients' location and how can this build a wider picture to deepen our understanding?
- How can fundraising become a part of wider learning, rather than being a brief or isolated event?

Such issues will enhance activities undertaken as a part of charity projects. They can help to challenge stereotypical views that suggest that people in certain parts of the world live in poverty or are helpless without external intervention. They can also help older children to question the assumptions behind need and to begin to consider how it arises and the circumstances that sometimes cause it. This can help to create an understanding that development works in two ways: at times we may be able to support others, but also we can learn from their experience and ways of life.

Developing worldviews

The 1988 *Education Reform Act* made social, moral, spiritual and cultural development the concern of the whole curriculum. It should be implicit in a school's ethos and daily routine. Rudge (1993: 16 cited in Steele, 2004: 35) states that two things are essential to create that ethos: 'One [essential thing] is encouraging pupils to have a confidence in their own sense of identity. The second is developing a willingness to value diversity in others.' Measures of cognitive or child development must not restrict or limit how children develop this sense of identity. It is important to consider Bruner's concept of scaffolding – growing as it did out of Vygotsky's research on the zone of proximal development (1962; 1978). His notion of supporting children through experiences slightly beyond their current capabilities, and providing challenging concepts as important developmental tools, are both important aspects of helping to develop a sense of awe, wonder, mystery and otherness. That I am a part of something far greater than myself, which I cannot express, comprehend or rationalise, is a key aspect of such development.

Those engaged with the curriculum for history and geography know that there are no facts without interpretation. This interpretation essentially requires a sense of the collective others in society, for without this it is impossible to gain a sense of justice, fairness, the valuing of a shared humanity, our place in the continuum of history and our responsibility for that developing history. Our impact upon the environment (natural and built) and our consumption of the world's resources necessitate a developing understanding of how our own actions impact upon the whole enterprise that is the survival of this world in a state fit for human habitation:

> Far from promoting one set of answers, Education for Global Citizenship encourages children and young people to explore, develop and express their own values and opinions, whilst listening to, and respecting, other people's points of view. This is an important step towards children and young people making informed choices as to how they exercise their own rights and their responsibilities to others.
>
> (Oxfam, 2006b: 1)

This involves the development of personal convictions and principles to inform one's own life choices and relationships. Thus the curriculum needs to be broad enough to look at the links between ideas and to look beyond the confines of what is immediately apparent. The sense of all people being interconnected and of one's own actions impinging upon the lives of others goes beyond the tangible or measurable and into the realm of human values, in which there is a sense of oneness that is difficult to put into words. Without this overarching sense of a shared humanity, it becomes possible to fragment issues and concepts and to focus on specific incidents without considering the relationship between cause and effect. This overarching sense also supports the interconnectedness of ideas: for example, any discussion about caring for the world's resources needs to include a consideration of the power issues that contribute to resourcing problems (Shah, 1996). Globalisation, citizenship and cosmopolitanism provide three ways of seeing the world that can assist this process. The first two have been addressed earlier in this chapter, and we now consider the third.

Cosmopolitanism

Cosmopolitanism is concerned with the notion that all people are part of a single moral community. It stands in contrast to the ideologies of nationalism and patriotism (explored further in Chapter 2). It has its roots in Ancient Greece and the philosophy of the Stoics and their idea that people live within a series of concentric circles: for example the self, family, community, state and humanity (Nussbaum, 1997). Following the Holocaust of the Second World War (explored in Chapter 8), the concept of 'crimes against humanity' brought the idea into the modern world and developed the sense of individual responsibility that is deemed to exist between all people. The development of the *United*

Nations is one indication of such an international sense of global responsibility. Cosmopolitanism does not require a world parliament (although some would argue for this or for a strengthening of the UN); rather, it can involve feeling a sense of commonality and interdependence with people elsewhere, and thinking and feeling beyond the nation state. In this sense, it relates to many of the ideas about global citizenship outlined above.

The impact of developing worldviews

The experience of learning about the lives of others, of studying a distant place and of encountering different cultures in a local community may each provide opportunities for learners to experience

> different windows through which a new perspective can be gained on the familiar [and the unfamiliar], where wonder and awe can be seen, where before there was only the mundane, where appreciation can be gained that others are using different roads to access the same truths as oneself.
>
> (Bottery, 2002: 136)

Herein is reflected the importance of the local, as well as the global, in E4GC, for an appreciation of the diversity of one's own community or region can be as informative and challenging as an appreciation of wider cultural contexts. Global does not necessarily mean distant. Indeed, the windows need not only represent a metaphor for looking out into different local, national and global contexts, they can also represent the opportunity to look inwards and to reflect on our own values, perceptions and attitudes. Such reflection will help us to avoid leaving decisions and problems in the hands of others. Without this, it is possible to divert responsibility through:

- temporal displacement (where effects, risks and problems are left for a future generation to face); and
- spatial displacement (where a state or organisation imposes environmental harm on a less economically or politically powerful state or organisation).

Leaving the repercussions of our actions in the hands of those weaker than ourselves, or those living in the future, is unethical. This requires us to consider the issue of the sustainability of our choices and actions in the present. There needs to be a move to reduce the resource intensity of production (leading to sustainable production) and to change what is consumed, by whom, and the patterns of consumption (leading to sustainable consumption) (Baker, 2006). This brings us to a consideration of development issues, and the notion of *sustainable development.*

Issues of sustainability and caring for the environment

It is essential to consider what we mean by the term *development.* It means more than economic growth or prosperity, which, at times, have come at the expense of care for the environment. Whilst traditional models of development have led to threats that include biodiversity loss, climate change, deforestation, desertification and water shortages, 'development must include a consideration of its social impact which can affect social cohesion and social and political stability' (Baker, 2006: 211). Development needs to be seen in terms of both environmental and social consequences (details about trends in the UK and a range of data relating to environmental matters can be found in DEFRA, 2008). We can help children to consider what it means to live in the *developed* world: does it involve having more resources than others, additional technologies, increased leisure time, enhanced happiness, or intense stresses and pressures? Considering what constitutes quality of life plays an important part in this process.

The term *sustainable development* can be applied in two ways. First, it is development that can be maintained over time: development that is sustainable. Any project or activity must have the capacity to become ongoing and self-perpetuating. If it will only run whilst aid is being provided and cannot be taken on by local people, it will inevitably be short-term. Second, it is development that gives the planet a chance of survival: development for sustainability. If activity depletes the world of its natural resources to the point where destruction of the environment is irreversible, the planet will become unable to sustain itself. Deforestation, global warming, water consumption and mineral extraction are all examples that may lead to resource poverty and unsustainability. This section will explore both aspects; I contend that both interpretations are required in order to build a full picture of the implications of human actions on settings in various parts of the world. The two are not mutually exclusive by any means, but the nuanced difference is important. The term *sustainable development* is fraught with complexity and there are myriad definitions (for example Dobson (1996) records over 300): even its staunchest advocates are not clear whether it is a means to an end or an end in itself (Scott & Gough, 2003: 3).

Sustainable development is concerned with the requirement to meet human need in the present whilst preserving the environment so that needs can be met in the indefinite future. The term was used by the Brundtland Commission (WCED, 1987), convened by the United Nations in 1983 to consider the consequences of the deterioration of the human environment and natural resources; it developed possibly the most common definition, that sustainable development 'meets the needs of the present without compromising the ability of future generations to meet their own needs' (UN, 1987). In a general sense, sustainability is the capacity to maintain certain states or processes indefinitely. It may relate to three elements, identified as the 'interdependent and mutually reinforcing pillars' of social development, economic development, and ecological or environmental protection (WHO, 2005):

- social contexts relate to the need to ensure that meeting the requirements of the present will not compromise the ability of future generations to meet their own needs;
- economic contexts relate to businesses that have developed their practices to use renewable resources and to be accountable for their environmental impact; and
- ecological/environmental contexts relate to the ability of an ecosystem to maintain its processes, productivity and biodiversity into the future.

It has been argued that a fourth strand should be added to the idea of sustainable development: that of culture. Culture is essential to human emotional, spiritual, moral and intellectual development. It is as important to humankind as biodiversity is to nature (UNESCO, 2001). This understanding adds to the notion of development, stressing that it is concerned with more than economics. This points to the importance of human relationships and interrelatedness as being a key element of sustainability. I would question whether development that is not sustainable is in fact development at all. Indeed, it would appear more to be disaster or folly than development. Development means more than change; it suggests a sense of progress, refinement or improvement. Valuing people's backgrounds, heritage and cultures is fundamental to this process.

Brundtland (WCED, 1987) suggests creative ways forward that go beyond the common assumptions that protecting the environment can only be achieved at the expense of economic development: 'It presents an optimistic view that humankind can work together in constructive and cooperative ways to bring about a sustainable future' (Baker, 2006: 22). Education for global citizenship provides a vehicle to work towards such ends. In order to consider how this can be achieved in practical terms, we now turn to explore issues relating to child development.

A developing sense of environment

From birth, children have a sense and an understanding of their environment. In the first year of life they develop skills in moving their hands, feet, limbs and head, and increasingly learn about their situation and its attributes. From around the age of eight months, children become more mobile and are able to develop curiosity through an interesting environment with age-appropriate resources. Being taken to the park or sitting by a window and being able to watch people go by both provide a chance to gain a sense of the wider world and to realise that we do not live in isolation (Broadhead et al., 2010). Between 22 and 36 months children are usually able to enjoy active play with others and begin to learn about dangers and safe limits as they climb, walk and run. By the age of five they have a stronger sense of their own identity and their place in the wider world (DCSF, 2008a).

During their first years of formal schooling, in the Early Years Foundation Stage and Key Stage 1, children learn increasingly more about their dependence on others, understanding that their clothes and food come from a variety of locations around the world (as illustrated at the start of this chapter) and that they depend on a vast array of different people for everyday items and experiences. Gaining a sense of responsibility for this dependence can be developed further in Key Stage 2, understanding that our over-use of resources and pollution of the air affect people that we will never meet in a variety of locations. Children also become increasingly aware that other people have life experiences very different to their own and come to understand that natural disasters, farming methods, the use of water and human conflict can contribute to famine, homelessness, disease and death. It is not possible to shield children from such knowledge without denying them all access to media sources and censoring their conversations; childhood innocence does not extend to a lack of knowledge about suffering in the world and it is important to help children to overcome any sense of distress and powerlessness.

Case study

Our environment is made up of different factors, including the ecological, social, economic and cultural. These are not discrete facets of the environment but are interlinked and interdependent. Some children develop a natural interest in one or more aspects of the environment and caring for the world around them. In one Year 6 class I taught, a boy cared passionately about animal welfare. I discovered that he was bringing pictures into school, downloaded from the internet and printed at home, showing examples of animal cruelty. He was selling the images during break times and donating the money raised to a local animal rescue centre. Whilst his intentions may have been admirable, his approach was causing distress to some children. We were able to talk about the issues that he cared so passionately about and organised a fundraising activity to channel his energies. We invited a representative from the welfare centre to speak with interested members of the class to act as a catalyst for the fundraising project and wrote a brochure to keep in the school library, advising children how to care for their pets.

The actions outlined in this case study show a concern for the environment and give an example of active citizenship. That the child addressed all four issues of sustainability is remarkable:

- ecological – caring for living things;
- economic – seeking to provide financial support;
- social – engaging others in his quest; and
- cultural – educating others.

On a small scale this shows how one person can make a difference to a situation, and may encourage us to consider how small-scale activities within our own schools and communities can have an impact. Current government initiatives are focusing on issues relating to the environment, development and global citizenship through what is termed education for sustainable development.

Education for sustainable development

The period 2005–2015 has been designated by the United Nations as the decade of education for sustainable development. The *Ahmedabad Declaration* (ICEE, 2007) provides one indication of what this involves, stating that education for sustainable development is essential in order to transform needs created by inequality, loss of biodiversity, increasing health risks, poverty and the climate crisis. It suggests that individuals and communities need to change the ways in which they live in order to address these issues: 'With creativity and imagination we need to re-think and change the values we live by, the choices we make, and the actions we take' (ICEE, 2007).

To address these issues in schools, the DCSF has introduced a range of materials emphasising the importance of education for sustainable development:

> We would like all schools to be models of global citizenship, enriching their educational mission with activities that improve the lives of people living in other parts of the world. There is a global dimension to every aspect of our lives and communities. Sustainable development isn't just about the environment – and it isn't something we can achieve in isolation. The air we breathe, the food we eat and the clothes we wear link us to people, environments and economies all over the world. The decisions we make on a daily basis have a global impact.
>
> (DCSF, 2008c: 1)

It is encouraging schools to develop the global dimension across the curriculum, to consider how its purchases affect those in distant places, to make international links with diverse cultures and to explore the work of the UN and UNICEF with children and young people. Through a national framework for sustainable schools, the government has identified eight 'doorways' that it would like schools to address by 2020:

- food and drink;
- energy and water;
- travel and traffic;
- purchasing and waste;
- buildings and grounds;
- inclusion and participation;
- local well-being; and
- global dimension.

Whilst it is impossible to explore each aspect in detail in this chapter, details of the framework are available on the Sustainable Schools website (included in the resources at the end of this chapter). It is possible, however, to consider some general approaches that can be taken in schools with regard to their environment.

Developing the school environment

Government policy is promoting the idea of sustainable schools in which children learn through direct experience:

> Schools have a special role to play in securing the future for young people. As places of learning, they can help pupils understand our impact on the planet. And as models of good practice, they can be places where sustainable living and working is demonstrated to young people and the community. Tomorrow's solutions to the world's problems may be found by the children in our classrooms today.
>
> (DfES, 2006a: 2)

Developing practice

Teaching about sustainability and care for the environment is not likely to have much impact if it is not supported by strategies to model effective practice in the primary school. Schools can introduce strategies to help children to think about the impact they have on the environment and to reflect on the responsible use of resources, for example:

- organising the collection and recycling of waste (paper, plastics, etc.);
- stressing the need to turn off unused lights;
- collecting rainwater to use on the school garden;
- making sure that paper and other resources are used with care and consideration;
- cultivating produce to be used in the school kitchen;

- composting grass clippings from the playing field and sharing compost or clippings with the local allotment association;
- investing in solar or wind power technology and getting children to analyse heat wastage (though external doors, draught proofing and wearing appropriate clothing so the thermostat can be turned down);
- encouraging children to walk to school together, rather than travelling by car;
- considering how to offset carbon emissions from an educational visit by planting a tree in the school grounds or sponsoring a tree elsewhere; and
- calculating the distance the ingredients in a school meal have had to travel and comparing this with the use of local produce.

Whilst it must be acknowledged that not all schools have green space, and the location of some schools mitigates against safe or easy pedestrian access for some or all children, the process of encouraging children to reflect on, and take responsibility for, small contributions that care for the environment is an important part of nurturing their overall concern for the use of resources. Such considerations form an important part of developing the sense of being a global citizen and including a global dimension in learning.

In order to develop effective practice, we need to consider:

- how we utilise and value issues about which our learners care;
- whether we seek to nurture a sense of interconnectedness with others;
- how our curriculum and resources avoid stereotyping groups of people;
- how we help our children reflect on the idea of responsibility without feeling inappropriate guilt;
- whether we integrate social, moral, spiritual and cultural learning into our planning;
- how sustainable our school is, and whether can we introduce strategies to increase this;
- whether our children are encouraged to care about/for others in local, regional, national and global settings; and
- what the notion of cosmopolitanism can add to our learning setting.

Summary and key points

For the global dimension to find a secure place within the primary school curriculum:

> Teachers need to be equipped to have an understanding of the issues relating to global citizenship, to believe in its relevance for children, to be equipped to select appropriate content, resources, and methods, to appreciate the significance of non-formal education within their schools and to have the skills necessary for self-development.
>
> (Shah, 1996: 55–56)

This requires a focus on process and skills development (DCSF, 2009), rather than on product, outcomes and the confines of a curriculum pigeon-holed in subject areas. Teachers, and the children with whom they work, need to be enabled to make choices and decisions, to design and develop their own approaches to areas that need to be studied, and to be allowed to explore questions that go beyond the formal curriculum and that enable them to develop their own world-views and sense of being a part of humanity in a wider sphere. There is a need to focus on human, rather than state, security, going beyond the mindset of nation to a consideration of global citizenship:

> Only through governance structures that are invigorated through the sense of partnership and shared responsibility, through the expression of empathy for the needs of the many over and above the wants of the few, and through the acceptance of humans as part of, not dominant over, nature, can the conditions be created to bring this development model to fruition.
>
> (Baker, 2006: 218)

This approach needs to be non-tokenistic. The global dimension cannot be addressed as a bolt-on to the curriculum, nor can it be given justice only through occasional special weeks when global issues come to the fore. It is a matter for the whole of the school curriculum, both formal and hidden. All our relationships, reactions, values and attitudes exhibit the sense in which we feel ourselves to be global citizens. Our world-views and, from this, the ways in which we treat others, reveal our sense of being a part of something greater than ourselves and thereby show the construction of our reality.

Useful resources

Council for Environmental Education: www.cee.org.uk
Development Education Association: www.dea.org.uk
Eco-schools: www.eco-schools.org.uk
Global Teacher Project: resources and weblinks - www.globalteacher.org.uk/resources.htm
Healthy Schools: www.wiredforhealth.gov.uk
Oxfam Education: www.oxfam.org.uk/education
Sustainable schools web service: www.teachernet.gov.uk/sustainableschools
The Geographical Association: www.geography.org.uk/eyprimary
The Global Dimension website provides a useful search engine for resources about controversial issues: www.globaldimension.org.uk.
TIDE~ (Teachers in Development Education): www.tidec.org

Further reading

Bignold, W. and Gayton, Liz (eds) (2009) *Global Issues and Comparative Education*, Exeter: Learning Matters.

DCSF (2008) *Top Tips to Develop the Global Dimension in Schools*, London: Department for Children, Schools and Families.

DfES (2006) *Sustainable Schools: for pupils, communities and the environment*, London: Department for Education and Skills.

Hicks, D. and Holden, C. (2007) *Teaching the Global Dimension: key principles and effective practice*, London: Routledge.

Oxfam GB (2006) *Education for Global Citizenship: a guide for schools*, Oxford: Oxfam.

Pickford, Tony (ed.) (2008) *Get Global!: a practical guide to integrating the global dimension into the primary curriculum*, Stoke on Trent: Trentham.

Chapter 5

Democracy, politics and cooperation

Involving children in decision-making and collaboration

> In one school where I applied for the post of head teacher, part of the interview process involved being shown around by a small group of children. These members of the school council showed a real pride in their school and were able to answer many of the questions I had about its ethos and workings. Later in the day, the children met with members of the interview panel to share their views on the interviewees. Whilst I am not aware of the weight that was put on the views that the children expressed, their involvement in the process was an important indication that their voice had some role in the selection process. It made an important impression about the way in which the school worked and what and whom it valued.
>
> (Jeremy, head teacher)

The *UN Convention on the Rights of the Child* (1989) outlines how children and young people should be enabled to have a voice and to express their views and opinions. In the setting of the school it can be difficult to establish practices that truly involve children and avoid tokenism. This chapter explores strategies to develop children's skills in decision-making and collaboration so that they can engage in genuine dialogue within their schools. In addition, it explores how they can appreciate the democratic process in its different forms and develop a voice in matters of social concern. This chapter provides a discussion of generic skills and issues, which are explored in more specific detail in other parts of the book.

What is democracy?

Democracy can be a difficult term to define. On first consideration, it may be described as the way in which the political system works in the UK. However, this is to neglect the different workings of systems in various parts of the world. Political systems may be regarded in two ways: first, the formal structures of governance and second, a values base that informs personal opinion and action. These two approaches may be characterised by structures and a values base.

The structures involve:

- representative and accountable government, elected from a choice of political parties;
- protection of human rights and by the rule of law; and
- freedom of speech and expression, including free and diverse mass media.

The values base includes:

- mutual respect between individuals and groups, including valuing diversity;

- willingness to be open to changing one's mind, and basing one's opinions in evidence; and
- regarding all human beings as having equal rights.

Pause for thought

Consider the notion of democratic values in schools:

- How might stakeholders (for example children, carers, parents, staff, governors, members of the community) be involved in democratic processes?
- Can schools be truly democratic or do they need strong and direct leadership?
- What might be the risks and benefits of developing democratic values in schools?

The term democracy can be linked closely to notions of citizenship and participation. This is often termed *active citizenship*. This term, for many of us, will be something of a tautology. However, in contemporary society it is necessary to emphasise the active nature of citizenship in order to address the interconnectedness of rights and responsibilities. Whether one can be a citizen without being involved in community and society, at whatever level, may be something the reader wishes to consider as the chapter progresses.

The *Crick Report* (QCA, 1998: 44) outlines eight key concepts that children should understand by the end of compulsory schooling:

- democracy and autocracy;
- cooperation and conflict;
- equality and diversity;
- fairness, justice, the rule of law and human rights;
- freedom and order;
- individual and community;
- power and authority; and
- rights and responsibilities.

Whilst these concepts permeate the whole of this book, it is important to consider elements specifically in this chapter. In primary schools it is not appropriate to consider issues in a partisan or party political manner with children. Indeed, this is against the statutory requirements of the Education Act (1996) and is thus illegal. A teacher taking such a politically committed stance would be open to complaints made to the head teacher and governing body:

> The Education Act 1996 aims to ensure that children are not presented by their teachers with only one side of political or controversial issues. Section 406 of the Act requires school governing bodies, head teachers and local education authorities to forbid the promotion of partisan political views in the teaching of any subject in schools; and to forbid the pursuit of partisan political activities by pupils under age

> 12 while in school. Section 407 requires them to take all reasonably practical steps to ensure that, where political or controversial issues are brought to pupils' attention, they are offered a balanced presentation or opposing views.
>
> (QCA, 1998: 56)

The nature and complexity of controversial issues was explored in some detail in the introduction to this book. It is important here to restate the need for balance and for a non-partisan approach. It is also important to consider the nature of the term *political* and what its implications are for primary schooling.

The word politics derives from the Greek word for city, *polis*. In contrast to the contemporary use of the word (which conjures images of offices, shopping malls and skyscrapers), the city was the people and, as such, politics may be defined as being of or about the people. This definition may be useful when considering the issues that are discussed in schools and the structures and procedures by which schools operate. Those of us who define a school as being the community of its members, rather than the buildings, will identify with this term. Whilst we may choose not to use the term with our children, the nature and breadth of its concerns will be a part of what we believe education to be all about. Some people may argue that primary education lays the basic foundations for later learning and life, and is thus pre-political. However, children are already forming their own opinions and ideas, learning about the nature of fairness, questioning rules and taking on roles and responsibilities in their classrooms and schools (Klein, 2001). They have a sense of whether their school is democratic in its processes and whether their voice is heard and valued. Some children will also be aware of the working of political parties and pressure groups. They thus bring a wealth of ideas and viewpoints to the classroom and, I would argue, they should be encouraged so to do. Allowing and supporting discussions, when children bring issues to their classrooms, is a part of developing democratic schools where they all are valued and their opinions can be heard, explored and developed.

Tackling issues

Principles and rights

The principles underpinning democratic approaches to education can be found in documents produced by the United Nations (UN). Article 1 of the *Universal Declaration of Human Rights* (UN, 1948a) states that:

> All human beings are born free and equal in dignity and rights. They are endowed with reason and conscience and should act towards one another in a spirit of brotherhood.

Whilst this statement appears dated in its lack of inclusive language, the assertion that all human beings must have equal dignity and rights is inclusive and all encompassing. The second section of Article 26 of the declaration (UN, 1948a) relates directly to education and to the issues addressed in this chapter:

> Education shall be directed to the full development of the human personality and to the strengthening of respect for human rights and fundamental freedoms. It shall promote understanding, tolerance and friendship among all nations, racial or religious groups, and shall further the activities of the United Nations for the maintenance of peace.

Furthermore, Article 12 of *The UN Convention on the Rights of the Child* (United Nations General Assembly, 1989) states that:

1 Parties shall assure to the child who is capable of forming his or her own views the right to express those views freely in all matters affecting the child, the views of the child being given due weight in accordance with the age and maturity of the child.
2 For this purpose, the child shall in particular be provided the opportunity to be heard in any judicial and administrative proceedings affecting the child, either directly, or through a representative or an appropriate body, in a manner consistent with the procedural rules of national law.

The importance of children being able to express their views is key to these two statements. I argue here that the education system is one part of the formal administrative processes affecting the child, and that the experience and expertise of teachers and other members of staff in schools is fundamental to ensuring that their views are given due weight, in age appropriate ways, in schools. Such elements are reflected in the recent focus on 'children's voice', to which we will return later.

Power and powerlessness

Schools can be places where children learn about hierarchies and power. They will be aware that the head teacher has overall responsibility for the running of the school and is ascribed particular status for this role. The head teacher may be approachable and friendly or a more distant figure concerned with matters relating to finance and management. Similarly, teachers will exercise power in a number of ways. At times this is crucial, for example when making sure that children and others are safe. They will use their power in a variety of ways, and may vary this according to the situation in which they find themselves. One teacher told me that the best compliment he had ever received from a colleague was that, 'In all your time in this school I have never heard you raise your voice.' He felt this indicated the respect that he had for the children.

It is essential that teachers, and other adults in schools, consider their position of power and authority. Not only do they have the potential to be role models with particular influence on children, they also have the ability to make a child's experience of school positive or negative (Merideth, 2007; Lundy, 2008). They are not alone in this, and children do not arrive in classrooms as a blank canvas on which teachers can develop views and attitudes. Some children will already have a well-developed sense of what they can and cannot do, what they like and dislike and whether or not they will enjoy their schooling. It is against this background that teachers are charged to achieve the first aim of *The National Curriculum* for England, namely that all children should be enabled to learn and to achieve (DfEE and QCA, 1999). Whether we take an autocratic or a collaborative approach to our learners will impact significantly on the ways in which we are able to develop a sense of democracy in our classrooms.

Democracy in schools

The *Crick Report* (QCA, 1998) considered how whole-school approaches could contribute to the development of active citizenship and an understanding of democracy. It suggested that such issues needed to be understood in terms of the whole-school ethos, the ways in which a school is organised, its structures and daily practices:

> In particular, schools should make every effort to engage pupils in discussion and consultation about all aspects of school life on which pupils might reasonably be expected to have a view, and wherever possible to give pupils responsibility and experience in helping to run parts of the school. This might include school facilities, organisation, rules, relationships and matters relating to teaching and learning. Such engagement can be through both formal structures such as school and class councils and informal channels in pupils' daily encounters with aspects of school life. To create a feeling that it is 'our school' can increase pupil motivation to learn in all subjects.
>
> (QCA, 1998:36)

Crick also identified three strands that make up effective education for citizenship, with the intention that these should develop progressively as children move through the school system, namely:

- social and moral responsibility;
- community involvement; and
- political literacy.

Whilst a curriculum for citizenship may help to promote the knowledge, skills and understanding necessary for becoming active citizens, this is not enough in itself. Citizenship cannot be marginalised to discussions in assemblies, circle time or single lessons. It is modelled throughout a child's time in school through relationships, the ways in which they are listened to and heard, and the ways in which their views, values and opinions are taken into account. Social and moral responsibility cannot be an occasional focus on a curriculum plan; it is an ongoing way of establishing positive relationships and caring for the school environment. Similarly, in order to be involved in a community, one needs to have more than an occasional role: by its nature community involves ongoing relationships. Political literacy involves the ability to read these relationships, to consider how communities work in effective ways and to explore issues of justice and equality (Hine, Lemetti and Trikha, 2004). One way in which these issues are modelled is through the ways in which parents and carers are welcomed into a school and how their views are considered. White (1999) argues that the ways in which schools work in partnership with carers and parents will affect children's perceptions of how far a school is truly working in democratic ways. Mutual trust, exercised through partnership, is one way of judging the effectiveness of a school's ethos and its commitment to democratic values.

As with all issues considered in this book, this aspect cannot be approached as a bolt-on to the curriculum; by its very nature it is implicit and explicit to all that we seek to achieve through our lives together in schools. This is an approach that was supported by the *Ajegbo Report* (DfES, 2007). Stobbart (1991) suggests that human rights should permeate the whole of the life of a school, including its ethos and how it is organised. By promoting dialogue, showing solidarity with the range of stakeholders, and exhibiting respect and consideration for their views and needs, the school shows that citizenship is concerned with far more than the formal curriculum. This is done in ways that reflect both the formal structures and the values base outlined earlier in this chapter.

Case study

Children in Key Stage 2 held a mock election to coincide with the general election. Pupils in Year 6 volunteered to be candidates and prepared manifestos based around issues that they felt were important in the school community. They devised their own logos and party names, and held hustings in the school hall during break times. On the day before the national election, children voted for their choice of candidate in a secret ballot, with each class visiting the school hall in turn and using the polling booths set out for adult use the day after. An official count was organised by children in Year 5 and the returning officer (the head teacher) announced the winner in a special assembly. It was agreed that key issues raised in the winning candidate's manifesto would be discussed at the next meeting of the school governors.

Justice, freedom and autonomy

> Citizenship equips pupils with the knowledge and skills needed for effective and democratic participation. It helps pupils to become informed, critical, active citizens who have the confidence and conviction to work collaboratively, take action and try to make a difference in their communities and the wider world.
>
> (QCA, 2007)

White (1999) considers how democratic values and practices can be explored and exercised by children. Whilst it may be thought that children need to learn the skills necessary for democracy before being able to engage in it, this is not the case. Democracy is learned through practice. Harber (1998) suggests that democratic skills are learned through action. Whilst this brings the risk of making mistakes, without such a risk there is a danger that schools remain authoritarian. Harber suggests that children need teaching about processes so that they are clear about the nature of their role, can communicate effectively, are able to manage a group, can give a democratic lead and are able to handle conflict (Carter, Harber & Serf, 2003). Waiting until the theoretical foundations of democracy are fully understood will lead to schools never implementing democratic values. Whilst it may, in some senses, seem rational to get the theory right before implementing the practice, this is not how democracy works. If children are given opportunities to question how and why systems work, and to evaluate them in the light of changing circumstances, they will develop the ability to affect circumstances and to help to work towards change.

Democracy is essentially an imperfect system in which people work together to explore options and possibilities through debate, discussion and dialogue. They repeatedly evaluate and hone their practices – working towards a common good in increasing ways. Democracy is never perfect and Utopia will not be achieved. However, people's engagement in the process empowers them to make a difference.

Pause for thought

Consider the vignette at the start of this chapter.

- How might this situation help to give a sense of worthwhile involvement and empowerment to the children?
- What might the children's role add to the overall process of appointing a new head teacher?
- To what extent do you feel the children's views should be considered in this process?

I suggest that if children are given such a role they also need to be debriefed so that they are aware of the outcome of the process and some of the reasons for it. This is particularly important so that the children understand that lots of views and factors affected the choice of candidate. Without this, there is the possibility that they may feel that their view was not really taken into account and this will undermine any future participation.

Working together in community is one means of working towards living a positive and fulfilling life. It is not sufficient to live a good life on one's own. Callan (1997) suggests that the process of seeking what may constitute such a life is fundamental to establishing a shared way of public life and developing respect for fellow citizens. Whilst a textbook or a series of lessons might be able to present key elements including trust, care, respect, appreciation of others and the need to listen, such skills can only be truly learned and internalised through practice, trial and error. A school or early years setting may not only exercise democratic values – it is distinctive because it can nurture them. They are probably the first places where children come together in any number and have to work out how to relate and work together. Certainly they may provide the first experiences of having to cooperate and compromise with those with whom they have not chosen to associate. Learning to listen to others' points of view, coping with disagreement and conflict, learning how to respond when we are misunderstood, and learning to accept others as they are (rather than stereotyping them) are all key elements of this experience.

Primary schools cannot be concerned solely with moral education – issues of right and wrong – leaving the political until later. All human relationships are political to some degree as they impact on the building of an effective sense of community. Being able to handle diversity, understanding the nature of fairness and learning to compromise are all essential facets of a democratic society: this may be society at a local or a national level, and for younger children it will be concerned primarily with their most immediate surroundings. These spheres of interest and influence will grow as they mature. This is an ongoing process that requires persistence and a willingness to work together for the good of all. It requires education professionals to be persistent and to support children in considering the values and attitudes that will help develop a sense of togetherness and mutual appreciation in the classroom.

Key elements

Gregory (2000: 447, drawing on Gilligan, 1993) outlines six elements that contribute to an ethic of care and, thereby, I argue, the building of communities: acquaintance, mindfulness, moral imagining, solidarity, tolerance and self-care (to which I add my own interpretations):

- *Acquaintance* is concerned with the ways in which we develop contact with others, noticing their existence, naming and communicating with them. It is difficult to measure the ripple effects that acquaintance has on others, but it is important to note that our contact and reactions have impact.
- *Mindfulness* considers the ways in which our conduct affects others. It includes developing respect for others because they are fellow humans, whilst also appreciating that they are unique and individual. Thus it is fundamentally concerned with equality, understanding that this does not mean that we all have to be the same. It considers the attention we give to those around us.
- *Moral imagining* provides the opportunity to develop pro-social behaviours such as empathy and altruism. It provides the opportunity to think about what it might be like to be in someone else's position and to face their circumstances, without actually becoming like them.
- *Solidarity* involves helping others to achieve their goals and dreams and exercising a commitment to work on behalf of others. It implies that we are acquainted with and mindful of them. However, we are also able to empathise with and care for strangers.
- *Tolerance* may be viewed as a negative virtue: 'Behaviourally, tolerance is evidenced as much by the absence of repressive actions as by the practice of non-discriminatory procedures' (Gregory, 2000: 450). It provides opportunity to work towards inclusiveness and to accommodate each other's divergent needs and aspirations. However, I feel that the term *respect* encompasses these attributes and find this a more positive (and less begrudging) word.
- *Self-care* stands in contrast to the notion of being selfless. To be selfless implies that one does not matter oneself (it is not the direct opposite of selfishness). Being able to articulate one's own wants and needs is a part of caring for oneself and negotiating this with others is a fundamental part of existing in relationship with them. Citizenship does not require people to deny themselves; it requires the development of a sense of people's equally valuable contribution and place in society.

Gregory suggests that these facets provide the *soil* in which both personal and communal growth can take place through the development of mutual care. They suggest a set of values to be promoted in citizenship education in schools with children of all ages and, importantly, balance the needs of community with those of individuals.

Case study

Samina has been discussing the harmful effects of drug misuse with her Year 5/6 class. The children suggested reasons why people might misuse drugs, including peer pressure, low self-esteem, escapism and addiction. The children identified strategies that they might use to take care of themselves in a situation where they felt pressured to try a substance that had not been prescribed to them and that they thought to be harmful or illegal. Using Sam, a *persona doll,* Samina explored a situation in which Sam needed to say no to older friends who were experimenting with cannabis.

Consider how Gregory's six elements may have helped Samina to explore values with her learners:

- How might the situation help to develop positive contact with others (*acquaintance*)?
- How might the children understand that their own conduct, and that of others, has an effect on wider circles of people (*mindfulness*)?
- How might the use of a *persona doll* help the children to prepare for difficult situations (*moral imagining*)?
- Might the situation help to develop shared values and principles and to understand that saying 'No' is not just based on a personal view held in isolation (*solidarity*)?
- How might the situation support an understanding of the needs of others and an appreciation of the ways in which they behave (*tolerance*)?
- How can Samina reinforce the need to stay safe and healthy (*self-care*)?

The importance of practice

When considering the political nature of education it is important to understand that it is a form of enculturation: it is never value free. It is essential that we do not approach moral education in a didactic manner and impose our values on children. If they are not enabled to understand the reasons for moral and societal values, they will not accept them for themselves; without internalising, such learning values will not be fully embraced. We may be introducing them to common values in society (enculturating them) but they still need to think for themselves. Encouraging children to consider how best to treat one another and to question how they would like to be treated themselves provides a means of developing supportive and inclusive relationships. The example provided by Samina in the case study shows how children can be supported in developing reasoning. It is far more effective for them to explore a hypothetical situation and consider their responses and actions than to be told that drug-taking is wrong and must not be engaged in. Where children present views that are contrary to those generally accepted in a moral and caring society, it is important to help them to evaluate these and consider the reasons for their views. This has to be more than manipulation or imposition: there has to be a real sense of learning in which the values of care, respect and understanding are modelled by the teacher.

To take an authoritarian stance would be to present the antithesis to democracy. For Harber (2002), this would be marked by repression, censorship, intimidation and a lack of openness. Authoritarian education is therefore characterised by a series of negatives – the lack of, or absence of, participation, debate, responsibility and critical enquiry. Indicators of such an approach include rote learning, teacher-centred discipline and a climate of fear. It often involves the subordination or silencing of some groups of learners, including very young children and girls, and the exhibiting of extreme masculinity or compulsory heterosexuality (issues discussed further in Chapter 6).

What kind of democracy?

Who decides what democracy is? How is it defined and introduced? Who has the power to monitor or evaluate its effectiveness?

> Are all definitions equally valuable? If one country – or school – defines democracy in a particular way, is that acceptable as long as it is creating change in some direction, and opening up the debate?
>
> (Davies, L., 2002: 265)

One of the valuable contributions of *comparative education* is to generate discussion to see how different definitions and initiatives may combine to make a powerful force towards a democratising society. It is interesting to note that in South African society, for example, the terms *educator* and *learner* are used in place of *teacher* and *pupil.* After the end of apartheid, many terms, such as these, were changed in order to give a fresh start. This still causes discussion and some controversy. However, it provides one example of how decisions are made in order to move on from past injustices and abuses of power and to seek to emphasise the need for a fresh approach that is free from discrimination. The use of more active words focuses on the individual's roles and, particularly, implies the child's active role in the process. These terms may provide a focus to enable us to consider how roles in a school support democracy in practice. Readers may note that for this reason I often use the term learner, rather than pupil, in this book.

Roles and responsibilities

Parents and carers

It is important to remember that parents and carers are the primary educators of their child. They provide the setting in which early learning takes place and they model skills of decision-making, conflict resolution and negotiation. They also display attitudes towards others and children will learn from these. Those working with children in schools will come across children's expressions of parental/carer attitudes: 'My dad says if Jack is being unkind to me I should hit him before he hits me ... ' or 'My mum says I mustn't play with Sarah because her house is dirty.' Parents' shaping of children's wants, feelings and behaviours is very significant, particularly in the early years. This experience can be individual for a child and may, therefore, be concerned more with the development of personal identity and morality rather than a sense of social or civic responsibility.

Schools

A school may provide a child's first formal experience of a public social institution. Whilst they may have learned about rules and responsibilities in the home, and have gained a developing sense of what constitutes acceptable or appropriate behaviour, the school will provide a context in which shared values and behaviours are outlined to foster a sense of order, calm and safety. This may also be the first place outside the family setting where a child identifies him or herself in terms of being part of a collective: as a member of the school, a class, or subject or ability group.

School may be a place where a child finds that they are regarded as one amongst a group, rather than an individual. They may be in the 'Red Group' for maths or 'Eagles' for literacy. They may have a sense that their ability defines how they are viewed and how they are grouped. They may or may not identify with other children in their group(s) and may gain feelings of self-worth or lack of ability from the ways in which they are classified and categorised.

School councils

In recent years the presence of *school councils* has grown significantly. At best, they provide a way for children to share their views on the running of the school and to express their needs and wants. In some schools, *class councils* feed into this process. As with all structures in schools, it is important to consider how they operate and the ways in which they provide freedoms for the children and ways of expressing their views. If those managing the school limit discussion to minor issues, they limit the contribution that children can make and undermine any sense of a democratic process being in operation.

Case study

Lynn Davies (2002: 262) notes that school councils can often be seen as ineffective. If they are given little or no power they become formulaic:

> A telling example is of one primary school where the council simply decides the 'aim of the month' for students. Such aims include 'walk the corridor silently' and 'roll up your umbrella when you put it in the umbrella rack'. A survey of primary children asking them about who *should* make decisions found them citing only instances where they have been permitted in the past – choosing menus and class leaders.

If children are not given the opportunity to make decisions and to contribute effectively to the life of the school, their past experience is likely to affect their current and future spheres of influence. Thus, if their role has centred on commenting on the menu in the school dining room, the effectiveness of the litter collection team or whether balls should be allowed on the school field at both morning and afternoon break times, their interest and skills are likely to have been stifled. It is unlikely that they will request greater democratic involvement, given that this aspect of their learning has been neglected.

Circle time

The practice of circle time, now common in many primary schools, is one further way in which children can be encouraged to share their view, take turns, listen actively to one another, and share in giving advice and showing empathy. It can feed into the discussions undertaken by class representatives at a school council, or can provide a wider process in which all children in a school can contribute to discussion. The process involves setting and adhering to guidelines and provides the opportunity for adults to model democratic processes (for more detail see White, 1991; 2008; and Mosley, 2005a; 2005b; 2006).

Developing 'children's voice'

Section 38 of the *Education and Inspections Act* 2006 places a duty on schools to promote children's well-being and to take regard of their Local Authority's children's and young people's plan. At the Local Authority level, Section 53 of the *Children Act* 2004 requires due consideration to be given to the views of children and young people before determining what (if any) services to provide where these may impact on children and young people (DCSF, 2008b: 5). Each of these requirements and entitlements is underpinned by *The UN Convention on the Rights of the Child* (United Nations General Assembly, 1989) and the *Every Child Matters* agenda and, in particular, two of the five ECM outcomes (DfES, 2004):

- enjoying and achieving – getting the most out of life and developing the skills for adulthood, and
- making a positive contribution – being involved with the community and society and not engaging in anti-social or offending behaviour.

They can provide the opportunity for children to engage in the process of education, to have a voice and be heard, and to contribute to processes in democratic ways. While there is now widespread agreement with the principle of participation, there is no single right way of supporting children's and young people's involvement. The principles and practices set out in the guidance document *Working Together: listening to the voices of children and young people* (DCSF, 2008b) were identified through consultation as key aspects of involving children and young people and offer a point of reference for Local Authorities and schools in developing their practice. The guidance falls into four main categories, the content of which I summarise here.

Children's rights and well-being

Participation can give practical expression to children's rights and supports their well-being (DCSF, 2008b: 7) by:

- sending a powerful message that children and young people of all ages are citizens too;
- recognising children and young people as major stakeholders in society with important contributions to make to their community;
- enabling children and young people to influence decisions and services that affect them, in order to make them more sensitive to their needs; and
- helping every child to fulfil their potential.

Active citizenship

Participation can support and encourage active citizenship (DCSF, 2008b: 7–8) by:

- offering first-hand experience of how decisions are made and how to contribute to them;
- providing the opportunity to experience how rights go hand-in-hand with responsibilities;
- providing real-life opportunities for engaging with the taught citizenship curriculum;
- developing skills of participation and responsible action, including personal, learning and thinking skills; and
- increasing confidence, self-esteem and aspirations.

Community enhancement

Participation can strengthen communities (DCSF, 2008b: 9) by:

- providing a means of engaging with socially-excluded groups of children and young people;
- improving provision, uptake and cost effectiveness of services targeted at children and young people;
- enabling young people to take action on issues in the community that impact on them;
- giving children and young people the opportunity to mix with, and learn from and about, those from different backgrounds and generations;
- highlighting to children and young people how they can act as positive role models;
- encouraging volunteering; and
- helping young people prepare for the world of work.

Children and young people have equality of opportunity to be involved

Participation can enable equality of opportunity (DCSF, 2008b: 11) by ensuring that:

- no-one is excluded or prevented from participating on grounds of age, gender, ethnicity, disability, religion, culture, language (and I would add sexual orientation), or the area in which they live;
- children's and young people's age, maturity and understanding is taken into consideration when deciding how to support their participation;
- ways are found to involve those who may appear to lack confidence or motivation;
- support is provided to help 'hard-to-reach' groups, for example disengaged young people, looked-after children, and those facing the greatest barriers (e.g. some pupils with special educational needs); and
- children and young people understand that they share responsibility with others for helping to support and promote effective participation.

This guidance shows the government's stress on children's participation and the importance of *children's voice* in schools and society. It draws together elements of personal responsibility, rights, citizenship, and a contribution to the community. It is limited by its consideration of equal opportunity as opposed to equality (a concept that is discussed further in Chapter 3). However, it does provide a broad range of considerations to help facilitate inclusive and democratic classrooms.

Pause for thought

Consider the ideas presented in the guidance given above.

- How do you respond to the range of elements involved in developing 'pupil voice'?
- Are there elements that currently do not form part of your classroom practice?
- Might some elements cause individuals to feel pressured? Could some aspects lead to negative responses or reinforce stereotypes?
- Undertake a SWOT analysis of the four headings used in the guidance, identifying the strengths, weaknesses, opportunities and threats that might arise from implementing these values in your classroom practice.

Considering real life experience

Hughes and Sears (2007) consider how suitable situations for exploring ideas can arise from everyday situations. They suggest that some examples can serve as 'anchors' that provide a context to study, or 'springboards' that launch us beyond the facts, helping us to evaluate our own personal values and beliefs and to test our views against those of others. Using stories of Emmeline Pankhurst and the suffragette movement, Florence Nightingale's and Mary Seacole's transformation of nursing, or Rosa Parkes' contribution to civil rights in the USA, it is possible to consider real life examples of people who have made a stand against injustice and inequality.

Such examples provide the opportunity to consider how people faced issues in their own contexts and how their insight and persistence led to dramatic and long-lasting changes in society. Clearly, they need to be handled in sensitive and age-appropriate ways. They can also provide a catalyst for considering how we approach issues in the present day and to consider what active citizenship really means in a society where we have the opportunity to exercise democratic rights. By studying real life examples, children have the opportunity to ask questions and to formulate their own views. Lessons in which an autocratic teacher presents what children should believe are likely to have little impact on helping them to form their own values. Being able to raise one's own concerns, participate in debate and engage in problem solving are far more likely to have long lasting consequences. 'Doing citizenship' in this way will help to give the sense that you can make a difference (Claire, 2001).

One approach that is growing in popularity is *Philosophy for Children*. Here, children reason and explain their thinking using the Socratic method, with the teacher acting as a facilitator rather than a repository of knowledge. They are able to listen to, and build upon, the ideas of others and so develop a 'community of enquiry'. The teacher helps by challenging assumptions and helping children to take their questioning to deeper levels. The resulting dialogue enables children to develop their own views on the stories and questions being explored; they can also assist in the development of an understanding of democratic rights and responsibilities. Further details can be found at the end of this chapter.

Developing practice

In order to develop effective practice, we need to consider:

- how we plan to develop and support *children's voice*;
- whether schools can be democratic without this being tokenistic;
- how we support our learners in being active citizens;
- how we foster the idea that the school is its members rather than the building;
- what place learning about human rights and responsibilities has in our classroom;
- what strategies we use to learn democracy through practice, trial and error;
- how we support collaboration with carers and parents;
- whether we model democratic values in our relationships with stakeholders across the school; and
- how the ethos of our school supports this practice. Which elements help and hinder the development of democratic practice?

Summary and key points

This chapter has considered the place of democracy in the education system, drawing particularly on key government documents and initiatives. Fundamental to any discussion about developing democracy and citizenship in primary schools is the need to acknowledge that it is concerned with more than preparing children for future life. Learners can only understand what democracy entails by trying it out; it is not a collection of information, or facts to be learned now and applied later.

Creating genuine opportunities for children to voice opinions is central to this process, whether it be through class and school councils, circle time, dialogue between children and staff or some other means. This needs to be non-tokenistic and to relate to more than insignificant discussions and decisions. In addition, democratic practices need to involve a wide range of stakeholders in order to ensure that they all feel involved in the life of the school and so that its ethos is consistent with the values it is seeking to promote.

Sharing power is not always an easy experience, particularly for those who have come to enjoy the status and privilege it brings. However, if we want our children to understand the nature of democracy, they must be active participants and recognised partners in decision-making. How this translates into practice may not be easy, but that is the nature of democracy: it is about imperfect people exploring how to develop an imperfect system, and doing so collaboratively. This is a worthwhile journey on which to embark with our children.

Useful resources

Association for Citizenship Teaching (ACT) - a professional subject association for citizenship teaching: www.teachingcitizenship.org.uk

Philosophy for Children: www.childrenthinking.co.uk www.philosophyslam.org

The Citizenship Foundation: www.citizenshipfoundation.org.uk
The Institute for Citizenship: www.citizen.org.uk/Democracy/democracy3.html

Further reading

Claire, H. (2001) *Not Aliens: primary school children and the Citizenship/PSHE curriculum*, Stoke on Trent: Trentham.

Cremin, H. (2007) *Peer Mediation: Citizenship and Social Inclusion Revisited*, Buckingham: Open University Press.

DCSF (2008) *Working Together: listening to the voices of children and young people*, London: Department for Children, Schools and Families.

Hughes, A. and Sears, A. (2007) 'Teaching the contested and controversial nature of democratic ideas: taking the crisis out of controversy', in H. Claire and C. Holden (eds) *The Challenge of Teaching Controversial Issues*, Stoke on Trent: Trentham.

Ross, A. (2007) 'Political learning and controversial issues with children', in H. Claire and C. Holden (eds) *The Challenge of Teaching Controversial Issues*, Stoke on Trent: Trentham.

White, M. (2008) *Magic Circles: self-esteem for everyone through circle time*, London: Sage.

Chapter 6

Gender, identity and acceptance

Together everyone achieves more

> We lost the cup final last night. I was gutted. Year 5 had made it right to the end of the under-11s tournament for the first time ever. We were going to draw until the last minute, and then one of them got past me and ran for the goal. Afterwards I tried to joke it off. Mr Evans said, 'It was a team effort and we lost as a team.' I know that I lost the game for everyone and I carry the responsibility as team captain. I went round to thank everyone for playing so hard and even went to thank the staff and parents for coming to support us. I thought, 'If I can just keep busy, I will get through this.' But inside I was crying my eyes out. I didn't go straight home. I sat in the park and cried until I couldn't do it any more.
>
> (Gary, aged 10)

Children, like all people, are continually wondering how they fit into the world. Who are their friends? Are they popular? How do they feel about others? Developing a sense of one's own identity is implicit in many chapters in this book. Here, the issues are considered through gender, considering how boys relate to boys, girls to girls, and how the genders relate to one another. Gender stereotypes are explored along with strategies to question, challenge and address them. The chapter encourages education practitioners to think about their own views and biases and to develop ways of supporting the development of individual identity in their classrooms. This provides an additional dimension to the consideration of how to appreciate myriad different others, covered at several points in this book.

Gender issues are commonly thought about in primary schools. However, issues of diversity in identity and sexuality are looked at less frequently. This chapter is significant in its reflection on the ways in which schools reinforce and challenge stereotypes about gender roles and sexualities. This chapter considers how gender roles develop in the early years of schooling, and progresses to look at ways in which they can be considered in appropriate and supportive ways later in primary education. In addition, it considers issues of self-image including eating disorders. Essentially, all these areas relate to a child's mental health and well-being: it is thus important to explore strategies for dealing with issues of identity, difference and stereotyping in our classrooms.

What is gender?

The term gender has come into common usage in recent years. One only has to look at surveys and statistics to see it used as a synonym for biological sex. As the word 'sex' has become problematic, so the term 'gender' has come to replace it. This undermines or marginalises the original use of gender, which referred to the social construction and societal judgement of roles, expectations and experiences related to people's biological sex. Claire and Holden (2006: 1) argue that:

> The importance of resurrecting the original meaning of 'gender' is that it draws attention to the ways in which inequalities between the sexes are based on social constructions and not on biology and are thus open to challenge and remediation.

Traditionally, society has been patriarchal; male has been the norm and woman has been the 'other' (Paechter, 1998). By discussing gender, and not biological sex, possibilities are opened up for a transformation of society (or at least for its evolution) to address inequalities that have grown up over generations. Gender roles are learned and have varied throughout history according to time and place. What is seen as an acceptable style of dress or behaviour for males or females is different according to place, time and culture. In addition, people have refused to conform to the expectations or 'norms' of society throughout history and continue to do so. The definition of gender outlined above, and used in this chapter, includes a range of ways of being female or male, including identity relating to sexuality. Furthermore, the notion of *societal judgement* includes the use of common stereotypes including those relating to traditional power relationships, heterosexuality and heterosexism, and thereby opens up possibilities for change.

Gender and child development

From their earliest years, children have an awareness of gender. By 36 months most children can correctly label their own or another person's gender and are said to have achieved gender identity (Smith, Cowie and Blades, 2003). This is followed by gender stability (at around four years of age), when children understand that gender is normally stable, and gender constancy (by around seven years of age) (Papalia, Gross and Feldman, 2003), when they understand 'conventional' sex role behaviours and have developed fixed gender role ideas. Gender will play an important part in a child's sense of self as they mature; having security in their gender identity as a part of their overall sense of self will help to give them the confidence to be themselves. Williams and Best (1990) found that in over 30 different countries boys are expected to show instrumental traits (e.g. competitiveness and assertiveness) and girls are expected to show more expressive traits (e.g. care, sensitivity and being considerate). As professionals, we need to be aware of those who do not conform to traditional gender roles or stereotypes, as this is a common cause of bullying, which can crush self-esteem (DfES, 2000; DCSF, 2007b). We need to consider how to get beyond such stereotypes so that children can be themselves without restriction and we need to challenge stereotyping when it occurs.

The *Gender Equality Duty*, which came into force in 2007, is a result of Britain signing up to the *Millennium Development Goals* (UN, 2000; EOC, 2007). It requires all public bodies, including schools, to promote gender equality and to eliminate discrimination. The third of the eight millennium development goals is:

> to promote gender equality and the empowerment of women as effective ways to combat poverty, hunger and disease and to stimulate development that is truly sustainable.
>
> (UN, 2000)

Thus schools not only have a moral duty to work towards equality but a legal duty to eliminate gender discrimination.

Gender, socialisation and the family

From birth, children are characterised according to their biological sex and come to understand the associated traditional gender stereotypes. One only has to browse the greeting cards available in any shop to see that newborn girls and boys are imbued with expectations relating to gender. Browse further to see that each year of childhood has a birthday card signified with stereotypical images. Even later in life, greetings for aunts, uncles and grandparents are tinged with blue or pink, racing cars or flowers, footballs or kittens. There is an expectation that we will each behave according to societal 'norms' and fulfil certain expectations. Thus, when Stuart can iron his own shirts and Laura can mend the engine on her motorbike people comment, even in the twenty-first century.

Each child has a culture defined by their community, and more uniquely by their family:

> Gaining knowledge and understanding of their own culture and community helps children develop a sense of belonging and strong self-image … A positive self-image and high self-esteem gives children the confidence and security to make the most of opportunities, to communicate effectively and to explore the world around them.
>
> (QCA, 2000: 29)

Knowing that one has the unconditional love of parents/carers helps to make it possible to be confident in one's own identity and in exploring how to express that identity. Of course, such a level of care does not remove the possibility that family members will disagree with a child's decisions or behaviours, but it allows for critical discussion within a secure and supportive environment. For a child to know that they are loved and accepted, no matter who they are, is a potent and powerful experience that can bring the confidence to find out more about themselves.

Families communicate a great deal about gender through their behaviour and expectations. From an early age comments by parents/carers inform children of the path that is anticipated for them:

> 'He's always been good with his hands … he'll easily get a trade when he's older.'
>
> 'She'll be a real catch for someone one day, she's a real stunner and she'll turn heads.'
>
> 'She's an advanced reader for her age. We have high hopes that she'll get a profession and do us proud.'
>
> 'We don't mind what he does in life – so long as he is happy.'

Comments such as these sow seeds of expectation that children interpret and evaluate. They gain a developing sense of whether they are going to fulfil parental/carer hopes and begin to sense whether their evolving identity fits in with the expectations of those around them. The ways in which family members model gender roles, and how children are encouraged to play, work and socialise alongside their parents/carers, play an important part in the socialisation of children.

Case study

It is Jenny's birthday. She has brought small cakes to share with her class and explains how she made them herself, with help from her dad. Her teacher, Mrs Stopes, asks Jenny whether her mum helped: 'My mum works away most of the time. She is always jetting off to Canada or Brazil. She brings me back great presents, but dad looks after me and he is a great cook. When I grow up I want to be just like him.' Mrs Stopes says that she wishes she could cook as well as Jenny's dad.

Consider how this situation might provide an opportunity for the class teacher to discuss gender roles with the children.

- Do you anticipate that the discussion would be wholly positive?
- Might it raise any sensitive or difficult issues?

Gender inequalities

Statistics collated by the *Equal Opportunities Commission* (EOC, 2006; see also ONS, 2005b; 2005c) indicate that in Britain there are:

- 7 million families with dependent children, of which 5.2 million families are headed by couples; and
- 1.6 million families headed by a lone mother and 180,000 headed by a lone father.

Thus, around one-quarter of families are headed by a single parent, with a 9:1 ratio of female to male. Issues concerning families are explored in some detail in Chapter 3. However, whatever a child's experience of family life, it is important for schools to consider how children can access positive role models of both genders and how a variety of gendered behaviours are presented in classrooms.

Gender inequalities also exist in the workplace. Overall, 67 per cent of women and 79 per cent of men aged 16–64 are in employment (EOC, 2006: 12). Of these, 42 per cent of women and 9 per cent of men work part-time, and 58 per cent of women and 91 per cent of men work full-time. In 2005, average hourly earnings for women working full-time were £11.67, and for men were £14.08. This gave a gender pay gap of 17.1%. Women working part-time earned £8.68 on average and men £9.81, a pay gap of 11.5%.

Pause for thought

In some homes gender roles conform to traditional or stereotypical 'norms'.

- Is it the role of schools to present a range of gender roles?
- How might this reinforce or conflict with children's learning in their homes?
- How can schools avoid stereotyping gender and ensure that all children have positive aspirations?

Reflecting on the statistics about patterns of work and family life (above), consider how your learners might respond to this information.

- What questions might your learners raise and what attitudes might they exhibit?
- How could you enable the children to challenge gender stereotypes and to question any assumptions or misconceptions they already hold?
- Why, after legislation over past decades, do such inequalities still continue between men and women?

Gender and achievement

The increasing success of girls in the English school system is reflected in the now annual debate and comparison between genders when SATs, GCSE and GCE results are published. These bring into question how it is possible to engage boys and to encourage them to see learning as being important. Belying this view is the sense that men have traditionally identified themselves in terms of dominance and superiority, but now find themselves achieving at lower rates than their female counterparts. Bunting (2000) questions how males will accommodate women's equality, when so often their identity has been built on the subordination of women. Traditionally, male identity has been derived from a sense of power and from power-relationships. This power can be exerted through bullying, sometimes with a homophobic edge, that serves to normalise certain ways of being masculine and to determine where a boy is positioned in a hierarchy of masculinities (Mills, 2001a).

In a setting where some boys and men are finding themselves achieving less than their female peers, it is important to explore how men develop a sense of maleness and a sense of personal identity now that the tradition of dominance is undermined and untenable. Skelton (2001) suggests that what is required is a move away from stereotypical understandings of what constitutes masculine and feminine in order to transcend the limitations of sex-role theory and to appreciate that the gender identities commonly enshrined in male and female bodies are restrictive and now discredited. It is important to remember that people not only differ in terms of gender, but also differ a great deal in ethnicity, location, age, socialisation, family structure and cosmology (Morrell, 2005). This is developed further in the next section. Being a human is a diverse, individual and unique experience and both male and female learners need to be able to explore this in their own ways.

Gender, class and ethnicity

It is important to understand that gender is not an isolated factor affecting equality; it is also necessary to take into account ethnicity and social class (which reflects the discussion in Chapter 2). In addition, other factors such as sexual orientation, disability, age and religion/belief impact on how people are perceived and treated and are the causes of discrimination. Cole (2008b: 14) uses the term 'ism/phobia' to encompass the range of causes of discrimination, including racism, xeno-racism, sexism, classism, disablism and homophobia, transphobia, Islamophobia and xenophobia. This approach, he argues, is more sociological than the psychological concept of prejudice. Whatever our backgrounds, be they in the social sciences or not, this provides an interesting means through which to explore standing against such discriminatory mindsets.

Such isms/phobias can be interlinked. A Bangladeshi lesbian may be discriminated against because of her biological sex, gender, sexuality, ethnicity and/or social class. There is a danger that any or all of these facets may be stereotyped: discrimination comes in a variety of forms and must be considered from many angles (Claire and Holden, 2006). Similarly, gender must not be seen as an homogenous issue: for example, the experience of black or white women from middle- or working-class backgrounds and of different ages will vary considerably and will involve very different discriminatory practices. When discussing discrimination it is important to ensure that we do not fall into the trap of stereotyping those whom it affects. Similarly, boys' achievement is often considered in terms of gender, but the factors may be more complex. Whilst headlines may proclaim that boys are not achieving sufficiently high standards in English, it is not all boys who are underachieving but particularly those from lower socio-economic groups (Francis and Skelton, 2005; Coultas, 2007).

Case study

John developed a role play area in his Year 2 classroom to link with a topic on healthy eating. The 'Garden Centre' role play area included a range of tools, seeds, plant pots and compost, items of produce and a sales area. He had observed that some elements of play had been affected by gender stereotypes in the past and thought that this situation was more gender neutral. To encourage all the children to access all the different activities in the area he provided role cards – each identifying a job or task in the garden centre. To join in, each child took a card at random from the pack and joined in the activities accordingly. John reflected that this provided the children with the opportunity to try out roles that they might not otherwise have chosen and ensured that, over time, they accessed a range of experiences. 'I also saw that children who often take on the quieter or less-active roles in play were given additional confidence, because the pack of cards decided their place in the group. They became the head gardener or the shop manager and I was surprised to see how some of them rose to the occasion.'

When considering issues relating to identity, it is useful to be aware of the scale of diversity within the population. The Equal Opportunities Commission (EOC, 2006: 4) outlines that in a population of approximately 58 million people there are around:

- 29,690,000 females and 28,435,000 males (a ratio of 51:49);
- 10 million disabled people (i.e. those reporting a limiting long-term illness or disability that restricts daily activities) (17% of the population);
- 4.6 million people from minority ethnic groups (8% of the population);
- 3.1 million belonging to a non-Christian religion (over 5% of the population); and
- 2.3–3.2 million gay, lesbian or bisexual adults (4% – 5.5% of the population).

Whilst some of these figures may vary between surveys, depending on how terms are defined, whether people are willing to share information, and how they identify themselves, they still show large segments of the population in groups that commonly experience discrimination. Each of these areas impacts on gender identity.

Gender and the media

Whilst family and close personal relationships may be the main socialising factors affecting children, the media plays a key role in the secondary socialisation of children (Marsh, 2005). One only has to survey commercial breaks in-between children's television programmes to appraise the messages that are being promoted about clothing, toys and gendered behaviours.

A wealth of information and images about gender and gender roles are readily available to children and young people through magazines, the Internet, and television. Many children are able to view television channels where music videos demonstrate a sexualised culture and where reality television shows participants discussing and demonstrating their sexuality and sexual desires. Some will have access to a whole host of information via the Internet, sometimes without the supervision of their parents/carers. This may include being able to view materials with varying degrees of pornographic content. Some children will access pornographic magazines or videos owned by their parents, carers or siblings, with or without their knowledge or permission. On mainstream, prime-time television, a wide range of 'soap operas' has addressed issues of divorce, homosexuality, incest, rape and, more recently, paedophilia (Woolley and Mason, 2009). Children thus receive a great deal of information and see a range of role models, without necessarily having the maturity or experience to interpret them. These relate to a range of gendered identities.

One example is that through media representations and social relationships, boys are pressured to exhibit certain behaviours. Francis identifies that they are expected to show displays of 'hardness' (1999: 100), 'having a laugh' (1999: 65), sporting achievement, an interest in pastimes and subjects construed as masculine, showing off (Francis, 2000) and non-studious behaviours (Skelton & Francis, 2003). Whilst this may be the position in the playground, at times the media appears to embrace diverse ways of being male. Masculinities work at different levels: the national and international level of identifying with heroes and role models, and the local level of finding acceptance and one's place in friendships and community relationships. Sometimes the two conflict and boys come to understand that what may be acceptable in the media is not as acceptable in their community or family, and vice versa. They also come to understand what is acceptable in school, both from peers and staff.

Identity perception

This section considers in more detail the notion of masculinity as an expression of gender. In the past, many inequalities have been created and perpetuated by men and their use and abuse of power. In a variety of dominant roles (whether in government, communities or the family) men have exercised positions of control. It is necessary to consider the legacy of this history and how it can be addressed if gender equality is to be achieved.

Whatever progress has been made in terms of attitudes or legislation, society has not become as progressive as it sometimes wishes to appear. It still remains important to boast about sexual activity in order to posture within hegemonic (heterosexual) masculinity and apparent difference is only accepted against the background of a certain sense of what it means to be a man. Connell defines the leading pattern of masculinity as being hegemonic: in other words, that which is 'culturally exalted' or 'idealised' (1990: 83). It is certainly an example of how gender is commonly perceived, using the definition outlined earlier in this chapter. This notion of male potency derives from traditional stereotypes of the heterosexual man. Despite moves towards greater equality under Blair's *New Labour* government (1997–2007), including the equalisation of the age of consent and the introduction of civil partnerships, there are still dominant expectations for what constitutes maleness within society (Woolley, 2007b).

Case study

Dan and Andy were the only two boys in the Year 5/6 choir. Dan decided to stop attending because he was being called names in the playground, and Andy soon followed because he felt awkward in the group. The head teacher invited students from the local performing arts specialist college to attend an assembly, including the Year 10 guitar group and sixth form jazz choir, both of which have an equal gender balance. As a result, students from the sixth form started to visit the school once each week to lead a lunchtime music workshop. The head commented that, 'We wanted to support both boys and girls in their musical talents and interests. By bringing role models from the local secondary school we have been able to begin to address some of the stereotypes found amongst our younger learners and to encourage additional children to access music for enjoyment.'

- Consider how appropriate you feel the head teacher's response to be. What alternative strategies can you suggest?

Various typologies have been suggested to analyse male behaviours in school. The bravado of *macho* and *laddish* behaviours (Mac an Ghaill, 1994) is one means used by boys to protect themselves from those who seek to question or undermine their masculinity. Connell (1989) identified the *cool guys*, *swots*, and *wimps*; Mac an Ghaill (1994) the *macho lads*, the *academic achievers*, the *new enterprisers*, and the *real Englishmen*; and Martino (1999), using the pupils' own descriptive language to organise findings, the *cool boys*, *party animals*, *squids*, and *poofters*. Whatever the value of seeking to categorise masculinities, it is clear that there is a continuum. Such diversity is not fixed, and individuals may experience different aspects of being male, depending on the setting in which they are operating. It is essential for educators to be aware of this diversity and to consider how they will address such variety in their quest to help each individual find ways of expressing themselves in their own community (Woolley, 2007b).

In the UK media, portrayals of men appear to show that diversity across a spectrum of masculinities is valued. However, when a political figure admits to being gay, this media openness is revealed as being superficial. When a pop star is accused of being gay, he feels it may be necessary to take legal action in order to clear his name. In the media, diverse masculinities (and male sexualities) are not so much welcomed or embraced as tolerated, found conveniently interesting or sensationalised (Woolley, 2007b). Publicity about one's sexuality (and thereby, for some, one's perceived masculinity) can still be an unwelcome intrusion or even a threat to one's career.

Gender conformity

The risk of being seen as different exerts a great pressure on children to conform to social norms and expectations. This is illustrated by the story of Gary that is outlined at the start of this chapter:

> ... both heterosexual and homosexual boys who do not conform to the requirements of hegemonic masculinity always have the potential to be subordinated within the social organization of masculinity. The fear of this happening leads many boys to become complicit in maintaining existing gendered power relations.
>
> (Mills, 2001a: 142)

The threat of being treated differently and of being identified as 'different' causes some boys and men to live within the general confines of society's expectations: 'Homophobia and misogyny are two of the most important policing mechanisms of dominant masculinities' (Mills, 2001b: 63). Men who have a different view of masculinity from the perceived norm are pressurised into conforming, or at least appearing to conform, to the expectations of those around them. Gender can be used as a tool of social control, and this may be the most important consideration, rather than biology, psychology or spirituality (Baird, 2004). Violence and abuse perpetrated by men is thus a mechanism in asserting power over others and in seeking to ensure that others conform to stereotypical norms. The need to posture within the hierarchy of power relationships leads men to seek dominant positions over others. For male pupils, teachers and trainee teachers this can lead to a culture of secrecy and silence about their private lives if they do not conform to the stereotypes expressed by colleagues.

Some children are open about their sexuality at school (NUT, 1991; Epstein, 1994) and identify themselves as gay, lesbian, bisexual, transgendered, transsexual, questioning, curious or heterosexual. Some, if not all, staff will identify as being in one of these categories, whether openly or not. Virtually all children will be aware of issues relating to sexuality and will know people in real life, or through the media, who talk about their sexuality. It is important to remember that it is illegal to discriminate on the grounds of sexual orientation and that homophobic remarks, 'jokes' or insults need to be tackled.

Pause for thought

Jason is in Year 6. After a lesson delivered as a part of a sex and relationships programme, he approached his teacher to ask a question when the classroom had emptied for playtime. 'What about if I like another boy?' he asked. 'I haven't got a boyfriend but what if I want one? ... I have got some great friends but I don't know if they really like me. If I ask them and get it all wrong they will ... I don't know ... what might they do? You didn't tell me about liking boys.'

Consider Jason's questions:

- How might you respond if a child approached you with similar questions?
- How could you value Jason's honesty whilst also helping him to stay safe and offering him support?
- What concerns might you have about Jason's situation and how would you address these?

Jason's teacher told him that he was too young to know whether or not he was attracted to boys. She told him: 'It might be a phase and if you tell someone you might regret it. You might change your mind.'

- Is it appropriate to educate children about sex and relationships whilst presuming that they are all heterosexual?
- What messages does this communicate to children with other sexual orientations?
- What role models do children have, derived from published and broadcast media? How can their awareness of a range of sexualities be addressed in age-appropriate ways in primary schools?

A positive response to Jason's situation would be to say how special it is that he has decided to share his question with you. You could offer to speak with him again if he wants to talk about any issues, or if he has any problems, and you could affirm that your care for him is unconditional. As with all children, you will want to make sure that Jason is happy in school and positive about his learning and relationships with others. In this, he is no different to any other child. Should any issue arise with regard to bullying, your school's policies and procedures should be followed as normal: intolerance, discrimination and bullying are not permissible for any reason and this is enshrined in law in the UK. The more difficult question many teachers will ask themselves is, 'What should I do now about what Jason has told me?' I suggest that this is best approached through a conversation with Jason. Clearly he trusts his teacher and for her to tell others without asking him first (unless she has reason to believe he is at risk of harm) will undermine the relationship. It may be that he is happy to have asked his question and wishes to do no more about it at the moment. It may be that he is happy for his teacher to ask the school nurse, his parent(s) or someone else to give him advice. To act without speaking to him first could put him in a position where he feels pressured and loses control of the situation. It may also be appropriate to reassure him that the content of the lessons on sex and relationship education about self-respect and staying healthy and safe apply equally to boys and girls, whoever they feel attracted to. Legally, all must wait until the age of consent is reached (16 years in England) before engaging in sexual activity. We can also ensure that our classroom is a safe and accepting environment, where all needs and differences, whether known or not, are treated with respect.

Case study

A case from James, a Year 5/6 teacher, provides an example of how respect was encouraged in one classroom.

In my classroom there was a brief set of 'class rules' agreed during circle time at the start of the academic year. These included: *We respect each other's property; we keep our hands and feet to ourselves;* and *we use kind words and quiet voices.* If there was an incident in class, I was able to refer to the rules and to ask a child how we had agreed to behave. When a child called another a hurtful name, I was able to ask, 'Was that a kind word to use?' The rise of the use of the word 'gay' to indicate dislike (for example, 'That coat is so gay,' or, 'I hate football, it is so gay') challenged this rule. I amended it so that it was not the word that was inappropriate, but its usage. I could now ask, 'Did you use that word in a kind way?' This meant that the child's motivation, rather than a word itself, was questioned and they were encouraged to have positive attitudes to one another.

Self-image and health

Media images present a range of messages that pressure children and young people. Significantly, they convey notions of ideal body image that may affect children's sense of self-confidence and self-worth, and affect children's health (both physical and mental), which is a responsibility of schools (DfES, 2004). This is leading to the increasing occurrence of eating disorders amongst children. In 2006, NHS hospitals treated 58 children under ten years old for eating disorders. This included 35 boys (Disordered Eating, 2007). Over 13 months, 206 children under 12 years old were treated for an eating disorder in Britain and Ireland – including one six-year-old girl. Researchers at the British Paediatric Surveillance Unit asked 2,600 psychiatrists and paediatricians how many eating disorders they had diagnosed in children aged five to 12 years. From the results, they estimated that 3.5 children in every 100,000 in the UK are treated for an eating disorder, including anorexia, bulimia and binge eating. Around 18 per cent of cases identified were seen in boys, which is a higher proportion than in older age groups (BBC, 2007). Whilst it is beyond the scope of this chapter to explore these issues in detail, information about anorexia nervosa, bulimia nervosa and related eating disorders is available from NICE (2004). Further sources are included at the end of the chapter. Sarah Teather, when Liberal Democrat Shadow Education Secretary, commented:

> Sadly these figures only represent the tip of the iceberg. Many more children are suffering in silence and trying to appear as if everything is fine. Teachers have a key role in recognising and supporting pupils that are struggling in school because they are coping with hidden mental health problems. This is especially true where the parents may be unaware of their child's condition. As childhood becomes increasingly commercialised, young people are forced to grow up much quicker. It isn't surprising that this manifests itself in larger numbers of young children with mental health problems, including eating disorders.
>
> (Disordered Eating, 2007)

In addition, the rise in childhood obesity suggests that advertising may have an impact on children's consumption of unhealthy foods (see also Chapter 9). The presence of media resources (e.g. television, gaming consoles and computers) in their homes may also lead to a less active lifestyle. Childhood obesity in England has doubled in 10 years. A survey of 2,000 children by the *Health and Social Care Information Centre* found that one in four was obese. From 1995 to 2004, obesity among boys aged 11–15 rose from 14 per cent to 24 per cent and that among girls from 15 per cent to 26 per cent. The rate rose slightly in the two- to ten-year-old age group (BBC, 2006). This emphasises the importance of education in the primary phase and has become an area in which several initiatives have been introduced.

Case study

One large suburban primary school has introduced differentiated activities in PE to make it more accessible and interesting for a range of children. Having conducted a survey of children's interests, it was discovered that nearly a third of the children did not take any exercise outside school hours and that a significant percentage did not enjoy PE lessons outdoors. Three activities were set up to replace the more traditional weekly games lesson: team sports, including tag rugby and football; a mini cross-country and orienteering group, based around the school grounds; and an indoor circuit training and music/movement group in which children recorded their own achievements on a weekly basis. The latter two had a particular focus on individual achievement, performance and improvement. The range of after-school clubs was also increased to include all three foci. Since the introduction of the new programme the number of children participating in extra-curricular physical activity has risen by 30 per cent.

In 2008, Alan Johnson, Health Secretary, and Ed Balls, Secretary of State for Children, Schools and Families, published *Healthy Weight, Healthy Lives: A Cross-Government Strategy for England* (DH, 2008); it was a new £372 million strategy to help everyone to lead healthier lives. It aims to support the creation of a healthy society from the early years, considering schools and food, sport and physical activity, planning, transport and health services. In addition, other cross-government schemes and initiatives have been developed to contribute to reducing childhood obesity, including:

- Healthy Schools programme (www.healthyschools.gov.uk/);
- Food in Schools programme (www.foodinschools.org/);
- School Fruit and Vegetable scheme (www.5aday.nhs.uk).

A great deal of consideration is being given to childhood obesity and its potential future impact on health services and government spending. The *National Child Measurement Programme* (NHS, 2008) is a key part of the Government's work to tackle obesity. The programme aims to record the height and weight of all children in the Reception class and Year 6. This data will help primary care trusts to plan services to support schools and target resources; it also provides vital data to analyse trends at national and local levels (for early results see www.ncmp.ic.nhs.uk/). It is important to consider how this initiative might impact on children's self-image and self-confidence and to ensure that it is a productive and positive process.

Pause for thought

Given the explosion in the media focus on children and young people:

- What role do you feel schools have in addressing children's self-image and self-confidence?
- What pressures do children feel as a result of media products (e.g. advertising, television programming and child-focused Internet content) and how can they be equipped to cope with these?
- Does the significant media output aimed at children effectively challenge traditional adult roles (as providers, decision-makers and nurturers)?
- Do issues differ according to gender or other factors?

Other factors relate to health and well-being and have a significant impact on the development of children. For example, there is a disproportionate number of boys who are excluded from schools or who attempt suicide (Cole, 2008b). This is one indicator of the pressures experienced by some children.

Acceptance

Whatever a child's stage in developing an understanding of their identity, the pressure to appear to conform to the 'norm' is reflected in the idea that:

> *Becoming somebody* is the primary motivation of boys' and girls' social behaviour at school ... many boys learn that they must establish their position in a hierarchy of masculinities to avoid being positioned as the marginalized.
>
> (Meyenn & Parker, 2001: 173)

Whilst elements of this chapter have focused on traditional pressures felt by boys, girls also feel significant pressures. They are also involved in positioning within the hierarchies of being female and those developed between female and male. They may be praised for being caring and selfless, but face competing pressures by having to be individualistic and competitive in order to maintain their successes in school. There can be considerable tensions between the different and conflicting pressures experienced by girls. A survey by Girlguiding UK and The Mental Health Foundation (2008: 13) found that girls aged 10–14 years felt:

- compelled to act older than their age;
- sexual pressures from boys on the school playground;
- pressure from magazines and websites concerning what they 'ought to be', for example thin, trying drugs or having cosmetic surgery; and
- that boredom led to aggression, including the possibility of self-harm.

The last point is particularly important in classrooms, where boys can often demand a significant and inequitable share of a teacher's attention. This has important implications for girls' understanding of gender and power roles. It is also important to note how many of the girls' perceptions relate to appearance and its impact on self-esteem. The pressure on girls to conform to the expectations of others, including peers, family and the media, is apparent from the findings of this survey. It sought to establish girls' understanding of mental health issues and mental health as a concept:

> Some of the younger girls felt that a mental health problem was something you were born with – rather than something that can develop over time – and therefore felt girls with mental health issues would be different from them. Younger girls in two groups were also confused about the difference between mental health problems and physical disabilities. A few also associated the term with phobias.
>
> (Girlguiding UK, 2008: 10)

Mental health for both girls and boys is a key aspect of the *Every Child Matters* agenda (DfES, 2004). One of its five outcomes is that children should be healthy, which includes mental and emotional health as well as physical and other aspects. The *Targeted Mental Health in Schools Project* (see ECM, 2008), a three-year pilot scheme, is one example of how such issues are being addressed in a range of Local Authorities. Mental health is one of the last remaining taboos in British society. It is important that children understand its importance, alongside knowing how to keep healthy physically. If we are to meet the needs of the whole child we need to prioritise mental health and well-being, which necessitates addressing issues of equality directly.

Gender and the citizenship curriculum

The National Curriculum (DfEE and QCA, 1999) provides a framework in which it is possible to address issues of inequality, difference, respect and diversity. Claire (2001: 106) argues that this should be used in creative and imaginative ways, as

> education should have a progressive agenda, which would equip children to critique the society they live in and become familiar with contemporary discourses and explanations about inequality so they can develop a range of ideas about solutions.

The aims and purposes of citizenship outlined in the *National Curriculum* (and discussed in more detail in Chapter 5) can be read with different priorities. First, citizenship education can seek to educate about public duty, community service and the rules of law and order. Second, it can seek to evaluate the values, aims and purposes of such activities, and to consider equality and justice on a local, societal and global scale. Thus it can be about helping children to take increasing responsibility for their own lives, considering how they can play an active part in their relationships and communities and evaluating how to work towards a more equal world. This requires schools to develop safe and secure environments in which all children can explore their identities, values and beliefs, and find acceptance.

Developing practice

In order to develop effective practice, we need to consider:

- any ways in which we stereotype gendered behaviours or expectations based on gender;
- how we monitor our own attitudes, language and expectations;
- how the resources in our classroom avoid and combat gender stereotypes;
- how confident we are in tackling 'isms' and phobias (Who can provide support to help develop our confidence and practice?);
- how we help children to evaluate images they come across in the media;
- how we develop a no tolerance policy for bullying resulting from real and perceived differences between children;
- how we support all children in developing a positive self-image;
- the role of education in challenging gender expectations and limitations commonly found in society; and
- whether our own gender and self-image affect the ways in which we relate to and support our learners.

Summary and key points

This chapter has explored a range of issues relating to gender and identity. Key to this discussion is an understanding that gender is a social construct:

> Gender roles are not fixed, but are relative to time and place. Boys do not *need* to do badly at school relative to girls. Sexism, where subordinate gender locations are reproduced for females, does not *need* to predominate in schools. Women's structural location in the workforce can be changed and teachers *can* do something about it.
>
> (Cole, 2008b: 6)

This issue of identity is important. Whilst I have not argued for the promotion of any particular kind of gender identity or sexuality, I do believe that schools must be welcoming and open places where all stakeholders can explore their identities, free from bullying and harassment. The notion of respect for others, and the understanding that all people are different, are key to this discussion. Whilst the issues are complex, for teachers and all those involved in a child's development the challenge is to engage in the debate and to promote equality.

Schools can be non-sexist or anti-sexist: that is, they can make sure that they do not promote sexism or they can actively stand against it. Given the disparities shown in the statistics included earlier in this chapter, it is necessary to take a stand and actively work to combat gender inequality. This requires repeated reflection and evaluation of our practices and policies so that complacency does not allow the status quo to be maintained. Fundamental to these notions is the moral and legal requirement to promote children's mental health and well-being. The ways in which we come to understand and appreciate the diverse identities of others are key to this process.

Useful resources

DCSF and NHS (2009) Healthy Schools programme: www.healthyschools.gov.uk/

Disordered Eating: www.disordered-eating.co.uk

Kids First for Health, by Great Ormond Street Hospital: www.childrenfirst.nhs.uk/kids/health/ask_doc/food_file/eating_disorders.html

Schools Out: working for equality for lesbian, gay, bisexual and trans people: www.schools-out.org.uk

Further reading

Claire, H. (2001) *Not Aliens: Primary School Children and the Citizenship/PSHE Curriculum*, Stoke on Trent: Trentham Books.

DCSF (2007) *Safe to Learn: embedding anti-bullying work in schools*, London: Department for Children, Schools and Families.

Francis, B. (2000) *Boys, Girls and Achievement: addressing the classroom issues*, London, Routledge-Falmer.

Skelton, C. & Francis, B. (eds) (2003) *Boys and Girls in the Primary Classroom*, Maidenhead: Open University Press.

Chapter 7

Grief and loss

Facing change, death and bereavement

> 'Has my dog gone to heaven?' It was a straightforward question in the middle of a maths lesson on fractions. Clearly the death of Jack's pet was on his mind. On a personal level, I could perform mental gymnastics considering whether dogs have souls, exploring different theological possibilities based on ideas from major world religions and reflecting on how my answer might be compatible with the views of his parents/carers. However, it was a simple question and required a prompt and honest response from me as his teacher. 'Some people believe that dogs go to heaven,' I answered. 'To be honest, I am not sure. What do you think?' It may not have been a perfect answer, but it was honest and it gave the child the possibility of developing the conversation, if he so wished. A simple 'Yes' might have brought short-term reassurance, or might have conflicted with what Jack already believed. A short 'No' might have brought disappointment, discomfort or distress and would have placed me in a position of authority that suggested that I knew the answers to the meaning of life, the universe and everything. Whilst I may have a personal opinion or belief, this does not mean that I am infallible.
>
> (Ian, Year 5 teacher)

Facing loss is a difficult area for many teachers to address with children. Yet children frequently face loss – the loss of a friend, the death of a pet, the separation of family members; loss and grief are implicit to the human condition and to life experience. This chapter addresses issues of loss and grief in a wide range of situations, considering strategies to prepare children and to support them. It considers how teachers can respond to children who sometimes ask difficult questions about death, heaven and why 'bad' things happen to good people. It considers how teachers can explore these areas without feeling the need to have all the answers and how they can facilitate children's questioning, appreciate their answers and ideas, and support children's ongoing emotional development.

Facing loss – preparing ourselves

Death is often a taboo subject. When the words death, loss or bereavement are used, they raise a range of emotions. We each have different experiences of death in our lives to date, whether linked to family members, friends, neighbours or others we have admired or cared about. We have each coped in different ways, and many of us will have a sense of grief that remains with us or returns to us periodically.

Our cosmic view will affect how we view death. Some will believe in an afterlife or heaven of some kind, some will believe in rebirth or reincarnation, and others will believe that death is the end. Some readers will believe that it is possible to contact the spirit of a person who has 'passed over', whilst others will not. Whatever our personal belief or perception, it is key that we do not impose this on the children in our care and that we allow them to think, question and grow in their own way. This can be a difficult and sometimes painful process, and children will ask personal questions about our own experiences and beliefs as they seek to develop their own views. It is important to consider in advance how we might address these, so that we can be honest with ourselves, and with the children, without being dogmatic or feeling vulnerable.

Pause for thought

Consider the situation in the short vignette that opens this chapter:

- What issues does this situation raise?
- How might you have responded?
- Do you feel the teacher's response was appropriate?

The feelings faced by children may be similar to those felt by adults who are bereaved. However, they can be complicated and compounded by being experienced for the first time. Hipp (1995: 31) sought to capture the complexity of children's reactions to loss in his description of a 'loss pot':

> When people hold back feelings about loss, the feelings get all mixed up inside of them. It is as if all those feelings and hurts go into a big holding tank I call a 'loss pot' … A loss pot is like a stew filled with unpleasant ingredients.

This image may be helpful when considering how children feel following a bereavement; it may also help us as adults to consider how we feel about loss, grief and death.

Children's experience and understanding

It is important to remember that children and young people mature at different rates. Their response to bereavement is more likely to be affected by their previous life experiences than by their chronological age.

Young children

Young children (aged five and under) may have an emerging concept of death but not yet understand its finality. They may need repeated explanations about what has happened and may ask when the person is coming back. Dyregrov (2008) suggests that pre-school children may respond by withdrawing from their surroundings or by repeatedly playing out events. They may show regressive behaviours such as wetting or soiling; experience disturbed sleep; or exhibit anxious attachment behaviours such as clinging more to adults, being wary of strangers or needing much reassurance. Euphemisms such as 'he has passed on' or 'she has gone to sleep' may cause difficulty, as at this age children tend to think in literal and concrete terms. It is important to consider that children's active imaginations at this age may cause them to fantasise and come up with scary scenarios, if they are not told clearly what has happened.

Case study

Jason was told that his mum had some sad news to share with him: 'Your gran has been taken to be with the angels. We're all very sad, but she will be happier now.' Initially, he liked the idea of his grandparent being happy, as she had often been in a great deal of pain and sometimes broke down in tears as a result of her mobility difficulties. However, the more he thought about it, the more he worried that she had been 'taken'. Who had taken her and where was she? If she was happy, why couldn't they visit her? How could she be happy, if she wasn't allowed to see them any more?

Using clear and age-appropriate language and checking that children understand what we say are important aspects of the explanation process. As adults working with children, we are extremely aware of this with regard to the learning process in general. However, when it comes to addressing death, it is possible to forget this process and to neglect to use our professional skills. This may happen for a variety of reasons, including our own reticence or sense of awkwardness in addressing such a sensitive issue. It is particularly important to consider what existing knowledge and vocabulary children have about death and to consider where some of their perceptions may stem from.

Some of a young child's perceptions of death will come through the media. They will, no doubt, have seen cartoons in which characters are killed or seriously injured, only to reappear (Leaman, 1995). They may also be aware of fictional characters who die in role, but who then appear in another film or television programme or are featured in magazines or on chat shows. This can be a source of confusion and may present inaccurate understandings of the finality of death.

Key Stage 1 (5–7 years)

By the end of the Early Years Foundation Stage, children should be able 'to respond to significant experiences, showing a range of feelings when appropriate' and to 'find out about past and present events in their own lives, and in those of their families and other people they know' (DCSF, 2008a: 12, 14). Exploring one's family and its past will inevitably involve speaking about people who have died, and for some children this experience will be a 'present' event at some point. The notion of developing an enabling environment (DCSF, 2008a) includes an emphasis on supporting effective transitions. Whilst, at first, reading this may suggest a smooth transition into formal education and an effective progression into Key Stage 1, implicit to this idea is the need to help children to cope with the different transitions they experience in life. Facing loss and dealing with grief are key transitional experiences and it is essential to face these in school if children are to be enabled to be healthy.

Key Stage 2 (7–11 years)

By the age of seven, most children accept that death is permanent and that it can happen to anyone. They may show curiosity about birth, death and reproduction and can express logical thoughts and fears about death. They will probably understand that a dead person's bodily functions cease and that they do not move, see, hear or breathe. This is what Piaget (1954) described as the concrete operational stage. Children at this age have a wider social circle and are developing independence as they move from the home into the wider world of school and activity outside the family. They may 'make inner plans of action' to help themselves feel less vulnerable (Dyregrov, 2008:73) and imagine the actions they could have taken to prevent events from having happened.

Whilst they are able to express their feelings, they may also conceal them and outwardly appear unaffected. They may have a sense that they are to be strong and not cry, they may daydream, they may become aggressive or depressive and they may feel guilt. At this age, being given the opportunity to ask questions can ensure that they have clear information and can check their understanding of a situation. However, denial or suppression may be evident and can make it difficult for children to share feelings with either their peers or with adults. In addition, from five to eight years of age, children can become very interested in the rituals surrounding death.

Case study

After attending her uncle's funeral, Sophie (aged 6) began to re-enact elements of the committal service with her toys. She would prepare a 'grave' at the bottom of the garden, and then take soft toys or dolls and bury them. It was only when her dad noticed that toys were going missing that he realised what was happening. 'I am taking the toys to be with Uncle Pete,' she explained. 'I want him to have something special.'

Sophie's actions show that she was aware that her uncle had somehow gone away from the family; she knew that he had died and she had seen his coffin lowered into the ground. Her way of grieving was to try to do something special that her uncle might appreciate, by trying to give him the things that she loved in the manner of the ceremony they had used to say goodbye to him. Her parents explained that they could do something special together as a family to remember her uncle, and they visited his grave to leave flowers each weekend over the following month.

Usually, bereaved children do not need formal counselling, but they do benefit from clear information provided in language that they can understand. They need complex medical terms to be explained to them in language that they can comprehend. Holland (2004: 11) suggests that children may find it difficult to understand how a heart is 'attacked' or that something as gentle as a 'stroke' can kill. It is important to explain technical language in age-appropriate ways, and to consider whether words that we take for granted need setting in context in order for them to be fully understood.

From eight years of age, children's understanding of death can be very similar to that of an adult (Monroe and Kraus, 2004). They may still find it difficult to grasp abstract concepts, but they do have a growing sense of their own mortality, possibly accompanied by a sense of insecurity and fear. By this age, they may have more experience of death through the loss of a family pet or one belonging to friends. They still need to know details and may ask very specific questions. This process will continue: at different stages in their development, bereaved children will revisit the death of a loved one in new and fresh ways. As they mature, children need to be able to ask questions again about the death and to work through their developing understanding of such a major event (Christian, 1997).

The cycle of life

It is interesting that an understanding of the main stages of the life cycle of humans does not appear in the level descriptors included in *The National Curriculum* for science until level 5 (Attainment Target 2: life processes and living things, DfEE & QCA, 1999: 19). There is no reference to death or dying in the programme of study, only to 'nutrition, movement, growth and reproduction' as key life processes (DfEE & QCA, 1999: 85). This is an interesting omission. The curriculum for PSHE identifies that during Key Stage 1, children should learn to 'recognise, name and deal with their feelings in a positive way' (DfEE & QCA, 1999: 137) and, at Key Stage 2, they should 'talk and write about their opinions. … on issues that affect themselves' and 'reflect on spiritual, moral, social and cultural issues' (1999: 139). Implicit to these ideas is the need to consider death and dying in order to address their feelings and the issues that affect them. Whilst issues relating to death and dying themselves are not named in the national curriculum for primary schools in England, its requirements are in sympathy with addressing issues of loss with children at appropriate times in their lives. Whatever the requirements of the curriculum, teachers additionally have a duty of care to their children that necessitates appropriate responses to death and bereavement. This will be explored later in the chapter. Here, it is important to note that this significant part of the life experience of some children must be acknowledged; and it is important to question why the national curriculum fails to do this and how life processes can be discussed (particularly in Key Stage 2), when such a fundamental aspect is missing.

No official statistics have been collected on the number of children bereaved, and so it is impossible to calculate the extent of the need in our schools. However, the Childhood Bereavement Network suggests that around 1 in 25 of those aged 5–16 have experienced the death of a parent or sibling and that a child is bereaved of a parent once every thirty minutes in the UK (Green et al. 2005; Childhood Bereavement Network, undated; Winston's Wish, undated). In a study of schools in Humberside, Holland (1993) found that over two-thirds of primary schools had a child on their roll who had experienced a significant bereavement in the previous two years. Although this study involved a relatively small number of schools (75 replied to his questionnaire), it does give some indication of the need for schools to be prepared to face issues relating to child bereavement. This is even more the case when one includes children experiencing the death of a grandparent, family friend or neighbour.

Professional approaches

When a child is bereaved, teachers need to communicate with family members to make sure that they know what has actually happened. This communication is also important to ensure that anything that is said will not conflict with the family's wishes. Whilst many of us may find death a difficult or painful subject to broach, for a range of reasons, it is important to acknowledge it. It may be necessary to explain the circumstances to other children. There can be nervousness about broaching the subject of death with a child, but not to mention it might lead the child to think that the situation is unimportant or not cared about.

Children may ask questions that make us feel awkward, and these need to be addressed honestly. At times, we may need to acknowledge that we don't have all the answers; we will also need to listen, sometimes regularly. As professionals working in schools, we have a duty of care, which extends to acting in the ways that would be shown by a responsible parent/carer. As such, we have a pastoral responsibility as well as caring for the child's academic development. Teachers need to give reassurance, informed by the available facts. They themselves may also need to express emotion or to talk about the dead person. Sharing memories, and listening, are important parts of valuing the person who has died and acknowledging that they existed and were special (Jackson & Colwell, 2002). It is important to acknowledge that sadness at loss is an acceptable part of life. For adults to pretend otherwise is to go against what they, and the children, know to be true (Leaman, 1995). Trying to cover up a situation that is charged with emotion and possibly confusion, or trying to pretend that all is well, or being overprotective of childhood innocence and happiness will all lead to a child sensing the falsehood of the situation. Although very young children may only appear sad for short periods of time, older children will have a more developed *sadness span* (Dyregrov, 2008). Finally, it is important not to judge: children may grieve in ways that do not conform to our expectations or stereotypes; each person experiences a different process of grieving according to a different time frame. There is no prescribed or normal pattern for grief.

It is important to remember that grief is always with us: in some ways, a child's loss will be with them for life. Thus it is key for teachers to give bereaved pupils time, and to consider that whilst they may begin to feel that the death is distant, in terms of time elapsed, this may not be the experience of the child. Worden (1996) adapted his four tasks of mourning to apply to situations faced by children, which may provide a structure to help a teacher to appreciate the process a child is experiencing:

- *accepting* the reality of the loss;
- *experiencing* the pain or emotional aspects of the loss;
- *adjusting* to an environment in which the deceased is missing; and
- *relocating* the person within their own life and finding ways to remember the person.

Many children will come to terms with their loss through a similar process and will adjust to life without the deceased person. Whilst this four-stage process may be useful as a guide, it is important to restate that the grieving process make take a variety of forms and that there is no standard pattern. It is also important to consider how young children can be supported in expressing their grief, as they may not have developed the vocabulary to discuss issues due to their limited range of life experiences or knowledge (Leaman, 1995). Whilst we must not insist that children discuss their feelings, we can support children as and when they raise questions or share ideas and memories.

At times, death will come very suddenly and unexpectedly. Even when a long-term illness helps friends or relatives to prepare for loss, the actual event may still cause shock and emotion. The death of David's father provides one example.

Case study

Although David's parents had recently had a trial separation, they had decided to undertake marriage counselling and his dad had moved back into the family home.

The news of dad's suicide was, inevitably, unexpected and shocking. We learned of the death after the end of the school day. The following morning we did not expect David to be at school, but he arrived as usual and it was as though nothing had happened. Discussion in the staffroom centred on how to react in an appropriate way. His class teacher felt that she should acknowledge the situation, but in a way that did not make David feel awkward. As he left for the morning break she said, 'I am sorry to hear about your dad.' He replied, 'Things have been horrible at home for weeks. Now me and mum can get on with things.'

In some senses David may have begun the grieving process when his dad initially left home. At this point, he saw the death as the resolution to the turmoil in his home life. This does not diminish his need to ask questions and, particularly, the need to explore different scenarios and issues as the years pass. This may not be a typical response to suicide, but it provides a reminder that each situation is unique and may have associated circumstances of which teachers, colleagues or friends have been unaware. Jackson and Colwell (2002) suggest that it is important to acknowledge when suicide takes place. If we invent alternative reasons why a person has died, in order to protect children, it is likely that they will hear the truth from a different source and that this will undermine our relationship of trust with them. Whilst it may be impossible to explain why a person ended their own life, acknowledging this may be one way of providing an honest explanation to children.

Collective grief

So far we have concentrated on deaths that relate particularly to individual children and their families. At times, children and staff will share bereavement experiences:

> A shared bereavement occurred when the school guinea pig, Squeak, died. It had been shared around each class for months, with groups of children taking turns in caring for it. When it died, children were upset across the school, and it was felt necessary to mark the occasion in an appropriate way. We decided that Squeak should be buried in the school garden, and the head teacher agreed to lead a short act of remembrance for any children who wished to attend.
>
> (Judith, Year 4 teacher)

The death of a pet can affect children in different ways. It is important to explain that some children will feel sad, some may become emotional, but some may not feel any particular impact. This is important so that children do not feel that there is a 'right' or expected response. Some children will not have felt any particular attachment and may thus feel little or no sense of loss.

National and international events

On a much larger scale, there are events that affect a nation, such as the death of Diana, Princess of Wales. At that time, I had children in my class who became fascinated by her life and increased iconic status. Whilst it was important to respect their views and emotions, there was a sense of needing to balance this with a sensitive managing of the intense media coverage to which the children appeared to be responding.

As I have explored elsewhere (Adams, Hyde & Woolley, 2008), those of us who were working or living with children and young people at the time of the attacks in the United States on 11 September 2001, or the London bombings of 7 July 2005 in the UK, know all too well the impact that such events have on children. Many readers will have experienced these, or other similar, situations. We observed, and experienced, a wide range of emotions around these times: fear, anger, insecurity, empathy, confusion and uncertainty. On the first of these occasions I observed the reactions of primary school children and on the second I was working with secondary school students. Both groups needed to discuss the situation and to articulate their feelings in order to begin to make sense of what they had seen. They felt emotions that were powerful and difficult to control or explain. In these situations there was no protection from the news of the events. The media coverage was extensive. The children and young people were extremely aware that a major event had taken place and felt a need to try to gain an understanding of its meaning. They were not innocent as to the implications that were drawn by the media or members of their own families, and they also reflected themselves on the pictures presented by the news media.

As adults, we need to listen carefully to the ways in which children respond to global issues and crises and to acknowledge that sometimes there are no easy answers in complex circumstances. We can also create the opportunity to reflect on ideas and to feel the sense of the moment. At times, words are inadequate and our feelings are too complex and immediate to express. Allowing space for silence – and sharing silence together – can help us to gain a sense of being together that brings a sense of security and wholeness in difficult times. These times also provide the opportunity for adults to model the sharing of feelings and to acknowledge that they too find the situation difficult (Adams, Hyde & Woolley, 2008). Such times need careful structuring: an introduction to explain to children what they are for, a focus (e.g. lighting a candle or listening to music) and a clear ending with the possibility of an opportunity to respond in some way (perhaps by making a card, writing thoughts to share in a 'feelings box' or planting bulbs as a memorial). These strategies can work in a variety of settings, and are by no means exhaustive. It is important to scaffold children's experience, as structure will help them to focus and to think about their emotional response.

The wider school community

Of course, it is not only children who can face bereavement in schools. When a member of staff loses a parent, partner or child, the whole school community can be very aware of the situation. In such circumstances it is often the children who give the most open and moving response. Their feelings can show genuine concern for their teacher, and can sometimes reflect their concerns about the love they experience in their own families. To receive expressions of concern from a large number of children can be a difficult and emotional experience for adults and they are all too aware of the need to respond in professional and supportive ways to the children in their care. Some children do not know how to respond, and do not have any past experience upon which to draw. It can be possible for them to overreact, showing behaviours that they feel should be exhibited, possibly influenced by media representations of grief. Other children will react because the loss makes them think of their own family and brings the implication that they too could lose a parent/carer or sibling at some point. It is important to understand that a child's reaction may stem from a range of experiences and be affected by many factors. It is also important to consider how teachers can find support within what can be a busy and already stressful working environment. Finding time to speak with one another and being able to share personal thoughts and feelings in a supportive and secure environment can be a way of feeling valued in one's personal circumstances within a professional setting. There can sometimes be a tension between being honest about our feelings and circumstances, and maintaining professional relationships and an appropriate sense of 'distance' between the personal and the professional. However, teachers may need the support of a reliable colleague to talk through feelings in order to gain the support they need themselves; they may also wish to keep their feelings private and may ask that colleagues do not approach them about their bereavement.

Attending a funeral

Holland (2004) suggests that attending the funeral, and being involved in the family events around the time after a death, should help children with the task of accepting its reality. If children are not included in these events, they may feel excluded or isolated and may even feel anger towards the wider family. However, children may not wish to be included. This situation can be complex and families often spend a great deal of time considering whether children should attend a funeral. Sometimes they seek advice from the child's class teacher as an 'independent' person who knows their child well.

Children will need to be supported if they are given the opportunity to consider whether they would like to attend a family funeral. They may have strong feelings about attending or not attending, or may feel ambivalent. However, as Holland (2004: 13) suggests, choosing not to attend may remove an important part of the grieving process:

> Tony was a junior aged child at the time of the death of his father. He did not attend the funeral, having no strong views at the time, and said that then he was not really 'bothered'. It was only fourteen years later, after the death of another close relative, that he began to have pangs of regret for not having attended the funeral, and of not saying a final goodbye to his father.

In Holland's research, none of the young people attending the funeral of their parent reported any negative effects and, on the contrary, most of them felt that it had been a positive and helpful event. Of those not attending the funeral, three-quarters, with hindsight, wished that they had taken part:

> It seems that there is nothing to lose, but much to gain, by children attending the funeral, with the 'golden rule' of giving children the choice, neither forcing them to attend, or forbidding or distracting them from attending. It also seems important to prepare children for the experiences of attending the funeral.
>
> (Holland, 2004: 13–14)

On occasions, it may not be possible for a child to say goodbye to a caregiver or close friend directly, either before their death or through attending a funeral. In such a situation, it may be possible to say goodbye in a more symbolic way, perhaps by writing a letter or drawing pictures showing special memories (Jewett, 1984). This approach may be particularly useful for a class of children when one of their peers dies. The children will all have known the child who died, but will have had a range of interactions and relationships with them of varying intensity. Creating a special book of memories may help children to say something special about their lost peer. Again, it is important to remember that not all children may wish to do this; some of them will have little or no sense of loss and may not have known the child well even if they were classmates. Such a book of memories could be presented to the child's family, or kept in school. It may be useful to have such a collection of memories that can be referred to on special occasions such as the anniversary of the death, the child's birthday and other times when some children may feel the loss more acutely.

Using children's literature

Some children may find it difficult to put their thoughts or feelings into words or may feel that they are the only child ever to have faced a loss like their own. One way of addressing this is to use children's picture books, which can present issues through a third party. This provides the opportunity to introduce ideas that are one step removed from the child's own experience: children can then talk about the characters rather than about themselves directly (Berns, 2004). Picture books can be appropriate for children throughout the Primary phase of education, although they are sometimes wrongly presumed to be solely for younger children. Teachers will wish to consult with parents and carers about the choice of books. It would be inappropriate to suggest a list for use with children, as each child's needs are different. However, some useful starting points are included in a resource cited at the end of this chapter.

Pardeck and Pardeck (1993) define four aspects of the process of using books in this way with children (which some experts term *bibliotherapy*) that they feel are essential in order for the process to be successful. Each aspect must be guided by an experienced adult and is equally important. The four aspects are:

- *identification*, which requires a sensitive appraisal of the child's needs and emotions by the teacher;
- *selection*, which draws upon appropriate materials to provide for the child's needs, chosen using the teacher's skills, knowledge and experience;
- *presentation*, which involves choosing an appropriate place and time to introduce the materials; and
- *follow-up*, which involves developing a response, through conversation, art or writing. This is probably the most important aspect of the process, as it seeks to help the child respond to the materials and consider their thoughts and feelings.

Whilst it would be inappropriate for teachers to provide *therapy*, as this requires training and expertise not always possessed by teachers, the process does provide an outline that may help those working with children in school to use picture books in a supportive and empathetic manner, or to provide them as a resource for parents and carers. The explanation of each of the stages provides my interpretation of how a class teacher may use the process, should it be appropriate for the child and their needs/wishes.

Other situations of loss

Grief and loss can come in many ways other than the death of a loved one. Children can lose friends when a child moves away from the area; some may lose a home through financial difficulties or migration; some children will experience divorce or separation in their families. Separation can come for other reasons, including the need for a parent/carer to work away or their imprisonment, and these also can cause a significant sense of loss.

Case study

Amir's mother used to work away from home for significant periods of time. Although he was cared for by an experienced and very caring *au pair*, his sense of loss was particularly acute during the first few days each time his mother left home. At such times, his behaviour changed and he often alternated between being quiet and withdrawn and exhibiting out-of-character and boisterous behaviour, which led to his teacher having to use a variety of sanctions. Having offered to talk with him whenever he felt the need, they began to establish a sense of openness in which Amir could express his sense of frustration.

It is not always appropriate to offer to 'talk whenever you need it', as some children will speak endlessly of their sense of loss, and perhaps anger, and one may wonder how beneficial or healing this is. However, such behaviours (often referred to as attention seeking) indicate the need for a replacement for the attention they have lost. This requires a professional judgement about the appropriateness of the attention seeking and the extent to which a teacher should respond. At some points in life we all crave and seek attention. Sometimes, taking on a classroom responsibility, or knowing that there are particular times when a listening ear is available, or having a special diary in which a child can record thoughts and feelings can address this. Those working in schools can help children to prepare for such situations of loss by acknowledging them, affirming that the child is special and valued, and by providing opportunities for them to express their thoughts through activities. They can also address such feelings for children who are new arrivals to a school by providing a warm welcome, helping them to settle into new routines, taking an interest in where they have come from and making sure that their contributions are welcomed and valued.

Transitions

Any significant change in life can bring a sense of loss and feelings of grief. Whilst some of the situations in this chapter cannot be anticipated, some change can be predicted or expected. The move from one class or school to another provides one such example. Teachers can prepare children for such change and help them to face transition with confidence (Fthenakis, 1998). Strategies to support children may include:

- visiting the new classroom or school and meeting with their new teacher;
- writing about or discussing their feelings about the transition and sharing hopes and aspirations;

- hearing each other's feelings so that children realise that they are not alone in the move;
- inviting staff from the new setting or school to visit (e.g. to contribute to sports activities, to share in an assembly or to bring students to present a concert); and
- inviting former pupils to return to the school (or older children to visit a younger year group) to share their experiences and answer questions.

Two studies in Scotland highlighted the importance of friendships in helping children to cope with transition (Stephen & Cope, 2001; Graham & Hill, 2003). Galton et al. (1999) found that certain groups of children may be more vulnerable to losing ground academically during transition, including those with special educational needs, those for whom English is an additional language or those who are in receipt of free school meals. Those with a wider circle of friends may be better equipped to cope with such change (Graham & Hill, 2003). Teachers need to be aware of potential difficulties as they plan for transition.

A question frequently asked by children moving to secondary school is, 'Will I have my head flushed down the toilet?' Such mythology is common and can cause unnecessary concern. Bringing misconceptions out into the open and discussing them can play an important part in myth-busting. Additionally, some schools have developed common units of work so that themes initiated in primary school are picked up at the start of secondary education. Bridging units, summer programmes and extended induction programmes can help support the move from primary to secondary school and lead to gains in positive attitudes (Galton et al. 2003). Such inter-school cooperation can be effective in smoothing the transition and helping children to feel a sense of continuity and security.

Developing practice

In order to develop effective practice, we need to consider:

- how we might react to bereavement in school and how our own experience might affect our reactions;
- how we approach difficult questions from our learners that have no answer;
- our knowledge and understanding of the school's policy on handling bereavement;
- the resources that are available in school to support a bereaved child;
- how proactive we are in preparing children for loss, in age-appropriate ways;
- how we can use stories and picture books to offer slightly distanced ideas for discussion;
- which colleagues have particular experience or expertise to support us;
- how effectively we handle transition and how we monitor its effectiveness; and
- what examples or strategies from this chapter might help us when facing situations that cause personal awkwardness or discomfort.

Summary and key points

This chapter has considered a range of situations in which members of a school community may encounter change, death and loss. Whilst not exhaustive, they provide insights into some of the situations that are faced by professionals in education settings. Whilst each situation will be unique, it is important that we have considered in advance how we may respond, possible strategies to employ and how our own experiences and world-views may impact on our reactions.

Jackson & Colwell (2002: 107) suggest four rules to bear in mind when working with children who are bereaved:

- Be honest. If you don't know, say so. Don't be evasive. Be clear.
- Use words carefully. Don't use euphemisms.
- Be prepared to answer the same question several times. The child needs time to make sense of new information.
- Be aware of your own anxieties and worries. Don't feel you ought to feel comfortable with talk of death if you don't.

These points provide a useful summary for reference. Each school should have its own policy for dealing with death and bereavement. The most difficult time to access this may be the very moment when it is most needed. Obtaining a copy and becoming familiar with its contents is an important part of preparing to offer care to children and of clarifying the expectations and procedures agreed by the school. It will also be helpful to identify any colleagues with particular expertise, and to be aware of sources of support and advice. As with all difficult situations in school, it can be most helpful to have a confidential and trusted source of support away from the workplace in order to gain advice and reassurance for ourselves. This can be invaluable in addressing the personal needs that arise from our professional role.

For some of us, death will be the most difficult issue raised in this book and the one that we have discussed least with colleagues, friends or family members. It is possible that we are more likely to discuss sex than death; one taboo seems to have been replaced by another in contemporary society. It is important that we do not impose our taboos on the children in our care and that we allow them the possibility of exploring difficult issues as they grow and mature.

Useful resources

Examples of children's picture books relating to transitions, death and bereavement can be accessed through a resource prepared by staff and students at Bishop Grosseteste University College Lincoln: www.bishopg.ac.uk/trr

Child Bereavement Charity: www.childbereavement.org.uk/

Childline (resources for children and adults): www.childline.org.uk

The Child Bereavement Network: www.childhoodbereavementnetwork.org.uk/

Winston's Wish is the charity for bereaved children. The website includes advice, strategies for supporting children of all ages and assembly ideas. www.winstonswish.org.uk

Further reading

Dyregrov, A. (2008) *Grief in Young Children: a Handbook for Adults*, 2nd Edition, London: Jessica Kingsley.

Jackson, M. & Colwell, J. (2002) *A Teacher's Handbook of Death*, London: Jessica Kingsley.

Monroe, B. & Kraus, F. (2004) *Brief Interventions with Bereaved Children*, Buckingham: Open University Press.

Chapter 8

Remembrance and remembering

Challenges and opportunities

> We sat in silence in assembly this morning to think about people who are different to us and how we need to respect them. Millions of people were taken from their homes [in the Second World War] and treated in horrible ways and killed because they were different ... Some said the silence seemed like forever, but all I could think about was my brother. He has been away from home for three months now and I can't wait for him to come home. I don't know if he will be back for his birthday, but I have started making his presents. Mum says that if he isn't back we will have another birthday when he gets home from Iraq. When they blew the candle out in assembly I was still thinking of him, and I think of him all the time. It was hard today thinking about the war but it's worse when I see the war on the TV.
>
> (Abbey, aged 11; Holocaust Memorial Day)

This chapter explores whether issues relating to past and present wars can be explored in age-appropriate ways in primary education and how older children can come to consider issues that arise from both historical and contemporary situations, including those that they view frequently in news bulletins. It suggests a continuum of learning that starts with Remembrance Day and gradually introduces themes and ideas from the Second World War, before children are introduced to wider learning from that history.

Issues in primary education

It would be inappropriate to expose young children in primary schools to the full horrors of conflict or warfare. It is important to consider children's cognitive and emotional abilities and to acknowledge that, whilst all children progress at different rates, and there are no absolute stages of development, theories suggest common patterns in the abilities of children in different age groups. These can help here in a consideration of how skills, values and attitudes might be approached with children in primary education and how these can be nurtured from their early years. Some children will have a range of questions that arise from the news media, whilst others will have little awareness of the conflicts taking place in the world at any given time.

The Early Years Foundation Stage

At the age of around four years, children are beginning to generalise and to reason. They can ask a good deal of who, what, when and why questions, which include those about birth and death. They are starting to notice differences between people, developing a sense of right and wrong and sensing some fears and anxieties. They have some sensitivity for others and their feelings; for example, they may be concerned when a friend is upset or hurt. There is a developing sense of yesterday and tomorrow.

At this age children will be aware of soldiers and contemporary warfare from the television news and some will include military themes in their collaborative play. However, the concept of the Second World War is too distant and abstract to be considered. Their developing sensitivity to the feelings of others may help them to understand that people are sad when a daughter or brother is injured or killed through warfare. They may have a straightforward understanding that fighting is wrong (and see this in stark terms). These abilities will help with an appreciation of the importance of Remembrance Day and can support discussions about why people buy and wear poppies and how this is significant. There may also be a more egocentric aspect of wanting to buy, own and wear a poppy. I have worked in classrooms where children have wanted to buy several and where they have brought money every day to gain a poppy when the tray is taken around school. This may provide an opportunity to suggest that making one donation to have a special poppy is appropriate, and to encourage children to look after their poppy as it symbolises a special way of remembering the needs of others.

The notion of remembering is important. For many children the act of remembering will be that of recalling information gained second-hand. With younger children, it may be more appropriate to focus on thinking about people who serve in the armed forces in the present day and those who have been injured that they may be aware of from the news media, and on remembering families separated because of service overseas. This is an important aspect of Remembrance Day and provides one means of making it accessible to younger children. This is particularly pertinent where those in a class have family members in the armed forces. These issues relate particularly to the *Knowledge and Understanding of the World* strand of the curriculum for the Early Years Foundation Stage (DCSF, 2008a: 14, 15), that children should:

- ask questions about why things happen, and
- find out about past and present events in their own lives, and in those of their families and other people they know.

Pause for thought

When thinking about the context of younger children, it may be useful to consider the following questions:

- What and who are the children remembering?
- How can remembrance be given an age-appropriate context for younger children?
- How can issues or situations be discussed without the need to introduce the horrors of war?

Key Stage 1 (5–7 years)

At five years of age children are asking interesting questions about the world around them. They are also interested in the answers that they receive and will remember and internalise some of this information, and can enjoy arguing and reasoning and using the word 'because'. They have a greater sensitivity to the feelings of others. At around six years of age children can begin to understand differences of opinion. They know the difference between right and wrong and are moving towards more abstract thinking. Children's attention spans are increasing and they are developing a sense of logic and skills to help with problem solving. Statements of personal points of view will accompany developing confidence: children may reject some of an adult's ideas and suggest their own alternatives. This is an appropriate age to begin to consider pro-social behaviours of *empathy* for those who have lost loved ones, or who have been injured or disabled through conflict, and *altruism* by giving to support others (Puckett and Black, 2001; Bee and Boyd, 2003). It may be possible to discuss why the *Poppy Appeal* is necessary and to find out how the money raised is used.

Key Stage 2 (7–11 years)

At around seven years old children are starting to reason more and can have strong emotional reactions to ideas, events and situations. From seven years onwards, a good understanding of everyday concepts will be grasped and an understanding of more abstract concepts will grow; children start to become more self-aware and self-conscious and start to think more independently. Children aged eight can be more extrovert than younger children, they are interested in the world around them and they seek to understand the reason for things. They can be fascinated with fire, storms, blood and violence and may 'experience' these through the television, video games and the Internet. These interests might lead them to inappropriate fascinations with elements of, for example, the Second World War or more recent conflicts. Their developing maturity opens up opportunities to consider historical accounts of children in the war, including those who were evacuated within the UK and to the UK through the *kindertransport*. Understanding some of the reasons why it was important for children to be relocated is possible, as is developing some empathy for the emotions that may have been experienced. Children cannot understand the thoughts or feelings of children in that setting; none of us can have that understanding without having had the experience ourselves. However, they may gain insights from carefully retold accounts. A particularly effective resource is *Journeys: Children of the Holocaust Tell Their Stories* (Whitworth, 2009), a collection of thirty short survivor testimonies written for children in Key Stage 2. These introduce a variety of experiences as refugees, *kindertransportees*, of surviving in the ghettos or living as hidden children. Used sensitively, they provide the opportunity to access age-appropriate autobiographical materials.

From around the age of ten, children's understanding of right and wrong informs decisions, rather than being motivated mainly by punishment avoidance (as younger children might be). They become more self-motivated and develop more abstract thinking. At this age it may be appropriate to consider accounts from the time of the Second World War in more detail. There will be a greater ability to consider some of the feelings experienced by those who were displaced in ghettos in mainland Europe and to consider why some groups of people were disenfranchised and dispossessed. Some children will have an emerging knowledge of 'the final solution' (Furet, 1989) and the Holocaust, but perhaps not necessarily of the terms or specific details. Despite their growing maturity, it is essential to consider how much detail to include in any programme of study. It may be appropriate to explore accounts of the war, including the Holocaust, to the gates of the camps, but not beyond (Wiseman, 2006). Examples are considered later in the chapter.

It is important to consider how to address direct questions from children at this age, especially as they may be rooted in an interest in the events surrounding the war derived from books, films, television documentaries or the Internet. There may be a variety of interest and knowledge within a class, and it might be appropriate to address questions from individual children in different ways according to their interest and maturity. They may have questions arising from films or literature such as *The Boy in the Striped Pyjamas* (Boyne, 2006; see also Bawden, 1973; Beresford and Mayhew, 1993; and Blake and Sheppard, 1998).

The example at the start of this chapter highlights how one school is choosing to mark Holocaust Memorial Day (HMD) with its pupils. Whilst the Holocaust is not a part of *The National Curriculum* for Key Stage 2 in England (DfEE & QCA, 1999), some schools include it in their planning for History or mark HMD (27 January). It is important, therefore, to consider whether aspects of Holocaust education can be explored in age-appropriate ways in primary schools. Some children may, themselves, have been displaced by war, be asylum seekers or have faced prejudice as a result of migration. It is essential to bear in mind children's backgrounds when introducing elements from the Holocaust in schools.

Why teach about the Holocaust?

Lindquist (2007: 22) argues that

> teaching the Holocaust involves unique demands, pressures, and potential pitfalls that make [secure subject knowledge and appropriate teaching methods] critical as teachers consider the *if*, the *what*, and the *how* of Holocaust education as well as the moral implications that arise from any meaningful and appropriate study of the event.

In addition to *if*, *what* and *how*, teachers need to consider *why*. If aspects of this genocide are to be addressed with children in primary education, why is this so? If the aim is to address issues of tolerance, respect and diversity with learners, why choose the Holocaust as the stimulus for this? Whilst it may provide issues to address through *Philosophy for Children* (discussed in Chapter 5), if learning objectives can be met through another means is it appropriate to introduce such a harrowing part of history to children and do they have the maturity to begin to consider its magnitude or appreciate its complexities? Landau (1992: 12) suggests that Holocaust education, taught with due concern to content and pedagogy, can 'civilize and humanize our students and perhaps more effectively than any other subject can sensitise them to the dangers of indifference, intolerance, racism and the dehumanization of others.' However, if taught badly it can, 'titillate, traumatise, mythologise and encourage a purely negative view of all Jewish history, of Jewish people and indeed of *all* victim groups.'

Speaking as Prime Minister about the events of the first *Holocaust Memorial Day* in Britain, Tony Blair commented that:

> [Holocaust Memorial Day is] … a powerful way of writing its lessons into our national conscience. We need to learn the lessons of the Holocaust as victimisation, racism and intolerance continue – both in our own society and in many parts of the new generation to enable us all to work towards building a safer, more just and tolerant world.
>
> (Blair, 2001: 4–5)

Most teachers will accept the values espoused by Blair. However, using the Holocaust as the means of addressing racism, intolerance and injustice is more controversial. In any setting, Holocaust education is a complex and difficult area that requires a great degree of subject knowledge and a significant appreciation of the context in which the Holocaust took place. Whilst the Holocaust is not in itself controversial, the idea that it can be addressed with children in primary schools is. There are dangers in simplifying and trivialising issues and reinforcing misconceptions and stereotypes. Some teachers will argue that without an appreciation of some of the issues the Holocaust raises it is impossible to study the Second World War (a common topic in History at Key Stage 2) or to understand Judaism in Religious Education. Others will argue that it provides a vehicle by which to explore issues of intolerance and hatred and to consider why people of difference can be marginalised in society.

The term and its use

It is important to be clear what Holocaust education is. It may be self-evident that it involves education about the Holocaust, but what this entails is very specific. The Holocaust was the attempt to totally destroy the Jewish people, which resulted in the murder of six million Jews during the Second World War, and can be regarded as including the associated political systems and societal pressures in the pre-war period. Other people were disenfranchised, persecuted and murdered at this time, including Gypsies, Travellers, Roma and Sinti, homosexuals and people with mental or physical disabilities. In addition, Soviet civilians and prisoners of war, Jehovah's Witnesses, ethnic Poles and political opponents of the Nazi regime were killed. Some writers suggest that this increases numbers to around eleven million people (USHMM, 2001). However, many scholars agree that the term Holocaust refers specifically to the murder of Jewish people. They were the only group that the system sought to wipe out in totality through a programme of deliberate extermination (Furet, 1989).

The word Holocaust comes from the Greek: *holos*, meaning 'completely' and *kaustos*, 'burnt'. Another word used to name the Holocaust is *Shoah*, a Hebrew word meaning 'disaster' or 'conflagration'. The Shoah or, with the addition of 'Ha' (meaning *the* in Hebrew), HaShoah, is a term commonly used to refer to the Holocaust, particularly by Jewish people. The word Shoah encompasses the whole historical event rather than focusing on the killing (and cremation or burning) of Jewish people. It also avoids the notion of a completely-burned sacrifice, which is associated with the term *holocaust,* and which has religious connotations reminiscent of the sacrifices offered in the Hebrew Bible. To suggest that the murder of Jews was a holy offering of a religious nature is wholly inappropriate and thus makes the term Shoah preferable. However, for the purposes of this chapter the word Holocaust will be retained as it is the term that is commonly used in schools and for *Holocaust Memorial Day*.

Pause for thought

Consider the term Holocaust and the definition outlined above.

- How does this reflect or contrast with your existing understanding of the word?
- Can you identify any benefits or difficulties in teaching about the Holocaust in primary school?
- Make a note of these issues for reference as you read the rest of the chapter.

An important consideration when including teaching about the Holocaust in primary education is the fact that it is a compulsory part of the curriculum in secondary schools in England. Short (2003a: 127) suggests that both proponents and detractors neglect to consider the possibility of 'Holocaust fatigue' when, if learners have covered part of the subject in primary school, they then encounter it again at secondary level. However, this argument is diminished when one considers that statutory coverage of the Holocaust in secondary schools can amount to just two or three lessons. Whilst the new curriculum for Key Stage 3 (ages 11–14) makes possible increased cross-curricular study, the limited coverage of such an extensive, complex and significant subject strengthens the argument for preparatory work in earlier years in order to ensure that children are ready to deal with both content and issues (as suggested in the earlier examination of key stages); it also strengthens the case for effective transition between key stages and schools. The Holocaust cannot be studied in isolation in terms of subject matter, skills development or pedagogy.

Furthermore, there is an additional danger of overexposing children and young people to the Holocaust. They may feel manipulated, which may lead to a degree of antipathy, 'which, in turn, could render Holocaust education not just ineffective but counter-productive' (Short, 2003a: 128). This is true when considering so many difficult and challenging issues in primary education. This highlights the point that it is not only the teacher who has to consider why the Holocaust is being taught. As with so many parts of the curriculum, children also ask 'Why do we have to learn this?' I have faced this question myself from children and know that the best answers are not, 'Because it is a requirement of the national curriculum,' or, 'It is on the school's curriculum plan for this term.' Such answers reduce teachers to the level of technicians, delivering what has to be done at the time it is decreed, rather than educators who have a philosophy for what is being learned: how, why and what it hopes to achieve.

The requirements of the curriculum

Whilst the Holocaust is not a statutory part of the history curriculum in primary schools, pupils in Key Stage 2 are required to study either *Victorian Britain* or *Britain Since 1930*. The latter involves a study either of the impact of the Second World War, or of the social and technological changes that have taken place since 1930, on the lives of women, men and children from different sections of society. It suggests that this may include, 'the Blitz and evacuation; rationing; serving in the land army or the home guard; new technologies such as code breaking; and the Second World War in the local area' (DfEE and QCA, 1999: 107).

This list is interesting in its omissions. There is no mention of the service personnel who fought in the different war zones around the world, why or how the war began or indeed any suggestion of conflict other than the Blitz (which itself is centred on the experience of those in some major cities). However, a wider consideration of people's experience may be included in the impact of the war on the local area, for example through speaking with families separated through National Service, identifying the names of the fallen on the local war memorial and seeking to learn something about them and their families, and speaking with evacuees (including *kindertransport* children) or the families with whom they stayed. Wiseman (2006) suggests that to discuss the war without reference to the Holocaust is a missed opportunity:

> We talk about teaching 'to the moment of need' and therefore we are doing our pupils a disservice if we do not address some of the issues concerning the Holocaust at the same time. It would be a missed, valuable learning opportunity.

The National Curriculum (DfEE and QCA, 1999) effectively suggests that learning about the Second World War in primary schools should be limited to the borders of Britain's beaches and go no further. However, this does not preclude children's questions about why the war took place or their making links to other parts of their general knowledge, which may include knowledge of the war derived from family stories, films or books. An unsatisfactory answer would be to suggest to children that they must wait until Key Stage 3 before exploring their questions. However, this is not to suggest that teachers should force such questioning, push children to explore issues for which they are not yet ready, or seek to create an interest or inquisitiveness where none arises.

Older children might consider the importance of homes and families, how they would feel if they had to leave home, and develop a sense of what they feel is important in their lives. On this level, accounts from the time of the Holocaust would provide a means of developing personal identity and values without exploring the horrors of the ghettos or camps (for example Abramski, 2007; Morgenstern, 1998, 2007). It is important to explore the normality of life for Jewish people pre-war, so that they are not solely presented or stereotyped as victims and to make clear that there are survivors of the Holocaust.

Tackling issues

Using the children's storybook *I Wanted to Fly Like a Butterfly* (Morgenstern, 1998), children in Year 5 explored the story of Hannah and how she and her mother went into hiding during the Holocaust. The story opens with an account of her experiences in Poland before the war. This stresses how ordinary life was and shows that she shared the same interests and pastimes as other children. As Hannah develops her story, she says:

> Then things began to happen that made me forget all the songs, poems, and games that I once knew so well. A terrible war broke out; my wonderful childhood came suddenly to an end. My life was to change for ever.
>
> (Morgenstern, 1998: 3)

After a time when the family expected to be deported, and a time in hiding, Hannah and her mother were able to escape to Warsaw where they went into hiding with the Skovroneck family:

> For two years we lived with them.
> For two years I did not leave the building.
> For two years I did not walk around the apartment.
> For two years I did not go near a window – I would always crawl underneath.
> (Morgenstern, 1998: 24)

The story introduces aspects of the persecution of Jewish people, without referring to the horrors of concentration camps. It provides part of the story, based in one family's experience, preparing for some of the issues that will be explored in Key Stage 3, whilst maintaining age-appropriate content for older primary school children. The story has a positive ending, telling how Hannah's mother remarried and the family moved to Israel. There Hannah became a nurse, married and now has grandchildren. Contact details at the end of the book make it possible for readers to write to Hannah with their thoughts about her story and any questions.

Consider:

- How can the story of one person help children to access an otherwise complex and huge series of events?
- How might the use of a factual account contrast with fictional stories (e.g. *The Boy in the Striped Pyjamas*)? Might the use of fiction suggest that the Holocaust is not a part of history? How would you address this?
- How might the positive elements in the ending of the story help to avoid upsetting or traumatising children?

Arguments against teaching about the Holocaust

Totten (1999) objects strongly to the exploration of the Holocaust by younger children. He believes that they will struggle because it is so complex and will suffer emotionally if exposed to its horrors. He contends that to teach the Holocaust to children aged 10 or 11 years old would involve watering it down to such a level that it becomes distorted. Furthermore, he suggests that to call moral lessons drawn from this genocide 'Holocaust education' is a misnomer and should more rightly be re-categorised as moral education, prejudice reduction or human rights awareness. Short (2003a) argues that Totten's critique is unconvincing on a number of grounds. First, it is limited by a misplaced emphasis on terminology and by a lack of evidence to support claims about the pre-adolescent's intellectual and emotional immaturity. Second, it ignores both relevant research findings and some important theoretical questions that arise from too early an acquaintance with the Holocaust. In Short's view, 'the priority is not to challenge the legitimacy of the term "Holocaust education" to describe lessons derived from the genocide; it is rather to question whether the derivations themselves are legitimate' (2003a: 121). There would seem to be a dichotomy between the views of Totten and Short, one considering learning *about* the Holocaust and one exploring learning *from* it. Nonetheless, this does not detract from the complexity of the issue or its sensitivity. There is also an assumption about the detail and extent of the teaching that will take place. The example of Hannah's story, explored earlier in the case study, shows how one person's experience of the Holocaust can be considered whilst avoiding many of Totten's concerns.

Glanz suggests that any study of the Holocaust is 'somber, huge, significant, and ultimately redemptive' (2001: 3). The first three points are self-evident. The fourth suggests that any study of the Holocaust should make a difference to the learner by helping them to become a better person and a more responsible citizen. Thus, Holocaust education should be transformative. Glanz argues that to teach the Holocaust without it making a difference in the life of the learner is to do a disservice to those who were murdered for they will become nothing more than facts and statistics, devoid of any right to empathy, understanding or compassion. Indeed, all those who were dehumanised or oppressed by their role in the Holocaust, whether victim, perpetrator, bystander or rescuer, need to be understood if they are not to be dehumanised further in the classroom. However, it is also important to consider our motivation in using the Holocaust to teach about values. People's stories of life and death must be handled with sensitivity to avoid using them solely as a means to an end, which would, in itself, do a disservice to their memories.

Planning and implementing Holocaust curricula are complex and problematic because multiple pedagogical concerns plague the teaching of the subject, leading to Wieser's stark statement: 'Teaching it can be like trying to find one's way through a minefield' (2001: 62). Wiseman (2006) suggests that the most common argument against teaching the Holocaust in primary schools is that children are too immature to face such depressing subject matter. However, she argues that children often encounter hate and violence through the media, which makes them remote and unreal. Their exposure to fictional violent heroes can lead to misconceptions about good and evil, which, Wiseman suggests, learning about the Holocaust can address. The notion of childhood innocence is interesting. In some situations adults invoke it in order to avoid having to face difficult or complex issues. This, in itself, is not a strong reason for avoiding the subject.

Possibilities for teaching about the Holocaust

Cowan and Maitles (2002) suggest that although Holocaust education is not a panacea for racism (explored in Chapter 2) and antisemitism, it has a significant contribution to make in developing young learners' attitudes to these contemporary issues. In the primary school, its contribution to citizenship includes developing pupils' understanding of justice, stereotyping and discrimination and provides opportunities for developing positive values of empathy, awareness of antiracism, and an understanding that the individual can make a difference (Short and Carrington, 1991; Maitles and Cowan, 1999; 2005; Cowan and Maitles, 2002).

Case study

Maitles and Cowan (1999) maintain that primary school teachers are more likely than their secondary counterparts to adopt a cross-curricular, multi-disciplinary approach to the subject and are better positioned to respond to pupils' concerns with flexibility and immediacy. The Scottish teachers they interviewed centred their approach to the Holocaust around the life of Anne Frank and, to varying degrees, made use of the teaching pack *Into Hiding* (Rendell, 1987). They employed role-play to good effect and found that their 9- to 11-year-old pupils benefited from watching videos and from listening to Holocaust survivors. The only criticism they had of the teaching pack was that it provided no description, detail or definition of the extermination camps. They found their own ways of dealing with this key omission and seem to have done so without difficulty, prompting Maitles and Cowan to conclude that the Holocaust is not 'too harrowing a study for primary pupils' (1999: 270). This inference is consistent with research carried out over recent decades showing that children are able to cope intellectually and emotionally with political topics previously thought suitable only for an older age group (Carrington and Troyna, 1988).

Whilst the experience of Anne Frank is well known, and her story is often used in primary schools, it is important to help children to understand that hers is but one story and that her experience was not the norm. It is also important to note that role-play must be used with great caution so that children do not gain an impression that they have sensed what it was like to live at the time of the Holocaust.

The teaching strategies used in primary education lend themselves to learning about aspects of the Holocaust. Teachers are able to develop effective cross-curricular links as they plan the whole curriculum for their class and are able to plan a thematic curriculum that makes it possible to spend an extended period of time based around a topic or subject. It may be argued that addressing prejudices of various kinds is more effective with this age group as in secondary education peer pressure can 'exert a powerful countervailing force' (Short and Carrington, 1995). Learning from the Holocaust can present opportunities to consider present concerns, including belonging, community, identity, loyalty and peer pressure. These are all issues that children encounter regularly in their daily lives. Considering how people make choices, and using the past as a stimulus to consider the present, may help children to consider how they can make a difference and to understand that one person's actions can have an impact.

Addressing misconceptions

When teaching about the Holocaust, it can be easy to lose any sense of individual tragedy or loss in the magnitude of the genocide. It is difficult for any person to appreciate the vastness of the death of six million people. Many textbooks focus on numbers in their Holocaust sections, 'causing students to view the topic as an aggregate event rather than as a circumstance that affected individual people' (Wilkins, 1996 cited in Lindquist, 2006: 215). The scale of the Holocaust is beyond comprehension and can lead to a sense of detachment from the reality of the events. To counteract this, learners need to consider the lives of individual people – the families, grandparents, parents and children – that are behind the statistics (USHMM, 2001). The account of Hannah, cited earlier, is one such example. It is only by considering loss on a personal level, focusing on individual people, that any understanding of the Holocaust can become accessible to children.

This sentiment is summarised in the inscription placed on the medals awarded to non-Jewish rescuers by Yad Vashem:

> Whoever saves a single life, it is as if he had saved the whole world.
>
> (The Talmud, Sanhedrin 4:5)

Similarly, it is possible to suggest that those who can begin to appreciate the plight of one person can begin to gain some glimmer of understanding of the wider impact of the Holocaust. Whilst this will be a fragmentary understanding, it still provides the opportunity to help children to develop their understanding and attitudes.

Teachers cannot and should never give their learners a sense of what it was like to live at the time of the Holocaust; it is not possible to understand fully or to feel what others endured: 'No simulation, regardless of its intensity, can give students a true sense of what it was like to have been a victim during the Holocaust' (Lindquist, 2007: 28). It is important to be realistic about what one is trying to achieve with learners and to help them to appreciate that their understanding is partial. Teachers can use histories, documentaries, memoirs, diaries, and other valid sources that allow students to hear the accounts of survivors and learn about their lives. Establishing a sound rationale for studying the events, setting the historical context, using reflective thinking, honouring the memory of the victims, and creating an emotionally secure environment for students as they study the Holocaust will help to ensure that learners benefit from their consideration of this 'watershed event in history' (USHMM, 2001: 2).

Case study

At *Beth Shalom*, the Holocaust Memorial Centre at Laxton, Nottinghamshire, in the UK, children of primary school age are able to visit *The Journey*, an age-appropriate interactive exhibition presenting the story of Leo, a young Jewish boy living in Nazi Germany. Through a series of rooms showing his home, classroom, his father's shop and the railway carriage in which he is evacuated as part of the *kindertransport* programme, they are able to consider his experience. By using technology so that Leo can 'address' the children, artifacts and displays, and a meeting with a survivor to hear a talk and ask questions addressed at a level appropriate to the maturity of the children, opportunities are provided to consider different stages in Leo's story. Leo is a composite character, chosen to represent children taking part in the *kindertransport*. This raises the question of how children learn history through fiction, albeit based in fact. Details of *The Journey* are included at the end of this chapter.

It is essential to provide a safe learning environment and to enable children to make sense of issues arising from the Holocaust in the light of children's own life experiences. Pupils may feel challenged at times, but any discomfort needs to be balanced by a sense of safety in the learning environment. One may conjecture that deep learning only takes place when one feels some discomfort as it is a part of challenging and changing one's knowledge and understanding. Many of us will find talking about prejudice and discrimination difficult. However, this can make discussions all the more worthwhile.

The need for wider knowledge and understanding

Considering context

Before studying the Holocaust, it is important to consider how to set it in context. To introduce the Jews at, for example, the time of *Krystallnacht* (9–10 November 1938) is to risk stereotyping them as a victim group. The lives of Jewish people before the war (and before the rise of Nazism) can provide information about ordinary and outstanding individuals and families; hearing stories, listening to music and reading poetry can all give a 'face' to Jews before the war. It is important that children learn about the Jews as people before they embark on a study of the Holocaust. This may be an important contribution to learning that can be made in Key Stage 2, in preparation for later studies in secondary education.

Case study

Wiseman (2006) illustrates the importance of having wider knowledge of Jewish people with an experience from an initial lesson on the Holocaust:

> A highly intelligent, highly indignant pupil [in Year 6] quite correctly challenged me with, 'I don't get it ... The last time I heard about the Jews was that thousands of them were being led out of slavery in Egypt through the wilderness by Moses and now I am hearing that it's the 1930s and millions of them are in Germany, Poland, etc. They sound like they are still in slavery ... Did nothing happen in between?'

In simplifying the history in order to make it accessible to children in Key Stage 2, there is a danger that we have to resort to stereotypes. To talk about the Nazis and the Jews is to simplify the experience of different individual people and to oversimplify the context in which the Holocaust occurred. Similarly, to learn about perpetrators, victims, bystanders and rescuers is to seek to pigeon-hole people who may have faced very complex decisions and engaged in a variety of roles at different times.

If children have little or no sense of Jewish culture and identity, they will find it difficult to consider the experience of Jews during the Holocaust. Common misconceptions include the idea that Jewish people are foreign, that they all come from Jerusalem, or that they cannot be British. They may have seen pictures of Hassidic Jewish men with beards and Homburg hats and have made assumptions from this (Grugeon and Woods, 1990; Short, 2003b). Children need to be able to understand that Jewish people can be regarded as a religious and an ethnic group and to appreciate that many people with different beliefs and lifestyles live side-by-side in the UK, as they did in pre-war Germany (this also links to an understanding of *xeno-racism*, outlined in Chapter 2). This degree of preparation, necessary before children can embark on a study of the Holocaust, may be felt to be so significant that it makes it unfeasible in primary schools.

Tackling Issues box

Tommy is a collection of drawings by Czech artist Bedrich Fritta that was created for his son's third birthday (Fritta, 1999). At that time, they were imprisoned in the Theresienstadt ghetto where Fritta was head of the technical department. His role, along with other artists, was to create propaganda materials for the Germans, although they also secretly made images of the grim realities of their daily lives. The book shows how people would have celebrated a birthday outside the ghetto, with pictures of presents and cakes. It also includes memories of the outside world to teach his son, Thomas, about trees, flowers, birds and animals in the hope that one day he would experience them for himself. Fritta died in Auschwitz and his wife, Hansi, died in Terezin. After the war, his father's friend and fellow artist Leo Hass and his wife, Erna, adopted Thomas. The album of drawings was recovered from its hiding place in the walls of Theresienstadt.

Lorna uses the *Tommy* drawings when working with children in Key Stage 1:

> We do not talk about the Holocaust, death or suffering; instead, I show them the special present of drawings that Tommy's dad made. I focus on life and teach about living. I lay out all the postcards on the carpet and the children choose one. They make up stories about each picture. Sometimes we look only at the cards showing transport, food or animals. I focus on different categories at different times. We get to know Tommy over a period of several days and I place the book [which includes all the pictures] in the class library. It usually becomes very popular and the children come to like Tommy. I stress that Tommy lived many years ago in a far away country: distancing techniques ensure that the children will not become scared or face personal discomfort as the story develops. I always smile a great deal and am positive about the pictures. I don't personalise pictures – we don't think about what pictures we would like or what our favourite animal is. I do this so that the children don't worry that what happened to Tommy might happen to them. The focus is all on Tommy, who lived many years ago and far away. I repeat these facts often.
>
> Once we have got to know Tommy, I explain that the pictures were made as a birthday present. At that time, Tommy's life was not very easy; he had to live away from home in a place that he was not allowed to leave. There was not much to eat and his parents had to sell what they had to buy food. I explain that when there was no cake for Tommy's birthday, his dad painted one for him. In later years, it is possible to return to the story of Tommy and to add more detail. I focus on the picture of him with his uncle, to show that he was cared for after the war. On Holocaust Memorial Day this provides some context, as we can remember Tommy's parents, who died. Each year, before Holocaust Memorial Day, the children return to Tommy's pictures and learn a little more about him.

This example suggests a spiral curriculum, which starts with the real-life character of Tommy and develops a sense of interest in and relationship with him. His likes, interests and needs are considered before any sense of life in the ghetto, the death of his parents or the Holocaust. The use of drawings means that both discussions and questions can be tailored to the cognitive and emotional abilities of learners. A key strategy is that children get to know Tommy as a person before they come to know more about his circumstances. This reflects the assertions elsewhere in this chapter that it is important to know about the normality of Jewish people's lives before the war in advance of learning about their experiences during it.

Consider:

- How might using such artefacts from the time of the Holocaust support children's learning and understanding?
- What are your feelings about the idea of returning to the story at different times to develop the narrative and raise new issues?
- How might the story of *Tommy* provide a basis for looking at further accounts (e.g. of Anne Frank) as children move into upper Key Stage 2?

Considering other genocides

We now move to consider more contemporary situations of genocide. Genocide, as defined by Article 2 of the United Nations' *Convention on the Prevention and Punishment of the Crime of Genocide* (UN, 1948b), means any of the following acts committed with intent to destroy, in whole or in part, a national, ethnic, racial or religious group:

- killing members of the group;
- causing serious bodily or mental harm to members of the group;
- deliberately inflicting on the group conditions of life calculated to bring about its physical destruction in whole or in part;
- imposing measures intended to prevent births within the group; and
- forcibly transferring children of the group to another group.

Older children may be aware of the term, which is complex and debated extensively by experts, and will have seen footage in news broadcasts and documentaries of families who have been displaced, of people who have been maltreated or murdered, and of mass graves. Again, it is important to consider why any discussion of genocide might take place with children:

> ... if the study of genocide is not also the study of humanity and inhumanity, if it does not add to our understanding of human behavior, then what is its purpose in the curriculum?
>
> (Drew cited in Totten, Feinberg, & Fernekes, 2001: 4)

As with the Holocaust, to focus on the atrocities involved in more contemporary genocides is inappropriate in primary school classrooms. However, children may bring questions or views into the classroom (as noted in the concluding chapter of this book) and teachers will need to respond to these. Teachers may need to consider with children whether it is ever acceptable to kill others; whether people should be discriminated against because of stereotypes or differences; and how power can be abused for the benefit of some and to the detriment, or destruction, of others. It is most likely that children encounter genocide when a public appeal is launched to address significant need. Responding to the needs of others can provide a positive way of reacting to the distressing information that children have come across, without needing to embark on a detailed analysis of the social and political causes.

Developing practice

In order to develop effective practice, we need to consider:

- how appropriate it is to explore aspects of war and conflict with learners in upper Key Stage 2, or before;
- whether other situations or examples are more appropriate to support the exploration of issues, values and attitudes;
- how we plan overtly to nurture respect, acceptance and tolerance;
- whether it is appropriate to study the Second World War without mentioning wider aspects of the conflict;
- how we use experiential learning with our children – encouraging them to self-reflect on their own values and attitudes;
- whether our curriculum promotes the prosocial behaviours of empathy and altruism;
- how we balance the desire to protect childhood innocence with the need to explore issues that children know of and are concerned about;
- how we address questions from individual children that other children may not yet be mature enough to consider; and
- how we deal with a situation when a child raises an issue or brings a resource to the classroom that is not appropriate for their age and maturity.

Summary and key points

It is not my intention to persuade teachers that Holocaust education should, or should not, be a part of the primary school curriculum. I have used it as a focus to explore some of the difficult issues faced by teachers when considering conflict and violence. This chapter has sought to raise some of the main difficulties and benefits, and to provide readers with the opportunity to make their own evaluation. With regard to the Holocaust, some key points arising from this chapter are:

- The term Holocaust is specific and needs careful explanation.
- The Holocaust or Shoah refers specifically to the genocide involving the Jews in the Second World War.
- It is important that the events of the Holocaust are not divorced from their context.
- Teachers need to have a clear understanding of why they are teaching about the Holocaust; could issues and skills be addressed through other events or situations?

- Teaching needs to be integrated within a larger framework of knowledge and skills development and include an awareness of what will be studied in Key Stage 3.
- Children should not come away from lessons thinking that they know what it was like to live during the Holocaust.
- A continuum of knowledge, skills and understanding needs to be developed so that children explore issues at age-appropriate levels throughout their schooling.

Teachers may find that they work in schools where the Holocaust is a part of the curriculum, or where Holocaust Memorial Day is marked by all or some of the children. There may be a sense that such opportunities ought to be taken because their focus is significant and relates to a defining event in the shaping of the modern world. However, to embark on such learning or commemorations because they seem to be the right thing to do is not sufficient in itself. The same applies to a variety of situations. If any learning about war and conflict is to take place in primary education, it requires a carefully structured rationale underpinned by teachers' sound subject knowledge, an appreciation of the complexities of the subject, and a sense of linkage to the wider curriculum (including progression into secondary education) and the ethos of the school.

Useful resources

Boyne, J. (2006) *The Boy in the Striped Pyjamas*, London: David Fickling Books.

Morgenstern, N. (1998) *I Wanted to Fly Like a Butterfly: a child's recollections of the Holocaust*, Jerusalem: Yad Vashem.

Sarah's Attic is an interactive website for children aged 8–12 years, provided by the Shoah Museum (Memorial de la Shoah), Paris. It is available in English and French: http://www.grenierdesarah.org/

The Holocaust Exhibition at the Imperial War Museum, London: http://london.iwm.org.uk/server/show/ConWebDoc.1454

The Journey, Beth Shalom Holocaust Memorial Centre, Nottinghamshire: http://hcentrenew.aegisdns.co.uk/?page_id=718

The Taskforce for International Cooperation on Holocaust Education, Remembrance and Research (ITF) website includes guidelines for teaching. Whilst these are aimed at secondary schools, the approach will be of interest to primary school teachers: www.holocausttaskforce.org/education/guidelines-for-teaching/

USHMM (undated) *Guidelines for Teaching About the Holocaust*, Washington, DC: United States Holocaust Memorial Museum. www.ushmm.org/education/foreducators/guideline/

Yad Vashem International School for Holocaust Studies, Jerusalem can provide lesson plans, resources and other materials to support teachers across all age phases:
www1.yadvashem.org/yv/en/education/index.asp

Further reading

Glanz, J. (2001) *Holocaust Handbook for Educators*, Dubuque, IA: Kendall/Hunt.

Grugeon, E. and Woods, P. (1990) *Educating All: multicultural perspectives in the primary school*, London: Routledge.

Jones, A. (2006) *Genocide: a Comprehensive Introduction*, London: Routledge/Taylor & Francis.

Wiseman, H. (2006) *Guidelines for Teaching About the Holocaust to Year 6 Pupils*, London: Imperial War Museum. http://london.iwm.org.uk/server/show/nav.1199

Acknowledgement

Permission to use extracts from *I Wanted to Fly Like a Butterfly* kindly granted by Yad Vashem. All rights reserved to Yad Vashem The Holocaust Martyrs' and Heroes' Remembrance Authority, The International School for Holocaust Studies, Yad Vashem.

Chapter 9

Learning and the market

Addressing values and consumerism

> For the past three months we have been monitoring the market. Working in groups with a set budget children had to decide how much to invest in a savings account and how many shares to buy from a choice of ten leading companies. They also chose a house from adverts in the local newspaper and have been monitoring mortgage payments for its advertised price. Every Friday we calculate the losses and gains. It has been fascinating to see the impact of the *credit crunch* [of 2009]. The children have been surprised as their mortgage payments went down and disappointed as their shares decreased in value and interest on savings diminished. It was been a valuable lesson in real-life experience.
>
> (John, Year 6 teacher)

Children face a barrage of attention from the media, and advertisers in particular. Their spending power, and their influence on adult spending, is highly significant. This chapter explores the influences faced by children and explores how they can develop the social and emotional literacy necessary to deal with the competing pressures upon their daily lives. It also explores how children can be supported in interpreting the media images and messages around them and how children can learn to question some of the assumptions and presumptions of contemporary society and begin to develop their own worldviews. This chapter also examines how market forces operate in schools, including target setting, league tables and success criteria that exert pressure on children to 'succeed' according to external measures. Throughout the chapter, I question some of the assumptions underlying these and explore alternatives.

Education and financial capability

In 2000, the Department for Education and Employment set out the case for the importance of financial capability as a skill within the education system. It argued that citizens in general are being faced by ever more complex financial decisions and that financial capability is thus an ever more important life skill for everyone. The context for this is an increasingly flexible labour market, short-term contracts, the increased age to which people are living and the stress upon lifelong learning. Indeed:

> Financial capability is an important life skill for everyone: the ability to make financial decisions is the key to identifying and making best use of the opportunities in today's changing world.
>
> (DfEE, 2000a: 4)

This relates directly to the fifth aim of the *Every Child Matters* agenda (DfES, 2004: 1): to enable all children to achieve 'economic well-being'. When working with children, it is important to remember that they come from a range of backgrounds, including those with different incomes and different ways of managing finances. Some children will be very aware of household finances and will be privy to discussions and decisions (and arguments) about money. How parents and carers spend their income will vary considerably, as will a child's awareness of how decisions are reached about earning, saving and spending. Some children will be conscious of the arrival of bills, and may be party to discussions about limiting water or electricity consumption in the home in order to save money. Other children will have no awareness of such expense or how utilities are paid for. The rise of direct debit as a means of payment and the use of paperless bills sent electronically via e-mail may both impact on a child's experience. The days of dreading the arrival of a postal worker and the thud of a bill on the mat are diminishing. In addition, the use of credit and debit cards to pay for shopping can limit a child's knowledge and understanding of the use of money; some children may not associate purchases with expenditure, as their parents and carers operate in a relatively cashless manner. DfEE (2000a: 12) suggests that 'one way round the issue of everyone having different home experiences is to provide a common experience in the classroom which will serve as a base of shared knowledge.' This approach is reflected in the example at the start of this chapter.

The DfEE (2000a:5) suggests that the main aims of personal finance education are:

- to develop financial capability for both girls and boys at all ages; and
- to enable children to make informed judgements and to take effective decisions regarding the use and management of money in their present and adult lives.

Such judgements and attitudes, it is claimed, will enable children and young people to move into adulthood 'with confidence in their ability to deal effectively and efficiently with the range of financial decisions' (DfEE, 2000a: 5).

It is important to stress here that these ideas form a part of the guidance issued by the DfEE for those in Key Stages 1 and 2, that is, for children aged five to eleven years. Some will wish to question how much awareness, responsibility and pressure children should face in these relatively early years. Whilst a fundamental aim of *The National Curriculum* for England is to prepare children for adulthood and to help them to make informed choices throughout their lives (DfEE and QCA, 1999), one may question the extent to which this should be the focus of education in the primary phase.

Pause for thought

Consider the vignette at the start of this chapter.

- How might this approach help to develop children's financial capability?
- Is this an appropriate activity for children to undertake in the primary phase of education?
- Do you have any concerns or doubts about the effectiveness of this approach?

- At what stage should the curriculum start to prepare children for adulthood, and when should it focus on developing them as children? Are the two different, or conflicting, aspects of learning?
- Is it appropriate to introduce children to capitalist systems at this age and to normalise such economic machinations?

Children's spending patterns and power

In past years, the print media have highlighted the spending power of children and young people in the UK. Their income may come from a range of sources, including pocket money, parental/carer rewards for success at school, birthday and Christmas gifts, and even from the tooth-fairy. Their combined wealth has been calculated to be £7.2 million (Firth, 2006), with an average of £800 per year including gifts. This equates to about £15 per week. It has been calculated that those aged 13 to 15 spend an average of £20.40 per week, compared with £11.30 for 10- to 12-year-olds and £7.00 for those aged seven to nine (Thornton, 2005). Jones (2007) suggests that the average weekly income from pocket money is £8.00. Some children supplement their income by selling old toys on eBay. Figures from high street bank the Halifax, gathered over twenty years from 1987, suggest that the amounts given to children have risen by 600 per cent in that time, compared with a rise in inflation of 99 per cent over the same period (Jones, 2007). This reinforces the notion of the growing significance of the spending power of children. Of those children questioned, most said that they did not save their pocket money for anything in particular, spending it on sweets, going out and drinks. Those who did save tended to have computer games or holiday times in mind (Office for National Statistics, 2005a).

Responsible spending

Writing in the *Daily Mail*, Poulter (2008) reported how high street banks are giving debit cards to children as young as eleven. Whilst in the past these might have been restricted to use in cash machines or at bank branches, Poulter reported that one fifteen-year-old boy used his card to buy cigarettes, Viagra and a fake adult ID via the internet. This raises the question of how younger children might be able to use such cards. The cards are Visa enabled, which means that they can be used widely. Poulter notes that whilst there are safeguards to ensure that children cannot use such cards on adult websites, one bank insisted that it is the responsibility of parents/carers to police how they are used. In this case, the parents only discovered how the card was being used when they received a demand from the customs authority for duty on cigarettes bought via an overseas website. The bank expected that children would inform their parents/carers that they had received the card.

Other banks offer a Visa enabled card to children of 11 and above, but require the written permission of their parent or guardian. It is now possible to buy such cards with a pre-loaded balance over the counter in many shops, which means that carers and parents may have no knowledge of their child's ability to buy online. When the fifteen-year-old's father complained to the bank, he was told that 'it was not down to them to monitor other people's children, and that teenagers who were brought up well would not abuse this facility.' Such examples provide the context for the consideration of children's exposure to financial pressures and practices.

The banks are not the only institutions giving children glimpses into the financial world of adults. In schools, 'enterprise' education helps children to explore the world of finance, to consider profit, loss and expenditure, and seeks to prepare them for life in the contemporary world. The appropriateness of this needs to be questioned, particularly in the primary school.

Case study

In one school, the head teacher introduced a *Dragon's Den* style initiative, using an idea developed from the popular BBC television series. Groups of children in Year 6 were asked to pitch business ideas for raising money at the school summer fair. Each group had to consider the costs of making games or other fundraising activities, suggest how much to charge other children to play or to buy the goods, and develop a projection of profit. The children had to request start-up costs (presented as a costed list of resources) and indicate the percentage profit anticipated. One group costed the ingredients needed for baking biscuits, another the costs for providing drinks to be sold at a realistic profit, one developed a small-scale sports tournament with prizes where the participants paid a fee to enter their team. The head teacher commented:

> The children were able to apply their mathematical skills, work with money and use skills of presentation when pitching their idea ... The activity pulled together a wide range of skills and gave them a realistic and purposeful context. When I announced that all the groups had the go-ahead the cheers were euphoric!

Such a situation provides a context in which children have to apply themselves to a problem and work towards a realistic and carefully formulated solution. However, the approach needs to be addressed with care:

- the outcome may give false expectations in the future, as all groups were successful;
- the situation may be stressful for some children and there is the threat of failure;
- competition may be divisive and, even with an apparently successful outcome for all, inevitably, some groups will raise more money than others.

In addition, the activity may overemphasise the financial aspects of the project, rather than valuing the need to provide a service to others through the sale of goods or the enjoyment of playing games. Whilst such values may stand in opposition to the workings of free-market economics, they are nonetheless important. Some aspects may relate directly to the school's curriculum in overt ways; however, it is important to consider the values inherent to the 'hidden curriculum', which are equally important in preparing children and young people to be active and responsible citizens. It is also important that, as teachers, we are fully aware of both hidden and overt messages that such activities purvey to our children and their impact.

Tackling issues

The DfEE (2000a: 6) sets out the foci of financial capability, using three strands.

Financial knowledge and understanding involve:

- helping children to understand the concept of money;
- developing insights into its nature and usage;
- preparing children to face everyday financial issues; and
- informing decisions and choices about personal finances.

Financial skills and competence involve:

- exploring personal situations and those beyond our control;
- considering day-to-day money management;
- being able to identify and tackle problems or issues with confidence; and
- managing financial situations effectively and efficiently.

Financial responsibility is concerned with:

- considering the wider impact of decisions about money and personal finance;
- exploring financial issues for an individual's future and for wider society;
- understanding that decisions can have an impact personally and on families and communities;
- knowing that decisions and actions are closely linked with value judgements of various kinds (social, moral, aesthetic, cultural, and environmental, as well as economic); and
- appreciating that decisions have social and ethical dimensions.

Consider which of these aspects form a part of your existing practice. Are there any that you feel are inappropriate in a school setting? How do they reflect your personal priorities for developing children's learning?

Sustainability, needs and wants

Areas such as the environment and sustainability are addressed in Chapter 4. However, here it is important to consider the transient and temporary nature of many things in contemporary society. In a world where acquisition is cumulative (in other words, where getting what we want leads to us wanting more), we must consider the difference between what we *need* and what we *want*. I may want the latest computer game, but once I purchase it my interest may fade quickly. Technology develops at such a pace that what was once seen as a luxury can quickly be seen as disposable. One only has to look at the latest mobile phone technology to find an example. The playground can all too often provide an environment in which keeping up to date with the latest gadgets and gizmos brings acceptance and status. Helping children to consider what they *want* and what they *need* is an important part of the education process. Helping them to appreciate the value of possessions, as opposed to their cost in financial terms, and enabling them to consider whether personal attributes can be worth more than ownership, is an important part of exploring who they are. The value of friendship, kindness, care and empathy cannot be commodified, but certainly must be valued: who I am is worth far more than what I own.

The notion of *ubuntu*, found in South African societies, provides one model for interpreting our humanity in the very different context of capitalist Western society. The word may be translated as 'I am – because you are' and suggests that we need other people in order to be fulfilled. The notion that my humanity is inextricably bound up in yours is important: if one member of our group is suffering, unhappy or in need, then this impacts on the experience of us all. It is a notion that has been taken up by many organisations and propagated by Archbishop Desmond Tutu (Tutu, 1999). It can help to put the notions of wants and needs in context, and help me to consider my own wants in terms of the needs of others. I may be the wealthiest and most powerful person on the planet, but, if I find tomorrow that I am its sole inhabitant, these attributes will be rendered worthless. My position in society depends on others, and my values and beliefs are shown in the ways in which I treat others. The very ways in which we define ourselves (as child, partner, friend, worker) are all bound up in relation to others and our lives are bound up in a complex and intangible connection to others (as is explored in more detail in Chapter 4). Whilst it is not the purpose of this chapter to discuss such metaphysical concepts in detail, they do impinge greatly on our relationships and, thus, on our spending choices, the ways in which we value the work and service offered by others and the ways in which we see the world. As such, they are political and economic in nature and must inform any market-based principles in our schools. They are fundamental to the two aims of *The National Curriculum* in England (DfEE and QCA, 1999): to provide opportunities for all pupils to learn and achieve, and to promote pupils' spiritual, moral, social and cultural development. As educators, we must consider the need to have ethical discussions with children so that they understand the difference between needs and wants and are able to evaluate a society that often portrays wants and desires as immediately attainable.

The power of children's spending

Children are an important and influential consumer group. In recent years, notions have developed about the 'child market' and the commercial practices used to reach the under-twelve age group. Market researchers follow the social trends that affect the buying habits of children and young people. Their findings directly influence manufacturers and advertisers. An example of market research in action is the recent use of the term 'tweenage', or 'tweens', to refer to older children or young teenagers between the ages of nine and thirteen. Market researchers *Datamonitor* (2006) indicate that the spending power of tweens in the UK is rising faster than that of any other group and their autonomous spending is increasing. This suggests that they are an important target group for advertising.

In general, advertising is seen by many children as informative rather than persuasive: as providing a helpful indication of what is available in the shops (Childwise 2003,

Young 2003). Before the age of twelve, children may be able to understand the motives behind advertisements and to differentiate between persuasion and information, but may be able to apply these skills only with adult support or reminders (Peterson and Lewis, 1988). If adults ask a direct question about what the advertisement intends to do, children are able to reflect on its aims and purposes. Dorr (1986) found that by the age of eight most children are capable of differentiating between television programmes and advertisements. Prior to this point they find it difficult to separate fact and fiction (DCSF, 2008a). Thus educators and parents/carers need to support children of primary school age in interpreting broadcast media so that they process and evaluate the messages they receive. This is particularly important when children aged 2 – 11 years spend around 17 hours per week watching television (Datamonitor, 2006).

Large stores have ranges of products such as cosmetics, CDs and magazines specifically targeted at children. Datamonitor (2006), however, asserts that the spending power of tweens goes further, to more expensive purchases such as cosmetic surgery, laptops, hand-held computers and mobile phones. The importance of children and young people as consumers increases dramatically if account is taken of their influence on the spending of carers and parents, particularly through what is termed as 'pester power' when children skilfully wear down parental/carer resistance. For example, 60 per cent of parents surveyed agreed that they give in to children's demands for food products in the supermarket (Turner et al. 2006). Thus, manufacturers and advertisers see children and teenagers as a primary and influential market in their own right, and a particular demographic to target.

Children's backgrounds

It is important to recognise that children in any class in a school will come from a range of backgrounds, including homes with contrasting levels of wealth. Children will have varying levels of awareness of how their home lives contrast with their peers. The clothing labels they wear, their levels of pocket money, the car their parent or carer drives and the holidays they take or do not take will all impact on how they perceive their life in comparison with those of others.

Schools often see having a uniform as being a great leveller, which helps to avoid competition in terms of having the latest designer label goods. However, this, in itself, does not eradicate difference. Some families will be able to afford new items of uniform more regularly than others and some families will pass down sweatshirts and other garments through the family as children grow. Short of schools providing free uniforms on demand, and laundry services, some children will always appear more smartly presented than others. This raises an important issue for schools: how can values be developed and promoted that appreciate individuals on more than the basis of appearance? How can friendship, loyalty, kindness, generosity of spirit and concern be valued more highly than other more superficial attributes? How can this be done within a free market setting that prizes material possessions and success?

Fundraising and charity

Undertaking fundraising activities to support others in society can be one way in which children are enabled to make plans to raise and handle money. In one school, an

'Enterprise Fair' was organised by pupils in Year 5. Using resources provided by the school, they made a series of games and charged other pupils small amounts of money to play. They had to calculate how much to charge and whether to fund small prizes from the proceeds, and they had to collect money, calculate change and provide a final total. This exercise provided a real-life situation in which money was handled and financial practicalities were discussed. The profits were donated to the local hospice.

There can be drawbacks. Such an event might reinforce notions of dependency: raising money for an orphanage in central Africa or for a television fundraising appeal can stereotype those in need and suggest that they are helpless or dependent on the charity of other, wealthier, people. It is important to consider the ethics surrounding the notion of charity: children may need to question why some people are wealthier than others and why some use far more of the world's resources than others. This sets the discussion in a wider context. Whilst it may be essential and appropriate in the short-term to provide aid for an area hit by a natural disaster, it is also important to consider the bigger picture. Doing this in a way that does not overburden children with a sense of guilt requires careful planning and execution.

The notion of charity and charitable works is commonly found in organisations working with children (Adams, Hyde & Woolley, 2008). A wide range of child-care settings receives regular approaches from non-government organisations asking for permission to visit their establishments to make presentations about their work, and often to leave fundraising materials. Whilst it might be necessary to raise funds for areas affected by disaster, where the prompt delivery of humanitarian aid may alleviate suffering or loss of life, what message does this send to the children and young people involved in such an enterprise? It is possible that it perpetuates an image of the powerful supporting the powerless, and of the relatively affluent supporting the needy. This does nothing to challenge the process or to question why it is that some people in the world have sufficient or a surplus, whilst others go without. A belief in the link between all humanity, in the spirit of *ubuntu*, necessitates that such challenging questions are asked. Why is it that, as a result of the coincidence of being born in an affluent and powerful country, we can be privy to a range of benefits and excesses denied to the majority of the world's population? How do we feel about this position? What do our values and beliefs lead us to consider doing as a result? The 'West' seems to accept the notion that the polarisation between rich and poor is acceptable, or at least tolerable, if there are systems in place to provide a 'conscience-salving safety net' such as fundraising (Davies, 2002: 116). We need to ensure that our fundraising activities do more than ease consciences. McGuinn (2002: 138) suggests that unless we rise to the challenge of engaging in education for a better world, which involves challenging inequality, we have no future:

> I am not convinced that we, as a society, actually believe in 'education for a better world'. If we did, our education system would not be dominated by the traditional, work-orientated, subject-discrete curriculum which now prevails. I fear that we are more interested in education – or perhaps I should say 'training' – for the world *as it is now* – a hierarchical world where people compete with each other for a finite and rapidly diminishing share of material resources.

This better world can only be achieved if we discuss the causes behind need, rather than organising events to obscure it (as discussed in more detail in Chapter 4).

In addition, some of us will be faced with dilemmas when it comes to fundraising. In responding to national television-based appeals that focus on raising funds for projects in our own countries and overseas, there may be a tension because some or many of the children in our care should be the beneficiaries of funds, rather than the contributors. However, the sense of supporting others, or being aware of wider needs and of working together to make a difference, make it important to become involved in projects. Involvement brings the opportunity to develop shared values, to cooperate and to empathise. At times, the local benefits, in terms of skills and learning, may outweigh the necessity to discuss the wider global and political issues. It can be difficult to reconcile some of these ideas.

The classroom and the market

We turn now to consider some different issues, exploring several ways in which the market impacts on the school system and particularly the processes commonly experienced by children and teachers. These issues are different from those relating to children's spending power and contribute different pressures that affect children's schooling.

Target setting

Target setting and review is one part of the assessment process, whether this be an assessment of learning or of behaviour. If it is addressed in a cooperative manner, with staff and children working together, and including parents/carers as appropriate, then it can foster greater independence and help children to set realistic expectations for themselves (MacGrath, 2000). Indeed:

> At its best, target setting can give a sense of purpose and direction, for individual pupils as well as for whole groups, especially if both pupils and teachers are party to the process, rather than the victims of it. At its worst, however, a sense of desperation to meet targets will override professional judgement about what needs to be done and will distort, rather than enhance, the educational process.
>
> (Wragg, 2001: 84)

Setting targets will not make a positive impact upon children's development unless it is supported by a collaborative process. It is essential that children feel the target-setting process to be realistic, achievable and fair. If they feel that decisions about their targets are unfair, or too lenient, this will undermine the process. By making success criteria overt, teachers make it possible for children to succeed; being assessed against hidden criteria can be demoralising, like trying to win a game without knowing the rules (Woolley & Johnston, 2007). This, in turn, can undermine the integrity of the teacher and destroy the trust between educator and learner.

At best, the teacher will also identify some of their own personal targets to work towards in the classroom, choosing content that is appropriate for sharing with the children, thus modelling the process so that their learners can support them and offer praise at appropriate moments. Agreeing clear expectations is an effective way of motivating children and of providing small steps to facilitate their learning: they are aware of what is needed for them to succeed and can work towards this success with greater confidence and independence (Jacques & Hyland, 2003). Teachers can model this process and can ensure that it becomes an accepted part of classroom routines. As I have argued elsewhere, at its best target setting provides a clear indication to all parties of what is to be achieved, and the reflection that follows helps to identify the next small steps in the continuum of learning (Woolley & Johnston, 2007).

However, teachers need to question the purpose and validity of setting targets. If the outcome is that learning is commodified and the classroom turned into a marketplace driven by competition, teachers need to consider the appropriateness of this and what messages it sends to children about their intrinsic value and the value of their learning. In contrast, if the process is about identifying next steps in learning and supporting progression and growth, it may have some validity. It is essential to have a clear philosophical standpoint to underpin the approach taken in schools so that they do not just become an extension of the market, or mimic it because it is presumed that this is what should be done. It seems that, increasingly, we live in an educational world where only what can be measured is seen as important (McGuinn, 2002). Schools that do not engage effectively in the assessment game, competing in a market-driven culture to attract students and, thereby, funding, find themselves in an increasingly untenable position.

Case study

When one school in the West Midlands gained a sudden and significant influx of children from the families of migrant workers, some existing parents/carers decided to transfer their children to a neighbouring school. They did this because they felt that such increasing diversity would lead to falling standards. Initially, the school struggled with some of the issues that the new pupils brought. Through effective management and the commitment of members of staff they maintained and raised standards and received awards acknowledging their success as an inclusive school. Some of the new children brought a work ethic that influenced the atmosphere in the school and their commitment to learning helped to support the efforts by staff. Market forces might have affected this school significantly, but now the school has a reputation for valuing diversity and is a first choice destination for carers and parents in the area.

The bigger picture

It is necessary to broaden the discussion to consider not only the forces of the market in the education system, but to consider how the systems of society work in totality. Here it is only possible to do this very briefly. Tony Blair's vision for the future was globalisation, with 'power, wealth and opportunity … in the hands of the many, not the few' (Ward 2001: 5); Gordon Brown (2005) was in agreement, stating that his vision was for 'a Britain made for globalisation – the location of choice and the place for business to be.' This globalisation, coupled with a commitment to the poor and the weak and a focus on justice, was to empower the majority of the population. Whilst this implied some kind of *redistribution* of power and wealth (although *New Labour* stalwartly avoided any association with this traditional plank of socialist policy), the fact that Blair spoke about power being in the hands of the many, not the few, still leaves the few without power. Can it be right to maintain injustice because it only affects a minority? It is also totally unrealistic, given the ascendency of capitalist market economics in the 1990s and beyond. Cole (2008a: 90) suggests that '[a]ny idea of putting the control of globalised capital into the hands of the many is … not viable.' He argues that capitalism is, by definition, a system in which a minority exploits the majority: where the capitalists exploit the working class. With a rise in the focus on the private rather than the public, greed, rather than human welfare, is the controlling factor in the market. Blair's idea to 'use the power of community to combine [globalisation] with justice' (Ward, 2001: 5) neglects to consider the power of unaccountable multinational companies.

Two changes in the popular mindset might alleviate this disparity. First, all working people need to realise that they are a part of the *working class* (by definition, the class of those who work) and need to build a sense of mutual dependence and solidarity in this. Second, and not unrelatedly, the popular mindset needs to take on some sense of *ubuntu* (described earlier in this chapter), where my well-being is inextricably tied up with yours. Whenever I allow the status quo to remain, and enjoy benefits and privileges gained at the expense of others, I am in effect a part of the oppression of other people (Woolley, 2007b). Being an oppressor is not the way to be truly human: it denies the full personhood of both those abusing power and those being violated. Until people's values, attitudes and practices seek to establish greater equilibrium, society will be subject to capitalist market forces, which are fundamentally unjust. Behind this discussion is a need to consider the interaction and balance between rights and duties. Cole (2009) claims that this is the 'last taboo' in the education system: whilst government strategies encourage schools to engage in enterprise education and to propagate the values of the capitalist free market, they do not balance this with any need to discuss or evaluate democratic socialism. This discussion is developed in more detail in Chapter 4, with a consideration of globalisation and 'global citizenship'.

This short discussion may seem distant and divorced from the experience of teachers in the education system. However, it may cause us to pause for thought to consider the values that underpin the policies, and the values that drive this system and that we may perpetuate in our schools and classrooms, knowingly or unknowingly, through our unquestioning acceptance of the latest strategies and dictats. Much of it relates to the need to help children to develop real financial responsibility and requires that we question the motivation for, and implications of, this 'need'.

Developing practice

The workings of the market have a varied and diverse impact on children. Their choices and spending power affect others, and the use of competition and target setting in schools affects them. In order to develop effective practice, we need to consider:

- how we support children in developing the social, emotional and visual literacy necessary to deal with pressure from advertisements and other media products;
- how we explore needs and wants in age-appropriate ways to support responsible decision-making;
- how we contextualise learning so that issues are explored in real-life situations;

- how we enable children to learn safely through vicarious means;
- whether we plan to ensure that children from different socio-economic backgrounds can access activities;
- whether we encourage children to question the norms of society and some of the assumptions about how wealth is gained and used;
- whether competition is healthy (Do we evaluate its impact on learning and self-esteem?);
- how we link personal choice with its possible impact on others;
- how we balance the need to prepare learners for their future lives whilst also addressing their needs in the present;
- how we can make the target–setting process useful, supportive and manageable (Do we avoid setting targets for their own sake?);
- how financial capability sits within the aims and purposes of education as we see them.

Summary and key points

This chapter has considered developments in recent years to nurture children's financial capability. Whilst we live in a society that uses money for many significant transactions, the question of what issues children should be made aware of, and at what stage in their development, is important. Understanding how to use money and how to save may be of consequence, but learning how to develop enterprise activities may be more questionable (unless they focus on team building and social skills). Part of the aim of the *National Curriculum* may be to prepare children for work and their future role as citizens, but we need to consider how and when this is introduced and what pressures children have to face. We also need to consider how this is balanced with a belief in learning for the sake of learning itself, and whether it is really moral to educate children so that they can become part of the production machine rather than educating them because they are children.

It is clear that children have significant spending power and great influence over the spending of adults. Being able to understand the purposes and intentions of advertisements may be one way of helping children to deal with their influence and to appreciate the difference between needs and wants. In a society that over past years has emphasised a 'buy now pay later' mentality, this is an important part of helping children to appreciate the value of things and to accept that sometimes people have to wait and to save in order to achieve what really matters. The pressures that the education system places on children, arising from unnecessary competition, testing and target setting, all contribute factors that will impact on children's health and well-being (see also Chapter 6). It is essential that we develop our approaches to such pressures so that we can provide the best support we are able to give.

The market system has had a huge impact on the education system since the advent of *The National Curriculum* (DfEE and QCA, 1999). The focus on targets, success criteria and league tables has placed significant pressures on schools, teachers and children. I am not so naïve as to suggest that these can be ignored and I know what it is like to work in a school that appears to be 'failing' according to such measures. However, the value that schools add to children's lives in terms of social skills, providing safe and secure environments, nurturing individual talents and aspirations, and dealing with the impact of many social issues must not be underestimated. As teachers, we need to speak up for what we believe to be the value of education, as well as evaluating the latest strategy presented by the system.

Useful resources

DfEE (2000) *Financial Capability Through Personal Financial Education: Guidance for Schools at Key Stages 1 and 2*, Nottingham: Department for Education and Employment.

PSHE Report from Ofsted: www.ttrb.ac.uk/ViewArticle2.aspx?anchorId=11860&selectedId=11884&ContentId=13595

The Citizenship Foundation: www.citizenshipfoundation.org.uk

The Institute for Citizenship: www.citizen.org.uk/Democracy/democracy3.html

Further reading

Cefai, C. (2008) *Promoting Resilience in the Classroom: a guide to developing pupils' emotional and cognitive skills*, London: Jessica Kingsley.

Woolley, R. and Johnston, J. (2007) 'Target Setting' in Johnston, J., Halocha, J. & Chater, M. (eds) *Developing Teaching Skills in the Primary School*, Maidenhead: Open University Press.

Wragg, E. C. (2001) *Assessment and Learning in the Primary School*, London: Routledge Falmer.

Chapter 10

Conclusion – towards inclusive practice

Tackling controversial issues

> It is difficult to meet the five outcomes of *Every Child Matters* (DfES, 2004) in education, which is an environment far removed from the realities of life in the community. Many of the things that ECM seeks to address arise from issues in the community: social, economic and political, which are beyond the scope of schools and educators to address. It can be confusing to establish where we have a duty to give children a 'complete' education, and where we cross the boundaries into parental responsibilities. We should be working together, but we are coming from different perspectives.
>
> (Undergraduate student teacher)

This final chapter draws together issues from previous chapters and considers teachers' responses. Using original research undertaken with those involved in delivering primary education at different stages in their careers, it raises further issues and suggests strategies to underpin the exploration of difficult issues in general. This widens the application of the book to other issues and provides a framework to support teachers in their work. As a conclusion to the book, it explores what makes an issue controversial, and considers how such issues change over time. It also addresses how to work with parents and carers who raise concerns when issues are introduced or discussed in classrooms. It seeks to give teachers, and those in the later stages of their training, the confidence to tackle issues and to help their children to explore questions about a challenging and ever-changing world.

Summarising core values

This book has explored a range of values in the context of specific controversial issues in primary education. Here, I draw together some key elements from across the chapters.

First, children are citizens. They are not the citizens of the future; they are living in society in the here and now. Whilst *The National Curriculum* (DfEE and QCA, 1999) has a focus on preparing children for adult life, schools also need to consider how they are supported in the present. The notion of the *polis* (city) outlined in Chapter 5 provides a basis for this: as members of the community children are inevitably affected by and concerned about political issues. They have rights, enshrined in national and international law, and need to be enabled to take on increasing responsibility for their own ideas, actions, attitudes and values. These are elements that are fundamental to developing a sense of citizenship, including global citizenship and cosmopolitanism (outlined in Chapter 4), through which they can contribute to the sustainability of the planet and care for its inhabitants.

Valuing both similarity and difference is a central element to such values. Appreciating the different identities of others, whether these relate to gender, ethnicity and 'race', family background, sexuality, social class or any other difference (whether real or perceived) is a fundamental value to be upheld and exhibited by all teachers and to be encouraged in our learners. The *Code of Conduct and Practice* introduced by the General Teaching Council (England) emphasises such an approach throughout its elements (GTC, 2007). Cole's (2008b) notion of *'isms' and phobias* (outlined in the introductory chapter) underpins a great deal of thinking in this regard. It stresses the need to make a stand against discrimination and inequality, actively seeking to make a difference. The idea that 'there is no —ism here' provides a breeding ground for complacency and for inequality to be tolerated. Whatever the circumstances outside the school, classrooms should be places where the highest standards of respect, value and inclusion are both exhibited and promoted.

Teachers need to be aware of children's needs, concerns and experience outside the classroom if they are ever to meet their needs within it. Whether this is through appreciating their home backgrounds (Chapter 3) and difficult situations they may be experiencing, or through helping them to deal with change and transition (Chapter 7), there is a need to nurture the whole child. Teachers are part of a very caring profession that is committed to the needs of individual learners. However, at times the education system mitigates against this through the pressures of market forces, including tests, performance criteria and league tables. As professionals, we can find ourselves hard pressed to deliver a curriculum that seems to leave little time for personal interaction and social care.

Two aspects are particularly important when considering controversial issues with our learners. First, there is the need to allow open discussion and to enable learners to evolve their own views and values without imposing our own (discussed in Chapter 3). Second, there is the need for issues to be explored in context rather than in isolation. Without a sense of the reality surrounding values children will not be supported in applying them to their own outlooks and behaviours. This has been considered particularly in Chapter 8, where the Holocaust provides a stark example of how an issue could be 'parachuted' into the midst of a busy curriculum without a proper sense of embedding learning and making links to children's broader understanding.

Social, moral, spiritual and cultural development

That there are things beyond our comprehension, or issues that perplex or confuse us, is a part of daily life for many people. Children, like all of us, are faced with questions of life and living: 'Who am I?' 'Why am I here?' 'What is the value and purpose of life?' Beginning to make sense of the world, identifying what is important to us and identifying core values are fundamental aspects of child development and of supporting children's personal, social and emotional well-being. For some people, organised religion in some form can play a part in these quests; for others, there is an equally important sense of spirituality. In England the spiritual dimension of childhood was included in one of the two fundamental aims of *The National Curriculum*, which was concerned with children's social, moral, spiritual and cultural (SMSC) development (DfEE and QCA, 1999: 11).

Spiritual development is the one aspect of this aim that has not been a main focus of this book, but without a consideration of its place and importance this book would be incomplete. Personally, I feel this is an important, even essential, aspect of education. However, this view is not universally shared. Spirituality is intangible and ethereal; it is difficult to define. As such it does not fit easily with the definition of a controversial issue as being open to reasoned argument (as set out in the introduction to this book). For this reason, I have left it aside until this point.

Watson (1993) identifies four strands as contributing to an emerging sense of what spirituality is all about:

- *inclusiveness*: a sense of the unity and interrelatedness of all things;
- *assurance*: concerning the way things are and the reason why we are here;
- *inspiration*: gaining a sense of being channels rather than engines (in other words, being enthused and stimulated by the world around us, rather than driven by it); and
- *acceptance of mystery*: glimpsing a 'power' beyond and other than ourselves (which might be some kind of deity, an invisible link through shared humanity or nature as a unifying force).

These strands reflect much of the content of this book, although they have not been referred to in overtly spiritual terms. Understanding that there are things beyond our knowledge, comprehension or influence is a fundamental part of being human. Indeed, accepting that one will never have all the answers is an important part of the maturing process and of dealing with the complexities and trials of human existence (Adams, Hyde and Woolley, 2008). Bastide (1987) identifies this as a part of the 'religious quest', but it is equally applicable to a broader search to understand the inexplicable and to gain a sense of one's place within the wider world order. In this sense, it is a social, moral and spiritual, rather than a specifically religious quest. This is a particularly important distinction, given the increasingly secular nature of society and the fact that the notion of formal religion is alien to many children. It is not my intention here to explore the role of religious education, although for some this is a contentious area of the curriculum (for reading in this area, see Ashton, 2000; Broadbent and Brown, 2002; Bastide, 2007; Watson and Thompson, 2007; and McCreery, Palmer and Voiels, 2008). However, in the world at the moment (and perhaps at all times) religious diversity can seem divisive or threatening. This is particularly acute when religion is associated with violence or war, and it is important to ensure that whole religions are not stigmatised by the actions of a small group of militants. Using discussion and questions, supported by the need for reasoned arguments, is one way to help children to work beyond any stereotypes or discriminatory views that they may have encountered.

Issues that student teachers expect to encounter

We now return to the survey of student teachers introduced at the start of this book. Earlier, the issues that they consider to be important were outlined. Now we turn to consider the issues that they expect to encounter early in their careers (see Table 10.1). Inevitably, the answers are a prediction and may well be modified as additional experience is gained. However, they provide an interesting perspective on the perceptions of the respondent group.

Of the 6.4 per cent of students who expect never to encounter children's developing sexualities, four were training to work with children aged 3–7 years, two with children aged 5–9 years and two with children aged 3–11 years. The others did not indicate an age-range. I suspected that there might be a correlation between the age of the children and the expectation of encountering developing sexualities, but across the sample as a whole this was not the case. It is also interesting to note that whilst 9 per cent of students do not expect to address children's developing financial capability in their early career, and 53.8 per cent expect to encounter it rarely, this is a fundamental aspect of the *Every*

Table 10.1 Student teachers' responses to the question: *Do you think you will encounter these issues in your first teaching job?*

% of respondents	*Frequently*	*Sometimes*	*Rarely*	*Never*
Multicultural and antiracist education	64.1	34.6	1.3	0.0
Issues relating to democracy (e.g. school councils, children's voice)	60.3	38.5	1.3	0.0
Issues about families (separation, divorce, same-sex parents etc.)	60.3	26.9	12.8	0.0
Environmental issues (e.g. sustainability, use of resources, climate change etc.)	46.2	51.3	2.6	0.0
Education for global citizenship	44.9	43.6	10.3	1.3
Children's spiritual development	39.7	38.5	19.2	2.6
Growing up (e.g. physical changes and puberty)	35.9	42.3	21.8	0.0
Addressing issues in the news (e.g. war, famine)	35.9	53.8	10.3	0.0
How to develop community cohesion	33.3	48.7	17.9	0.0
The impact of advertising and the media on children	31.2	54.5	14.3	0.0
Bereavement (e.g. supporting bereaved children and coping with loss in the school community)	11.5	59.0	29.5	0.0
Children's developing sexualities	10.3	41.0	42.3	6.4
Developing children's financial capability	3.8	33.3	53.8	9.0
Approaching Holocaust Memorial Day and Remembrance Day	1.3	43.6	43.6	11.5

Child Matters agenda (DfES, 2004). However, my phrasing of the question may have hindered responses and perhaps it should have addressed the outcome of achieving *economic well-being*. Whilst 87.2 per cent expect to encounter Holocaust Memorial Day or Remembrance day sometimes or rarely, which is a reasonable expectation given that they are both annual events, it would be interesting to explore why over one-tenth of respondents do not expect ever to mark either of these occasions in school with their learners.

The greatest divergence between the issues student teachers perceive to be of some importance (detailed in Table 1.1 in the introductory chapter) and those that they anticipate encountering in their first appointment are in addressing the Holocaust, financial capability, developing sexualities and bereavement. In each case, students identified the issue as having greater importance than its anticipated occurrence. Here, it will be interesting to consider our own experience. Which issues did we highlight as being important at the outset of this book? Have our views changed in any way as a result of its contents? And which issues have we encountered most often at this point in our training or career? This raises questions about how we design our curriculum: are we proactive or reactive in addressing difficult and controversial issues with our learners? How do we plan to prepare them for life's challenges and support them in developing skills that they can use to apply in a range of situations and when facing various challenges or controversies?

The views of teachers

The vignette at the start of this chapter shows the concerns of a student teacher about their remit and the complexity of addressing issues from outside the classroom within the setting of a school. In this section, I share some experiences from more established teachers. They bring us back from the theories and strategies of the earlier parts of the chapter to consider practical experience.

Case study

I discussed death and loss with my class last term. I was apprehensive about how some children would react and wanted to avoid making the issues too personal. So we used the picture book *The Princess and the Castle* (Binch, 2004). I asked how the characters might feel and, having gathered some ideas as a basis, a couple of children took part in a 'hot-seat' activity. They did really well. The other children asked them questions about how they felt. I was so proud of the way they got into role. At the end of the activity we talked about how we might feel if someone died, and I used the opportunity to explain that it is ok to be sad and upset – if that is how you feel. Shaun (aged 6) told us that his grandma had died a while ago and he still felt sad. He told us he missed her and it was nice to tell everyone about her. I really felt the lesson had helped one child.

(John, Year 2 teacher)

We have been following the presidential election [of 2008] in the United States in the British newspapers and online. Jason (aged 8) asked why we don't have a woman or a black man as Prime Minister (after reading about the contest between Hillary Clinton and Barack Obama). I was able to explain that we used to have a female premier and asked whether the children would mind who became Prime Minister in the future. The only strong opinion on the matter was from a small group of girls who felt that a woman might be more caring than a man. I decided not to comment on their observation but asked whether others agreed – and asked children to give an explanation for their opinions. We didn't reach any conclusion but we did have a discussion during which the children had to develop their views and justify what they said. I used it to reinforce the idea that we need to think through the reasons for our opinions.

Sharon (Year 4 teacher)

In a SEAL lesson with Year 3 we talked about bullying and how it might make people feel. Jody told the class that she sometimes gets picked on because she has freckles. 'I wish people would just leave me alone,' she said, 'they see me every day. It's not like I am ever very different. I don't mind someone noticing but not every day.' I did not pursue the issue (although I did speak with Jody after the lesson), but used the opportunity to talk about whether it is fair to treat people differently because of how they look. I gave each child a mirror and we had to suggest how we were the same and different to other children in the class. We talked about whether it was good to be different. One of our school aims is 'To respect difference'. I was really pleased that the children mentioned this in their conversation.

Caroline (Deputy Head)

> I faced an awkward situation when one of the children started to use what might be called racist language towards other children. He did it indiscriminately, not identifying any child's 'race' but using words he had heard at home to be unkind to any child he chose. I used circle time to talk about the times when we are called kind and unkind names and how this makes us feel. At the end there was a general feeling that we wanted to be called nice names at school because, as one child said, 'It's where we feel special together.' For the next few days we had a short circle time at the end of each morning session using the question, 'Who do I want to thank for saying something kind today?' It reinforced the concept and children started to make an effort to use kind words so that they would be mentioned in the circle. I am not sure that was the best motivation – but it worked and I addressed the situation without having to tackle racism head on, which, rightly or wrongly, I worried might be counterproductive.
>
> Andrea (Foundation Stage Coordinator)

Readers will reflect on the effectiveness and appropriateness of each of these experiences. They show how teachers are seeking to face both issues that arise in their classrooms and ideas that interest their learners. Whilst they are not intended as perfect templates for best practice, they do show how practitioners are trying to face some of life's challenges with their learners.

The changing face of controversial issues

Using *real-life* situations is a central part of developing children's social and emotional skills. If children are permitted and enabled to raise areas that concern them, then controversial issues are bound to arise. Inevitably, these issues will change over time as society and the world develops. The DfES (2005: 45) states that:

> Children should not be sheltered from such issues; through them, they can develop an important range of skills, including listening, accepting other points of view, arguing a case, dealing with conflict and dealing with difficult feelings.

The DfES (2005: 45) also identifies some of the issues that are likely to be sensitive or controversial, including:

- family lifestyle and values;
- physical and medical issues;
- law and order;
- financial issues;
- unemployment;
- environmental issues;
- bullying; and
- bereavement.

Many of these are reflected in the content of this book. However, I have focused more on the priority areas identified by student teachers in my survey. If this list had been devised 20 years ago, then no doubt the threat of nuclear war would have been on it. As a student teacher, I discussed with colleagues what I would do if the three-minute warning sounded; as a child, my discussions in the playground focused on where we might shelter and how we would survive an all-out attack. Whilst the purchase of weapons still hits the headlines, concerns about war and warfare change over time; children are now more likely to ask questions about terrorism. Technology has also made weapons smaller and supposedly more discriminating. It is impossible to guess what issues will come to the fore over the course of our teaching careers, particularly with current advances in technology. However, whatever changes come over time, many of the strategies and values outlined in this book will still have relevance, with thoughtful application and recontextualisation.

Research

Research undertaken by Davies, Harber and Yamashita (2005: 2) in primary and secondary schools in Birmingham found that learners wanted to learn about why wars happen:

> An outstanding mention in terms of what pupils wanted to know about was war – in the current context, and not 50 years ago. Pupils wanted to understand the reasons for war and the reasons for hate. They wanted to know precisely what was happening with Iraq, who was making decisions, why oil was such a big factor and why some countries fight and not others. They perceived hypocrisy in the rationale for the war, and displayed a keen sense of justice. They wanted to be exposed to different sides of the question …

The Local Authority (LA) told teachers to avoid discussing any issues related to the invasion of Iraq and there was a real fear of controversy from the LA and head teachers. However, learners wanted to explore and deepen their understanding of global issues.

This example serves to highlight how the perceptions of different stakeholders can vary when considering controversial issues. It stresses the importance of considering the needs, interests and concerns of our learners so that we can support them at the point of need when difficult and complex situations gain their attention. Indeed, at some times, the controversial issue may be the fact that we do not address some of our learners' concerns for fear of controversy.

Summary and key points

To remain silent on an issue does not remove it from one's consciousness. Indeed, children may wonder why the curriculum does not reflect their concerns and interests, particularly when it comes to a consideration of issues with a high profile in the news. Whilst one may conjecture that childhood innocence needs to be protected, children have access to a wider range of information than ever before and have an awareness of a broader range of issues. To ignore such facts is to deny them the opportunity to discuss their concerns and to develop informed, reasoned and coherent opinions. It has been argued for some time (Ross, 1987; Advisory Group on Citizenship, 1998; Cheung and Leung, 1998; Cowan and Maitles, 2002; Maitles and Cowan, 2005; Maitles and Deuchar, 2004) that issues relating to citizenship education should be introduced early in a child's schooling. Children of all ages are made aware of a range of issues by the media and other sources, and to suggest otherwise is to fail to acknowledge the wide range of information open to them. To ignore issues because they may prove controversial is to divert them to the playground and leave their consideration unsupported. As has been noted, issues can be controversial for two main reasons: because they can be viewed from varying reasoned standpoints; or because their inclusion in the setting of a school raises concerns about age-appropriateness and children's maturity. One indication of a child's readiness to engage with an issue is their ability to raise questions about it. As their understanding grows and deepens, they will be able to ask more focused and probing questions. A child may ask where a baby comes from and be satisfied with the straightforward answer that it grows inside its mother. However, if they are ready to understand more, and feel secure in their environment, they will ask a supplementary question that leads to further detailed learning. The same is true for other ideas and issues.

It is important to remember that all children are different and that they will react to issues in a variety of ways. Children from different backgrounds may show concerns and emotions differently and we should not expect conformity. Listening to children's responses and asking questions will help us to understand children's reactions. This is particularly possible in primary schools, where children have far fewer teachers in one day than those in secondary education. This special relationship also opens up both time and opportunity for cross-curricular and multi-disciplinary study. As Holden (1998) points out, it is entirely possible that these types of issues can be better discussed by younger pupils as these children tend to have a strong sense of social justice and they want to be active in working for change. In the context of a continuous and continuing close relationship, we are excellently placed to support children's learning.

The subtitle to this book provides a useful final focus. We are to face life's challenges with our learners. It is not our role to face the challenges for them, much as we may wish to, but to do so with them. This process of collaborative and cooperative learning, of learning alongside one another in an atmosphere that promotes mutual respect, is a strong way of tackling controversial issues.

Postscript

As this book reaches completion, the political scene in the UK has changed. A Conservative–Liberal Democrat coalition government has been formed and is beginning to announce its programme. One of its first actions was to rename the Department for Children, Schools and Families as the Department for Education. Inevitably, in the coming weeks and months further initiatives will be announced and implemented and the education system will continue to evolve in new ways. It remains to be seen how this will affect the curriculum for primary schools in England and their wider provision. The education system never stands still.

Whatever changes come about in the coming weeks and months, many of the needs of the children in our care will remain the same: the need to be respected and cared for; the need to learn in safe, secure and nurturing environments; the need to find acceptance for who they are and where they come from; and the need to develop the knowledge, skills and understanding to participate as citizens in local, regional, national and global environments. The issues addressed in this book will continue to be important for all those committed to supporting children with the difficult situations that they sometimes face and with the challenging questions they often ask. As ever, how we as teachers interpret the curriculum – and how we implement it – will be informed by our own philosophy of education and the values we bring to our professional role.

References

Abbott, D. (2008) *Speech on Black and Minority Ethnic Pupils, House of Commons. Hansard Column 224WH 1 April 2008.* Available: www.publications.parliament.uk/pa/cm200708/cmhansrd/cm080401/halltext/80401h0009.htm#08040154000587 (accessed 4 August 2009).

Abbott, L. and Langston, A. (eds) (2004) *Birth to Three Matters: Supporting the Framework of Effective Practice*, Buckingham: Open University Press.

——(2006) *Parents Matter: Supporting the Birth to Three Matters Framework*, Maidenhead: Open University Press.

Aboud, F. (1988) *Children and Prejudice*, Oxford: Basil Blackwell.

Abramski, I. (2007) *Three Dolls*, Jerusalem: Yad Vashem.

Adams, K., Hyde, B. and Woolley, R. (2008) *The Spiritual Dimension of Childhood*, London: Jessica Kingsley.

Advisory Group on Citizenship (1998) *Education for Citizenship and the Teaching of Democracy in Schools*, London: Department for Education and Employment.

Anti-Racist Alliance (undated) *Our Children and Anti-racism.* Online. Availablewww.antiracistalliance.org.uk/content/anti-racisteducation.htm (accessed 3 August 2009).

Argent, H. (2007) *Josh and Jaz Have Three Mums*, London: British Association for Adoption and Fostering.

Ashton, E. (2000) *Religious Education in the Early Years*, London: Routledge.

Baird, V. (2004) *Sex, Love and Homophobia: Lesbian, Gay, Bisexual and Transgender Lives*, London, Amnesty International.

Baker, S. (2006) *Sustainable Development*, London: Routledge.

Bastiani, J. (1989) *Working with Parents: A Whole School Approach*, London: NFER—Routledge.

Bastiani, J. and Wolfendale, S. (1996) *Home–School Work in Britain: Review, Reflection and Development*, London: David Fulton.

Bastide, D. (1987) *Religious Education 5–12*, London: Falmer Press.

——(2007) *Teaching Religious Education 4–11*, 2nd edn, Abingdon: Routledge.

Bawden, N. (1973) *Carrie's War*, London: Victor Gollancz.

BBC (2006) Childhood obesity 'doubles in decade'. BBC News online, 21 April 2006. http://news.bbc.co.uk/1/hi/health/4930264.stm (accessed 20 February 2010).

——(2007) Eating disorder in six-year-old. BBC News online, 27 March 2007. http://news.bbc.co.uk/2/hi/health/6498345.stm (accessed 20 February 2010).

Bee, H. and Boyd, D. (2003) *The Developing Child*, 10th edn, Boston, MA: Allyn and Bacon.

Beresford, E. and Mayhew, J. (1993) *Lizzy's War*, Hemel Hempstead: Simon Schuster Young Books.

Berger, K. (2000) *The Developing Person: Through Childhood*, 2nd edn, New York: Worth Publishers.

Berk, L. (2001) *Awakening Children's Minds: How Parents and Teachers can Make a Difference*, Oxford: OUP.

——(2006) *Child Development*, 7th edn, Boston, MA: Pearson Education.

Berns, C. F. (2004) 'Bibliotherapy: Using Books to Help Bereaved Children', *Omega: Journal of Death and Dying* 48 (4): 321–36.

Bignold, W. and Gayton, Liz (eds) (2009) *Global Issues and Comparative Education*, Exeter: Learning Matters.

Binch, C. (2004) *The Princess and the Castle*, London: Jonathan Cape.

Blair, Tony (2001) 'Holocaust Memorial Day', *Perspectives*, Summer: 4–5.

Blake, J. and Sheppard, K. (1998) *Sid's War: A Tale About Evacuation*, London: Franklin Watts.

Bonnett, A. (2000) *Anti-Racism*, London: Routledge.

Bottery, M. (2002) 'Globalization, Spirituality and the Management of Education', *International Journal of Children's Spirituality* 7 (2): 131–42.

Boyne, J. (2006) *The Boy in the Striped Pyjamas*, London: David Fickling Books.

Broadbent, L. and Brown, A. (eds) (2002) *Issues in Religious Education*, London: Routledge Falmer.

Broadhead, P., Johnston, J., Tobbell, C. & Woolley, R. (2010) *Personal, Social and Emotional Development*, London: Continuum.

Brown, G. (2005) *Speech at the CBI Annual Conference*, London, 28 November 2005, London: Labour Party.

Bunting, M. (2000) 'Masculinity in Question' in *The Guardian*, Monday 2 October 2000 http://www.guardian.co.uk/comment/story/0,376019,00.html (accessed 20 February 2010).

Callan, E. (1997) *Creating Citizens: Political Education and Liberal Democracy*, Oxford: Oxford University Press.

Carnie, F. (2006) *Setting Up Parent Councils: Case Studies*, Human Scale Education and Department for Education and Skills.

Carrington, B. and Troyna, B. (eds) (1988) *Children and Controversial Issues*, London: Falmer Press.

Carter, C., Harber, C., and Serf, J. (2003) *Towards Ubuntu: Critical Teacher Education for Democratic Citizenship in South Africa and England*, DEC: Birmingham.

Carter, V. (2006) *If I had a Hundred Mummies*, London: Onlywomen Press.

Cefai, C. (2008) *Promoting Resilience in the Classroom: A Guide to Developing Pupils' Emotional and Cognitive Skills*, London: Jessica Kingsley.

Central Advisory Council for Education (England) (1967) *Children and Their Primary Schools: A Report* (the Plowden Report), London: HMSO.

Cheung, C. and Leung, M. (1998) 'From Civic Education to General Studies: The Implementation of Political Education into the Primary Curriculum', *Compare* 28 (1): 47–56.

Childhood Bereavement Network (undated) *Briefing on Childhood Bereavement*. London: National Children's Bureau.

Childwise (2003) *Children and Advertising: Childwise Monitor Special Report*, Norwich: Childwise.

Christian L. G. (1997) 'Children and Death', *Young Children* 52 (4): 76–80.

Churchill, W. (1940) speech *Every Man to his Post* broadcast 11 September 1940, Ashland, Ohio: Teaching AmericanHistory.org. Online. Available: http://teachingamericanhistory.org/library/index.asp?document=1911 (accessed 8 August 2009).

CIC (2007) *Our Shared Future*, sine loco: Commission on Integration and Cohesion.

Citizenship Foundation (undated) Teaching about Controversial Issues: guidance for schools. Online. Available: www.citizenshipfoundation.org.uk/main/page.php?92 (accessed 1 August 2009).

Claire, H. (2001) *Not Aliens: Primary School Children and the Citizenship/PSHE Curriculum*, Stoke on Trent: Trentham.

Claire, H. and Holden, C. (2006) *Gender and Citizenship Education*, sine loco: Citized. Online. Available: www.citized.info/?strand=0andr_menu=res (accessed 3 August 2009).

Claire, H. and Holden, C. (eds) (2007) *The Challenge of Teaching Controversial Issues*, Stoke on Trent: Trentham.

Cole, M. (2006) *Education, Equality and Human Rights: Issues of Gender, 'Race', Sexuality, Disability and Social Class*, 2nd edn, London: Routledge.

——(2008a) *Marxism and Educational Theory*, London: Routledge.

——(2008b) 'Introduction', in M. Cole (ed) *Professional Attributes and Practice: Meeting the QTS Standards*, 4th edn, Abingdon: David Fulton.

——(2008c) 'Maintaining "The Adequate Continuance of the British Race and British Ideals in the World": Contemporary Racism and the Challenges for Education', Inaugural Professorial Lecture

Wednesday 29 November 2006 Bishop Grosseteste University College Lincoln. Lincoln: Bishop Grosseteste University College Lincoln.

——(2008d) 'Preface', in M. Cole (ed) *Professional Attributes and Practice: meeting the QTS standards*, 4th edn, Abingdon: David Fulton.

——(2009) *Critical Race Theory and Education*, London: Palgrave Macmillan.

Connell, R. W. (1989) '"Cool Guys, Swots and Wimps": The Interplay of Masculinity and Education'. *Oxford Review of Education* 15 (3): 291–303.

——(1990) 'An Iron Man: The Body and Some Contradictions of Hegemonic Masculinity' in M. Messner and D. Babo (eds) *Sport, Men and the Gender Order: Critical Feminist Perspectives*, Champaign, Illinois: Human Kinetics Books.

Connolly, P. (2003) 'The Development of Young Children's Ethnic Identities' in C. Vincent (ed.) *Social Justice, Education and Identity*, London: RoutledgeFalmer.

Cowan, P. and Maitles, H. (2002) 'Developing Poisitive Values: A Case Study of Holocaust Memorial Day in the Primary Schools of One Local Authority in Scotland', *Educational Review* 54 (3): 219–29.

Craft, A. (1986) 'Multicultural teaching', in J. J. Wellington (ed.) *Controversial Issues in the Curriculum*, Oxford: Blackwell.

CRE (2002) *The Duty to Promote Racial Equality: A Guide for Schools (Non-Statutory)*, London: Commission for Racial Equality.

Cremin, H. (2007) *Peer Mediation: Citizenship and Social Inclusion Revisited*, 3rd edn, Buckingham: Open University Press.

Datamonitor (2006) *Marketing to Kids: How to be Effective and Responsible*, sine loco: Datamonitor.

Davies, I. (2002) 'Education for a Better World', in I. Davies, I. Gregory and N. McGuinn (eds) *Key Debates in Education*, London: Continuum.

Davies, I., Gregory, I. and McGuinn, N. (eds) (2002) *Key Debates in Education*, London: Continuum.

Davies, L. (2002) 'Possibilities and Limits for Democratisation in Education', *Comparative Education* 38 (3): 251–66.

Davies, L., Harber, C. and Yamashita, H. (2005) *Global Citizenship Education: The Needs of Teachers and learners*, CIER University of Birmingham. Online. Available: www.education2.bham.ac.uk/documents/research/CIER/Global_Citizenship_Report_key_findings.pdf (accessed 4 August 2009).

Day, C., Kington, A., Stobart, G. and Sammons, P. (2006) 'The Personal and Professional Selves of Teachers: Stable and Unstable Identities', *British Educational Research Journal* 32 (4): 601–16.

DCSF (2007a) *Guidance on the Duty to Promote Community Cohesion*. Nottingham: Department for Children, Schools and Families.

——(2007b) *Safe to Learn: Embedding Anti-bullying Work in Schools*, London: Department for Children, Schools and Families.

——(2008a) *Statutory Framework for the Early Years Foundation Stage*, London: Department for Children, Schools and Families.

——(2008b) *Working Together: Listening to the Voices of Children and Young People*, London: Department for Children, Schools and Families.

——(2008c) *Top Tips to Develop the Global Dimension in Schools*, London: Department for Children, Schools and Families.

——(2009) *Independent Review of the Primary Curriculum: Final Report (the Rose Review)*, Department for Children, Schools and Families: London.

DCSF and NHS (2009) *Healthy Schools Programme*. Online. Available: www.healthyschools.gov.uk/ (accessed 3 August 2009).

DEFRA (2008) *The Environment in Your Pocket*, 12th edn, London: Department for Food and Rural Affairs. Online. Available: www.defra.gov.uk/Environment/statistics/eiyp/index.htm (accessed 3 August 2009).

DES (1985) *Education for All: Report of the Committee of Inquiry Into the Education of Children From Ethnic Minority Groups (The Swann Report)*, London: HMSO and Department of Education and Science.

DfEE (2000a) *Financial Capability Through Personal Financial Education: Guidance for Schools at Key Stages 1 and 2*, Nottingham: Department for Education and Employment.

——(2000b) *Remembering Genocides: Lessons for the Future*, London: Department for Education and Employment.

DfEE and QCA (1999) *The National Curriculum: Handbook for Primary Teachers in England (Key Stages 1 and 2)*, London: Department for Education and Employment and Qualifications and Curriculum Authority.

DfES (2000) *Bullying: Don't Suffer in Silence*, London: Department for Education and Skills.

——(2002) *Birth to Three Matters: A Framework to Support Children in the Earliest Years*, London: Department for Education and Skills.

——(2003) *Excellence and Enjoyment: A Strategy for Schools*, London: Department for Education and Skills.

——(2004) *Every Child Matters: Change for Children in Schools*, London: Department for Education and Skills.

——(2005) *Excellence and Enjoyment: Social and Emotional Aspects of Learning: Guidance*, London: Department for Education and Skills. Online. Available: publications.teachernet.gov.uk/eOrderingDownload/DFES0110200MIG2122.pdf (accessed 3 August 2009).

——(2006a) *Sustainable Schools: For Pupils, Communities and the Environment*, London: Department for Education and Skills.

——(2006b) *Making Sense of Citizenship*, London: Department for Education and Skills.

——(2007) *Diversity and Citizenship Curriculum Review* (The *Ajegbo Report*), London: Department for Education and Skills.

DfES and DH (undated) *Food in Schools Programme*. Online. Available: www.foodinschools.org/ (accessed 20 December 2008)

DH (2008) *Healthy Weight, Healthy Lives: A Cross-Government Strategy for England*, London: Department of Health.

Disordered Eating (2007) *Eating Disorders: Statistics*. Online. Available: www.disordered-eating.co.uk/eating-disorders-news/eating-disorders-statistics-children.html (accessed 30 January 2009).

Dobson, A. (1996) 'Environment Sustainabilities: An Analysis and a Typology', *Environmental Politics* 5 (3): 401–28.

Dorr, A. (1986) *Television and Children: A Special Medium for a Special Audience*, Beverly Hills, CA: Sage.

Dowling, M. (2005) *Young Children's Personal, Social and Emotional Development*, 2nd edn, London: Paul Chapman Publishing.

Draper, L. and Duffy, B. (2006) 'Working with Parents', in G. Pugh and B. Duffy (eds) *Contemporary Issues in the Early Years*, 4th edn, London: Sage.

Driessen, G., Smit, F. and Sleegers, P. (2005) 'Parental Involvement and Educational Achievement', *British Educational Research Journal* 31 (4): 509–32.

Dyregrov, A. (2008) *Grief in Young Children: A Handbook for Adults*, 2nd edn, London: Jessica Kingsley.

ECM (2008) 'Targeted Mental Health in Schools project', Department for Children, Schools and Families. Online. Available: www.everychildmatters.gov.uk./health/tmhsproject/ (accessed 4 August 2009).

EOC (2006) *Facts About Women and Men in Great Britain, 2006*. Equal Opportunities Commission. Online. Available: www.eoc.org.uk (accessed 25 November 2008).

——(2007) *Gender Equality Duty: Code of Practice for England and Wales*, Norwich: Equal Opportunities Commission.

Epstein, D. (1994) 'Introduction' in D. Epstein (ed.) *Challenging Lesbian and Gay Inequalities in Education*, Buckingham: Open University Press.

Epstein, D. (2003) *Gender, Sexuality and Identity: Violence and HIV in South African Schools*. ESRC Seminar Series, Warwick 15 February 2003. Unpublished typescript.

Epstein, J. (2005) 'School/Family/Community Partnerships: Caring for the Children we Share', *Phi Delta Kappan* 76 (9): May, 701–712.

Farrington, L. (1999) *Playground Peacemakers: A Working Manual on Peaceful Conflict Resolution for Schools Using the Mediation Way*, Plymouth: Loxley Enterprises.

Firth, M. (2006) 'Children's pocket money is £800 a year', *Independent* Monday, 6 March 2006. Online. Available: www.independent.co.uk/news/uk/this-britain/childrens-pocket-money-is-163800-a-year-468773.html (accessed 3 August 2009).

Francis, B. (2000) *Boys, Girls and Achievement: Addressing the Classroom Issues*, London: Routledge-Falmer.

Francis, Becky and Skelton, C. (2005) *Reassessing Gender and Achievement*, London: Routledge.

Fritta, B. (1999) *Tommy. To Tommy for his Third Birthday in Terezin, 22 January 1944*, reprinted by Yad Vashem, the Holocaust Martyrs' and Heroes' Remembrance Authority, Jerusalem: Yad Vashem.

Fryer, P. (1984) *Staying Power; The History of Black People in Britain*, London: Pluto Press.

Fthenakis, W. E. (1998) 'Family Transitions and Quality in Early Childhood Education', *European Early Childhood Education* 6 (1): 5–19.

Furet, François (1989) *Unanswered Questions: Nazi Germany and the Genocide of the Jews*, New York: Schocken Books.

Gaine, C. (2005) *We're all White Thanks: The Persisting Myth about White Schools*, Stoke on Trent: Trentham.

Galton, M., Gray, J. and Ruddock, J. (1999) *The Impact of School Transitions and Transfers on Pupil Progress and Attainment (DfEE Research Report 131)*, London: Department for Education and Employment.

Galton, M., Gray, J. and Ruddock, J. with Berry, M., Demetriou, H., Edwards, J., Goalen, P., Hargreaves, L., Hussy, S., Pell, T., Schagen, I. and Charles, M. (2003) *Transfer and Transitions in the Middle Years of Schools (7–14): Continuities and Discontinuities in Learning (DfES Research Report 443)*, London: Department for Education and Skills.

Gillborn, D. (2008) *Racism and Education: Coincidence or Conspiracy?* London: Routledge.

Gilligan, C. (1993) *In a Different Voice: Psychological Theory and Women's Development*, Cambridge, MA: Harvard University Press.

Girlguiding UK (2008) *Teenage Mental Health: Girls Shout Out!* sine loco: Girlguiding UK and The Mental Health Foundation. Online. Available: www.mentalhealth.org.uk/publications/?EntryId5=62067 (accessed 4 August 2009).

Glanz, J. (2001) *Holocaust Handbook for Educators*, Dubuque, IA: Kendall/Hunt.

Graham, C. and Hill, M. (2003) *Negotiating the Transition to Secondary School* (SCRE Spotlight 89), Glasgow: University of Glasgow, SCRE Centre.

Green, H., McGinnity, A., Meltzer, H., Ford, T. and Goodman, R. (2005) *Mental Health of Children and Young People in Great Britain, 2004*, London: HMSO.

Gregory, M. (2000) 'Care as a Goal of Democratic Education', *Journal of Moral Education* 29 (4): 445–61.

Grugeon, E. and Woods, P. (1990) *Educating All: Multicultural Perspectives in the Primary School*, London: Routledge.

GTC (2007) *Code of Conduct and Practice for Registered Teachers: Setting Minimum Standards for the Regulation of the Profession*, London: General Teaching Council for England.

Guardian, The, 13 January 2009, 'Strict Codes Bar Racism'. Online. Available: www.guardian.co.uk/uk/2009/jan/13/racism-workplace-codes-uk (accessed 3 August 2009).

Harber, C. R. (2002) 'Education, Democracy and Poverty Reduction in Africa', *Comparative Education*, 38 (3): 267–76.

Harber, C. R. (ed.) (1998) *Voices for Democracy: a North–South Dialogue on Education for Sustainable Democracy*, Nottingham: Education Now and British Council

Harber, C. R. and Serf, J. (2004) *Exploring Ubuntu. Education and Development: An Introduction to Theories and Debates*, Birmingham: TIDE~ Centre.

——(2006) 'Teacher Education for a Democratic Society in England and South Africa', *Teaching and Teacher Education* 22 (8): 986–97.

Harber, C. R. and Serf, J. (eds) (2007) *Comparative Education and Quality Global Learning: Engaging with Controversial Issues in South Africa and the UK*, Birmingham: TIDE.

Herlem, F. C. (2008) *Great Answers to Difficult Questions about Divorce: What Children Need to Know*, London: Jessica Kingsley.

Hicks, D. and Holden, C. (2007) *Teaching the Global Dimension: Key Principles and Effective Practice*, London: Routledge.

Hine, J., Lemetti, F. and Trikha, S. (2004) *Citizenship: Young People's Perspectives*. Online. Available: www.homeoffice.gov.uk/rds/pdfs04/dpr10.pdf (accessed 4 August 2009).

Hipp, E. (1995) *Help for the Hard Times: Getting Through Loss*, Center City, MN: Hazelden.

Hockey, M. (undated) *Where's My Teddy?* sine loco: Durham and Darlington Education Service for Travelling Children.

Holden, C. (1998) 'Keen at 11, Cynical at 18?', in C. Holden and N. Clough (eds) *Children as Citizens*, London: Jessica Kingsley.

Holland, J. (1993) 'Childhood Bereavement in Humberside Primary Schools', *Educational Research* 35 (3): 289–97.

——(2004) 'Should Children Attend their Parent's Funerals?' *Pastoral Care in Education*, March: 10–14.

Home Office (2001) *Race Relations (Amendment) Act 2000*, sine loco: Home Office.

hooks, bell (2003) *Teaching Community: A Pedagogy of Hope*, London: Routledge.

Hopkins, B. (2007) *The Peer Mediation and Mentoring Trainer's Manual*, London: Optimus Education.

Hornby, G. (2000) *Improving Parental Involvement*, London: Cassell Educational.

Hughes, A. and Sears, A. (2007) 'Teaching the contested and controversial nature of democratic ideas: taking the crisis out of controversy', in H. Claire and C. Holden (eds) *The Challenge of Teaching Controversial Issues*, Stoke on Trent: Trentham.

ICEE (2007) 'The Ahmedabad Declaration 207: a call to action', 4th International Conference on Environmental Education, *Education for Life: Life Through Education*, Ahmedabad, India: UNESCO. Online. Available: www.tbilisiplus30.org/Ahmedabad%20Declaration.pdf (accessed 3 August 2009).

Independent (2008) 'Notes on a small island: the things that really make Britain great'. Online. Available: www.independent.co.uk/news/uk/this-britain/notes-on-a-small-island-the-things-that-really-make-britain-great-910558.html?startindex=30 *Independent* (accessed 31 August 2008).

Jackson, M. and Colwell, J. (2002) *A Teacher's Handbook of Death*, London: Jessica Kingsley.

Jacques, K. and Hyland, R. (2003) *Professional Studies: Primary Phase*, Exeter: Learning Matters.

Jewett, C. (1984) *Helping Children Cope with Separation and Loss*, London: Batsford Academic and Educational and British Agencies for Adoption and Fostering.

Johnston, J. (2002) 'Teaching and Learning in the Early Years', in J. Johnston, M. Chater and D. Bell (eds) *Teaching the Primary Curriculum*, Buckingham: Open University Press.

——(2009) 'Working Together' in J. Johnston and L. Nahmad—Williams, *Early Childhood Studies*, Harlow: Pearson.

Johnston, J., Nahmad-Williams, L., House, A., Cooper, L. and Smith, C. (2009) *Early Childhood Studies*, Harlow: Pearson Education.

Jones, A. (2006) *Genocide: A Comprehensive Introduction*. London: Routledge/Taylor & Francis.

Jones, R. (1999) *Teaching Racism or Tackling it?* Stoke on Trent: Trentham Books.

——(2007) 'Pocket Money Rockets', *Guardian*, Saturday 21 July 2007. Online. Available: www.guardian.co.uk/money/2007/jul/21/moneysupplement2 (accessed 30 November 2008).

Katz, Y. J. (1996) 'Religiosity, personality and tertiary educational choice research' in L. Francis, W. Kay and W. Campbell, *Research in Religious Education*, Leominster: Gracewing/Smith and Helwys Publishing, 407–21.

Klein, R. (2001) *Citizens by Right: Citizenship Education in Primary Schools*, Stoke on Trent: Trentham Books and Save the Children.

Knowles, A. (1991) *The Mice Next Door*, London: Macmillan Children's Books.

Landau, R. (1992) *The Nazi Holocaust*, London: I.B. Taurus.

Lareau, A. (1989) *Home Advantage: Social Class and Parental Intervention in Elementary Education*, London: Falmer Press.

Leaman, O. (1995) *Death and Loss: Compassionate Approaches in the Classroom*, London: Cassell.

Lewis, A. (2001) 'There is no "race" in the schoolyard: color-blind ideology in an (almost) all-White school', *American Educational Research Journal* 38: 781–811.

Lindquist, D. (2006) 'Guidelines for Teaching the Holocaust: Avoiding Common Pedagogical Errors', *Social Studies* September/October: 215–21.

——(2007) 'A Necessary Holocaust Pedagogy: Teaching the Teachers', *Issues in Teacher Education* 16 (1): 21–36.

London Borough of Tower Hamlets (undated) *Citizenship Pieces*. Online. Available: www.citizenship-pieces.org.uk/anti-racism2003/multiculturalism.asp (accessed 12 December 2008).

Lundy, K. G. (2008) *Teaching Fairly in an Unfair World*, Portland, ME: Pembroke Publishing.

Mac an Ghaill, M. (1994) *The Making of Men*, Buckingham, Open University Press.

MacGrath, M. (2000) *The Art of Peaceful Teaching in the Primary School*, London: David Fulton.

Macpherson, W. (1999) *The Stephen Lawrence Inquiry, Report of an Inquiry by Sir William Macpherson*, London: Stationery Office.

Maitles, H. and Cowan, P. (1999) 'Teaching the Holocaust in Primary Schools in Scotland: Modes, Methodology and Content', *Educational Review* 51: 263–71.

——(2005) 'One Country, Many Cultures: Does Holocaust Education Have an Impact on Pupils' Citizenship Values and Attitudes?' *Scottish Educational Review* 37 (2): 104–15.

Maitles, H. and Deuchar, R. (2004) '"Why are they Bombing Innocent Iraqis?": Political Literacy Among Primary Pupils', *Improving Schools* 7 (1): 97–105.

Major, J. (1999) *Autobiography*, London: Harper Collins.

Marsh, J. (2005) 'Digikinds: Young People, Popular Culture and Media', in N. Yelland (ed.) *Critical Issues in Early Childhood Education*, Maidenhead: Open University Press.

Martino, W. 1999. '"Cool Boys," "Party Animals," "Squids"and "Poofters": Interrogating the Dynamics and Politics of Adolescent Masculinities in School', *British Journal of Sociology of Education* 20: 239–63.

Martino, W. and Meyenn, Bob (eds) (2001) *What About the Boys? Issues of Masculinity in Schools*, Buckingham: Open University Press.

McCreery, E., Palmer, S. and Voiels, V. (2008) *Teaching Religious Education*, Exeter: Learning Matters.

McGuinn, N. (2002) 'Response to "Education for a Better World?"' in I. Davies, I. Gregory and N. McGuinn (eds) *Key Debates in Education*, London: Continuum.

Merideth, E. M. (2007) *Leadership Strategies for Teachers*, 2nd edn, London: Sage.

Meyenn, Bob, and Parker, J. (2001) 'Naughty Boys at School: Perspectives on Boys and Discipline', in W. Martino and Bob Meyenn (eds) (2001) *What About the Boys? Issues of Masculinity in Schools*, Buckingham: Open University Press.

Miles, R. (1982) *Racism and Migrant Labour*, London: Routledge and Kegan Paul.

Mills, M. (2001a) *Challenging Violence in Schools: An Issue of Masculinities*, Buckingham: Open University Press.

——(2001b) 'Pushing it to the Max: Interrogating the Risky Business of Being a Boy', in W. Martino and Bob Meyenn (eds) *What About the Boys? Issues of Masculinity in Schools*, Buckingham: Open University Press.

Monroe, B. and Kraus, F. (2004) *Brief Interventions with Bereaved Children*, Buckingham: Open University Press.

Morgenstern, N. (1998) *I Wanted to Fly Like a Butterfly: A Child's Recollections of the Holocaust*, Jerusalem: Yad Vashem.

——(2007) *The Daughter we Had Always Wanted*, Jerusalem: Yad Vashem.

Morrell, R. 2005 (11 August) *Masculinity*, University of KwaZulu Natal.

Morris, J. and Woolley, R. (2008) *Family Diversities Reading Resource*, Lincoln: Bishop Grosseteste University College Lincoln. Online. Available: www.bishopg.ac.uk/fdrr (accessed 4 August 2009).

Mosley, J. (2005a) *Circle Time: ages 5–11*, Leamington Spa: Scholastic.

——(2005b) *Circle Time for Young Children*, London: Taylor & Francis.

——(2006) *Step-by-Step Guide to Circle Time*, Trowbridge: Positive Press.

NHS (2008) *National Child Measurement Programme*, National Health Service. Online. Available: www.ncmp.ic.nhs.uk (accessed 30 December 2008).

——(undated) *School Fruit and Vegetable Scheme*, sine loco: National Health Service. Online. Available: www.5aday.nhs.uk (accessed 30 January 2009).

NICE (2004) *Eating Disorders: Core Interventions in the Treatment and Management of Anorexia Nervosa, Bulimia Nervosa and Related Eating Disorders*, London: National Institute for Clinical Excellence. Online. Available: www.nice.org.uk/nicemedia/pdf/cg009niceguidance.pdf (accessed 20 January 2009).

Nussbaum, M. C. (1997) 'Kant and Stoic Cosmopolitanism', in *The Journal of Political Philosophy* 5 (1): 1–25.

NUT (1991) *Lesbians and Gays in Schools: An Issue for Every Teacher*, London: National Union of Teachers.

ONS (2005a) *Expenditure and Food Survey*, London: Office for National Statistics. Online. Available: www.statistics.gov.uk/cci/nugget.asp?id=1103 (accessed 25 January 2009).

——(2005b) *Focus on Families*, London: Office for National Statistics. Online. Available: www.statistics.gov.uk/downloads/theme_compendia/fof2005/families.pdf (accessed 5 August 2009).

——(2005c) *Population Trends 122 Winter 2005*, London: Office for National Statistics. Online. Available: www.statistics.gov.uk/downloads/theme_population/PopTrends122v1.pdf (accessed 5 August 2009).

Ofsted (2004) *Transition from the Reception Year to Year 1: An Evaluation by HMI*, London: Ofsted. Online. Available: www.ofsted.gov.uk/Ofsted-home/Publications-and-research/Browse-all-by/Education/Key-stages-and-transition/Key-Stage-1/Transition-from-the-Reception-Year-to-Year-1-an-evaluation-by-HMI (accessed 25 November 2008).

Oxfam GB (2006a) *Education for Global Citizenship: A Guide for Schools*, Oxford: Oxfam.

——(2006b) *Teaching Controversial Issues*, Oxford: Oxfam.

Paechter, C. (1998) *Educating the Other: Gender, Power and Schooling*, London: Routledge.

Papalia, D., Gross, D. and Feldman, R. (2003) *Child Development: A Topical Approach*, New York: McGraw Hill.

Pardeck, J. A., and Pardeck, J. T. (1993) *Bibliotherapy: A Clinical Approach for Helping Children*, New York: Routledge.

Passey, R. (2005) 'Family Values and Primary Schools: An Investigation into Family-related Education', *British Educational Research Journal*, 31 (6): 723–36.

Peters, M., Seeds, K., Goldstein, A. and Coleman, N. (2008) *Parental Involvement in Children's Education Survey 2007*, London: Department for Children Schools and Families.

Peterson, L., and Lewis, K. E. (1988) 'Preventive Intervention to Improve Children's Discrimination of the Persuasive Tactics in Televised Advertising', *Journal of Pediatric Psychology* 13 (2): 163–70.

Piaget, J. (1954) *The Construction of Reality in the Child*, New York: Basic Books.

Pickford, Tony (ed.) (2008) *Get Global!: A Practical Guide to Integrating the Global Dimension into the Primary Curriculum*, Stoke on Trent: Trentham.

Poulter, S. (2008) 'Visa debit cards cards for children of 11', *Daily Mail* 30 June 2008. Online. Available: www.thisismoney.co.uk/saving-and-banking/article.html?in_article_id=444104andin_page_id=7 (accessed 20 October 2009).

Puckett, M. and Black, J. (2001) *The Young Child: Development from Prebirth through Age Eight*, 3rd edn, Upper Saddle River, NJ: Prentice Hall.

Pyatt, J. (2007) 'School's veil ban £1/2m bill', *The Sun* newspaper 24 January 2007. Online. Available: www.thesun.co.uk/sol/homepage/news/article29578.ece (accessed 10 January 2008).

QCA (1998) *Education for Citizenship and the Teaching of Democracy in Schools: final report of the Advisory Group on Citizenship (Crick Report)*, London: Qualifications and Curriculum Authority.

——(2000) *Curriculum Guidance for the Foundation Stage*, London: Qualifications and Curriculum Authority.

——(2007) *Citizenship: programme of study for key stage 3 and attainment target*. London: Qualifications and Curriculum Authority. Online. Available: http://curriculum.qca.org.uk/uploads/QCA-07-3329-p Citizenship3_tcm8–396.pdf (accessed 10 December 2009).

Reay, D. (1999) *Class Work: Mothers' Involvement in Their Children's Primary Schooling*, London: University College Press.

Rendell, F. (1987) *Into Hiding*, Glasgow, Jordanhill College of Education.

Rose, S. and Rose, H. (2005) 'Why we should give up on race: as geneticists and biologists know, the term no longer has meaning.' *The Guardian*, 9 April 2005. Online. Available: www.guardian.co.uk/comment/story/0,1455685,00.html (accessed 15 October 2008).

Ross, A. (1987) 'Political Education in the Primary School', in C. Harber (ed.) *Political Education in Britain*, London: Falmer Press.

——(2007) 'Political Learning and Controversial Issues with Children', in H. Claire and C. Holden (eds) *The Challenge of Teaching Controversial Issues*, Stoke on Trent: Trentham.

Sage, R. and Wilkie, M. (2004) *Supporting Learning in Primary Schools*, 2nd edn, Exeter: Learning Matters.

Scott, W. and Gough, S. (2003) *Sustainable Development and Learning: Framing the Issues*, London: Routledge-Falmer.

Shah, S. (1996) 'Initial Teacher Education and Global Citizenship: the Context of Permeation' in M. Steiner, *Developing the Global Teacher: Theory and Practice in Initial Teacher Education*, Stoke on Trent: Trentham Books.

Short, G. (2003a) 'Holocaust Education in the Primary School: Some Reflections on an Emergent Debate', *London Review of Education* 1 (2): 119–29.

——(2003b) 'Lessons of the Holocaust: A Response to the Critics', *Educational Review* 55 (3): 277–87.

Short, G. and Carrington, B. (1991) 'Unfair Discrimination: Teaching the Principles to Children of Primary School Age', *Journal of Moral Education* 20 (2): 157–77.

——(1995) 'Anti-Semitism and the Primary School: Children's Perceptions of Jewish Culture and Identity', *Research in Education* 54: 14–24.

——(1996) 'Anti-Racist Education, Multiculturalism and the New Racism', *Educational Review* 48 (1): 65–77.

Sivanandan, A. (2001) 'Poverty is the New Black', *Race and Class* 43 (2): 2–5.

Skelton, C. (2001) *Schooling the Boys: Masculinities and Primary Education*, Buckingham: Open University Press.

Skelton, C. and Francis, Becky (eds) (2003) *Boys and Girls in the Primary Classroom*, Maidenhead: Open University Press.

Smith, P., Cowie, H. and Blades, M. (2003) *Understanding Children's Development*, 4th edn, Malden, MA: Blackwell Publishing.

Steele, K. (2004) 'In what ways can Religious Education contribute to Citizenship Education?' Oxford: Farmington Institute. Online. Available: www.farmington.ac.uk/documents/new_reports/TT165.pdf (accessed 10 July 2006).

Stephen, C. and Cope, P. (2001). *Moving on to Primary 1: an Exploratory Study of the Experience of Transition from Pre-School to Primary* (Insight 3). Edinburgh: Scottish Executive.

Stobbart, M. (1991) 'Foreword' in H. Starkey (ed.) *The Challenge of Human Rights Education*, London: Cassell.

Stradling, R., Noctor, M. and Bailes, B. (1984) *Teaching Controversial Issues*, London: Edward Arnold.

Sun, The (2006) 'Veil Row Teacher Sacked', *The Sun* newspaper 24 November 2006. Online. Available: www.thesun.co.uk/sol/homepage/news/article72598.ece (accessed 12 October 2008).

TDA (2007) *Professional Standards for Qualified Teacher Status and Requirements for Initial Teacher Training*, London: Training and Development Agency for Schools.

Teachers' TV (broadcast 24 November 2005) *School Matters: Challenging Homophobia*. Online. Available: www.teachers.tv/strandProgramme.do?strandId=6andtransmissionProgrammeId=212387 (accessed 15 December 2008).

Thornton, P. (2005) 'A Pocket Money Survey to Make Jamie Despair', *Independent* Thursday, 9 June 2005. Online. Available: www.independent.co.uk/news/uk/this-britain/a-pocket-money-survey-to-make-jamie-despair-493551.html (accessed 3 January 2009).

Tibbetts, G. (2008) 'Celebrate British Day "By Drinking and Watching Television"', *Daily Telegraph*, 15 September 2008. Online. Available: www.telegraph.co.uk/news/uknews/2958273/Celebrate-British-Day-by-drinking-and-watching-television.html (accessed 20 September 2008).

TIDE~ (2002) *Whose Citizenship? Report from West Midlands Commission on Global Citizenship*, Birmingham: Development Education Centre.

Tierney, A. (2007) 'Travellers and Gypsies', Presentation at a Conference to Launch the Local Authority Inclusion Strategy: Turning the Tables: Perception and Realities. North Lincolnshire Council 2 March 2007.

Tizard, B., Mortimore, J. and Burchell, B. (1981) *Involving Parents in Nursery and Infant Schools*, London: High Scope Press.

Totten, S. (1999) 'Holocaust Education for K-4 Students? The Answer is No!' *Social Studies and the Young Learner* 12 (1): 36–9.

——(2002) *Holocaust Education: Issues and Approaches*, Boston: Allyn and Bacon.

Totten, S., Feinberg, S., and Fernekes, W. (2001) 'The Significance of Rationale Statements in Developing a Sound Holocaust Education Program', in S. Totten and S. Feinberg (eds) *Teaching and Studying the Holocaust*, Boston: Allyn and Bacon.

Troyna, B. and Carrington, B. (1988) *Children and Controversial Issues: Strategies for the Early and Middle Years of Schooling*, London: Falmer Press.

——(1990) *Education, Racism and Reform*, London: Routledge.

Turner, J. J., Kelly, J. and McKenna, K. (2006) 'Food for Thought: Parents' Perspectives of Child Influence', *British Food Journal* 108 (3): 181–91.

Tutu, D. (1999) *No Future Without Forgiveness: A Personal Overview of South Africa's Truth and Reconciliation Commission*, London: Rider.

UNICEF (2007) 'UNICEF Report on Childhood in Industrialised Countries', news item 14 February. Online. Available: www.unicef.org.uk/press/news_detail.asp?news_id=890/ (accessed 2 October 2008).

United Nations General Assembly (1989) *The UN Convention on the Rights of the Child*, New York: United Nations.

UN (1948a) *Universal Declaration of Human Rights*, United Nations. Online. Available: www.un.org/Overview/rights.html (accessed 10 January 2009).

——(1948b) *Convention on the Prevention and Punishment of the Crime of Genocide*, sine loco: United Nations. Online. Available: www.hrweb.org/legal/genocide.html (accessed 10 January 2009).

——(1987) *Report of the World Commission on Environment and Development, General Assembly Resolution 42/187*. United Nations, 11 December 1987. Online. Available: www.un.org/documents/ga/res/42/ares42–187.htm (accessed 15 November 2008).

——(2000) *United Nations Millennium Declaration*. Online. Available: www.un.org/millennium/declaration/ares552e.htm (accessed 1 August 2009).

UNESCO (2001) *Universal Declaration on Cultural Diversity*. Online. Available: unesdoc.unesco.org/images/0012/001271/127160m.pdf (accessed 4 August 2009).

UNHCHR (1989) *Convention on the Rights of the Child*, Office of the High Commissioner for Human Rights. Online. Available: www.unhchr.ch/html/menu3/b/k2crc.htm (accessed 17 November 2008).

USHMM (2001) *Teaching about the Holocaust: A Resource Book for Educators*, Washington, DC: United States Holocaust Memorial Museum. Online. Available: www.ushmm.org/education/foreducators (accessed 12 January 2009).

Valentine, J. (1994) *One Dad, Two Dads, Brown Dads, Blue Dads*, Los Angeles: Alyson Wonderland.

Varma-Joshi, M. (2007) 'Speak No Evil, See No Evil: The Controversy about Saying "Hate" in Mainly White Classrooms', in H. Claire, H. and C. Holden (eds) *The Challenge of Teaching Controversial Issues*, Stoke on Trent: Trentham.

Vincent, C. (2000) *Including Parents? Education, Citizenship and Parental Agency*, Buckingham: Open University Press.

Visram, R. (1986) *Ayahs, Lascars and Princes*, London: Pluto Press.

Voiels, V. (1996) 'The Inner Self and Becoming a Teacher', in M. Steiner (ed.) *Developing the Global Teacher: Theory and Practice in Initial Teacher Education*, Stoke on Trent: Trentham.

Vygotsky, L. S. (1962) *Thought and Language*, Cambridge, MA: MIT Press.

——(1978) in M. Cole, V. John-Steiner, S. Scribner and E. Souberman (eds) *Mind in Society*, Cambridge, MA: Harvard University Press.

Ward, L. (2001) 'PM Sets Out his Global Vision: Action Needed instead of Rhetoric, Say Protestors', *Guardian* newspaper, 3 October 2001 p. 5. Online. Available: www.guardian.co.uk/politics/2001/oct/03/uk.afghanistan1 (accessed 15 November 2009).

Watson, B. (1993) *The Effective Teaching of Religious Education*, London: Longman.

Watson, B. and Thompson, P. (2007) *The Effective Teaching of Religious Education*, 2nd edn, Harlow: Pearson Education.

WCED (World Commission on Environment and Development) (1987) *Our Common Future (the Brundtland Report)*, Oxford: Oxford University Press.

Wellington, J. J. (ed.) (1986) *Controversial Issues in the Curriculum*, Oxford: Blackwell.

Whalley, M. (2001) *Involving Parents in their Children's Learning*, London: Paul Chapman Publishing.

White, M. (1991) *Self-esteem – its Meaning and Value in Schools: How to Help Children Learn Readily and Behave Well*, Cambridge: Daniels.

——(2008) *Magic Circles: Self-esteem for Everyone Through Circle Time*, London: Sage.

White, P. (1999) 'Political Education in the Early Years: The Place of Civic Virtues', *Oxford Review of Education* 25 (1 and 2): 59–70.

Whitehead, T. (2008) 'Brown Drops "Britishness" Day', *Daily Express*, 27 October 2008. Online. Available: www.express.co.uk/posts/view/68041/Brown-drops-Britishness-day (accessed 1 November 2008).

Whitworth, W. (2009) *Journeys: Children of the Holocaust Tell their Stories*, London, Quill Press.

WHO (2005) *World Summit Outcome Document*, World Health Organization, 15 September 2005. Online. Available: www.un.org/summit2005/documents.html (accessed 30 December 2008).

Wieser, P. (2001) 'Instructional Issues/strategies in Teaching the Holocaust', in S. Totten and S. Feinberg (eds) *Teaching and Studying the Holocaust*, Boston, MA: Allyn and Bacon.

Williams, J. E. and Best, D. L. (1990) *Measuring Sex Stereotypes: a Multi-nation Study*, Newbury Park, CA: Sage.

Winston's Wish: the Charity for Bereaved Children. Online. Available: www.winstonswish.org.uk (accessed 11 October 2008).

Wiseman, H. (2006) *Guidelines for Teaching About the Holocaust to Year 6 Pupils*. London: Imperial War Museum. Online. Available: http://london.iwm.org.uk/server/show/nav.1199 (accessed 7 September 2008).

Woolley, R. (2006) *Education for Global Citizenship: developing student teachers' perceptions and practice*. Paper presented at the 7th International Conference on Children's Spirituality. Winchester, 23–27 July.

——(2007a) *The Ethical Foundations of Socialism: The Influence of R. H. Tawney and William Temple on New Labour*, Lewiston, NY: Mellen Press.

——(2007b) 'What Makes Men … ? Masculinity, Violence and Identity', in C. Harber and J. Serf (eds) *Comparative Education and Quality Global Learning: engaging with controversial issues in South Africa and the UK*, Birmingham: TIDE.

——(2008a) 'Communicating Effectively' in M. Cole (ed.) *Professional Attributes and Practice,* 4th edn, London: David Fulton.

——(2008b) 'Development, Well-being and Attainment' in M. Cole (ed.) *Professional Attributes and Practice*, 4th edn, London: David Fulton.

——(2008c) 'Spirituality and Education for Global Citizenship: Developing Student Teachers' Perceptions and Practice', *International Journal of Children's Spirituality* 13 (2): 145–56.

Woolley, R. and Hanson, F. (2008) *Personal Histories*, Lincoln: Bishop Grosseteste University College Lincoln. Online. Available: www.bishopg.ac.uk/personalhistories (accessed 10 November 2008).

Woolley, R. and Johnston, J. (2007) 'Target Setting', in J. Johnston, J. Halocha and M. Chater (eds) *Developing Teaching Skills in the Primary School*, Maidenhead: Open University Press.

Woolley, R. and Mason, S. (2009) 'Sex and Relationships Education', in J. Sharp, S. Ward and L. Hankin (eds) *Education Studies: An Issues-based Approach,* 2nd edn, Exeter: Learning Matters.

Worden, J. W. (1996) *Children and Grief When a Parent Dies*, New York: Guilford.

Wragg, E. C. (2001) *Assessment and Learning in the Primary School*, London: Routledge Falmer.

Young, B. (2003) 'Does Food Advertising Influence Children's Food Choices? A Critical Review of Some of the Recent Literature', *International Journal of Advertising* 22: 441–59.

Index